RETHINKING THE SALES FORCE

Also by Neil Rackham

Major Account Sales Strategy

SPIN Selling

The SPIN Selling Fieldbook: Practical Tools, Methods, Exercises, and Resources

Getting Partnering Right: How Market Leaders Are Creating Long-Term Competitive Advantage

RETHINKING THE SALES FORCE

Redefining Selling to Create and Capture Customer Value

Neil Rackham

John R. DeVincentis

McGraw-Hill
New York   San Francisco   Washington, D.C.   Auckland
Bogotá   Caracas   Lisbon   London   Madrid   Mexico City
Milan   Montreal   New Delhi   San Juan   Singapore
Sydney   Tokyo   Toronto

Library of Congress Cataloging-in-Publication Data

Rackham, Neil.
    Rethinking the sales force : redefining selling to create and
capture customer value / Neil Rackham, John DeVincentis.
       p.   cm.
    Includes index.
    ISBN 0-07-134253-2
    1. Sales management. 2. Selling. I. DeVincentis, John R.
II. Title.
HF5438.4.R343   1998
658.8'1—dc21   98-47875
                                                      CIP

McGraw-Hill

A Division of The McGraw·Hill Companies

9 0 DOC/DOC   0 4 3 2

ISBN 0-07-134253-2

Printed and bound by R. R. Donnelley & Sons Company.

CONTENTS

v

CHAPTER SIX. THE NEW ENTERPRISE SELLING: FROM LARGE SALES TO DEEP RELATIONSHIPS

CHAPTER SEVEN. SALES PROCESS: LIGHT IN THE LONG DARK TUNNEL

CHAPTER EIGHT. RETHINKING CHANNELS TO CREATE AND CAPTURE VALUE

CHAPTER NINE. CHANGING THE SALES FORCE   249

ACKNOWLEDGMENTS

Sales forces are caught in the middle. On one side, their customers have changed dramatically in terms of how they purchase and what they expect. On the other side, their own corporations have shifted, going through downsizing, restructuring, and cost cutting. Traditional boundaries such as those between sales and marketing have crumbled. Sales people have to cope with more products, introduced faster with shorter life cycles, and less competitive differentiation.

CEO's and sales vice presidents we have worked with have felt an increasing frustration as existing models and methods have proved unable to cope with this changed world. As we've struggled with these issues in companies large and small, our own thinking has crystallized thanks to the hundreds of people who have given the time to share, discuss, and challenge. We owe them a deep debt and this book is the result of the intelligence and insights they so generously shared with us.

In particular we would like to thank Christine Bucklin, a principal in McKinsey's Los Angeles office, who helped shape and refine our thinking on channels; Tanuja Randery, who repeated the sterling research effort that she performed for Neil's earlier partnering book; Ann Roberston and her team, who coordinated the research and information effort to document examples and provide facts and figures used throughout the book. Walt Zyglinski and Richard Ruff of Huthwaite read and suggested changes to the drafts of earlier chapters. Renate Neely took the book through all its marketing stages. Trip Levis at Free Markets On Line gave us valuable insights into transactional selling, and Liz Webster helped in our early channel thinking.

Stephanie Stocker prepared illustrations, corrected and coordinated the draft text, and generally gave us an unreasonable amount of support. Yo Lynch undertook the thankless task of cataloging and checking the case references.

Finally, we owe a huge debt to Ava Abramowitz. She brought her marketing and sales experience to bear, convincing us to revise substantial areas of the text for the better. She also acted as our legal counsel. It was good to have a lawyer who understood what we were trying to achieve at every level, from the subtlest concept to the most prosaic hyphenation. Dennis Mankin, also a lawyer, provided unconditional support and encouragement throughout the project. Ava and Dennis, during our long writing sessions, also took on the heavy responsibility of looking after Capo, Digby, and Diggorie, who still don't understand what all the fuss was about.

Neil Rackham
Huthwaite, Inc.
15164 Berlin Turnpike
Purcellville, Virginia 20132

Tel: 540.882.3212
Fax: 540.882.9004
Email: Nrackham@huthwaite.com

John DeVincentis
3044 River Road
P. O. Box 353
Solebury, Pennsylvania 18963

Tel: 215.862.4874
Email: jdevincentisusa@
          netscape.net
Website: www.devincentis.com

THE NEW SELLING

From Communicating Value to Creating Value

Suppose some corporate Rip Van Winkle who fell asleep on the job 30 years ago was reawakening for the first time today. Looking sleepily around him, he'd find his organization so changed that it would hardly be recognizable. Wandering through manufacturing, he'd rub his eyes at the sight of strange new machines and unfamiliar technology. But, extraordinary as these innovations might be to Mr. Van Winkle, he would soon notice things that were even stranger. "Something's very different," he would mutter. The shop floor now looks more like a laboratory than the factory he remembers. The oil and grime have gone. So have the many piles of half-finished goods. But the biggest change isn't in the technology or the surroundings—it's in the work force. No rows of people working at single repetitive tasks. There's not one quality-control inspector to be seen. Where are the supervisors who should be giving orders? Who is worker, and who is manager? Instead of the old familiar hierarchy of command and control, people are working in teams; they seem to be making decisions for themselves. Groups are discussing problems and issues. That's a big change—talking on the shop floor was actively discouraged in his day. Nobody is standing around waiting for instructions on what to do next. In manufacturing, the fundamental nature of work has changed beyond all recognition.

It's a huge shift and more than Van Winkle can absorb on his first waking day, so off he goes in search of something more familiar. He heads for the typing pool, only to discover it no longer exists. He tries a succession of other departments, and the manufacturing story is repeated. Everywhere he finds new technology, new processes, and—above all—a radically different approach to the nature of work itself. Everywhere? Not quite. The sales department, where he used to work, is much as it was when he fell asleep 30 years ago. True, most people now have laptop computers—although, curiously, many of these devices seem to be more for decoration than for use. And there are more women in the department. He's now a "salesperson" rather than a "salesman." But most other things seem familiar. The sales function is still organized into three groups: small geographical accounts, larger major accounts, and a modest number of very large national accounts—the exact organization structure that had first been announced the year he fell asleep.

Van Winkle Rehired. The company decides to offer Van Winkle his old sales job back, so out he goes with his new sales manager to see how much selling has changed in 30 years. He's pleasantly surprised to find that, compared with other functions in the company, selling looks comfortingly familiar. There is certainly a wider product range now, and individual products do seem more complex. Competition is intense, and things are faster paced. Customers are more demanding, although he reminds himself that they weren't always a pushover 30 years ago. The hard sell now seems to be officially discouraged, but even in the old days he pre-ferred to sell through relationships rather than pressure. He's still expected to fill in call reports, although improved technology now lets him enter his lies and excuses electroni-cally rather than manually. He's paid more than before, but unlike his colleagues in manufacturing whose whole pay-ment structure has changed, he's still paid a base salary plus commission on sales volume. His sales manager coaches him in such familiar terms that it feels as if he'd never been asleep. She talks of features and benefits, of objection han-dling, of open and closed questions—ideas that were around 30 years ago. In fact, although Van Winkle doesn't know it, everything she advises him to do could have come word for word out of E. K. Strong's classic *The Psychology of Selling,* published in 1925. "Well," thinks Rip Van Winkle, "thank goodness that selling will always be selling. I could probably get away with it if I'd slept for another 30 years."

CHANGE AT EVERY LEVEL

That's where he would be wrong. Irresistible new forces are reshaping the world of selling. Sales functions everywhere are in the early stages of radical and profound changes comparable to those that began to transform manufacturing 20 years ago. If he'd slept for another couple of years, Rip Van Winkle would find himself in a very different world. Most telling of all, he might not even have a job to go back to. By some estimates, at least half of today's selling positions will be gone within five years. Every aspect of selling is changing. Customers, as we'll see in the next chapter, are fundamentally changing their expectations, changing their patterns of purchasing and changing what they want from a sales relationship. Sales organizations are changing too. Time-honored geographical territory structures are disappearing. The segmentation of the sales force by customer size that has been a central organizing principle for so long—with one group selling to small accounts and another to large—is no longer a sufficient model. The role and nature of sales management is undergoing a transformation too, with a new breed of sales managers beginning to emerge. Technology, of course, is also a major force for change, both within the sales function and at the interface with customers. And, as we'll see in Chapter 4, electronic commerce, with the ballooning and bewildering variety of Internet purchasing options, is fast developing a capacity to change not only selling but many other aspects of our lives. But one change outweighs all the others. The meaning of *selling* itself is shifting. The very purpose of sales is being rapidly redefined.

Crossing the Threshold. In most companies—and Rip Van Winkle's organization would be an example—these changes are just starting to be felt. The typical sales force today is at that uneasy juncture where it's clear that life is soon going to be very different, but it is not at all clear what those differences will be, or what they will mean. Some organizations have already crossed the threshold into this new selling world. Van Winkle wouldn't recognize the sales job in these companies. He might not even call it "selling." For example:

- *Microsoft* has a sales force that a few years ago was selling bulk software to corporate accounts in a typical business-to-business sale. Now they spend their time organizing and mobilizing a network of independent solution providers such as systems specialists, trainers, software designers, or installers. They are as likely to be selling with their competitors as against them. It's not even clear to a casual observer what they are selling or whom they are representing. The subject of Microsoft or Microsoft's packaged software products sometimes doesn't come up during sales calls, and when it does, it may sound more like an afterthought than the purpose of the call.

- *Enron,* the energy company that started out selling and transporting natural gas, now has a sales force that is just as likely to be offering sophisticated financial instruments such as options, swaps, caps, collars, floors, or firm forwards. Listen in to an Enron sales discussion and the salesperson sounds more like a high-level financial specialist than someone from a company that sells gas and electricity.

- *IBM* sent a team into Monsanto, the agricultural and pharmaceutical giant based in St. Louis. What were they selling? IBM hardware? Software? No, their purpose was to explore fundamental research issues on gene mapping in plant and animal cells. If you had been the proverbial fly on the wall during these discussions, they would hardly sound like selling. Yet out of these meetings came contracts to IBM worth several hundred million dollars.

- *Charles Schwab* was a pioneer in telephone selling of brokerage services—call them and you'd talk with a broker [a.k.a. salesperson] who would transact your business. Now, if you so choose, you can dial up on the Internet and place your own trades. It's a sale all right—Schwab gets a commission from the transaction. But there are no salespeople, or people of any sort, involved in the trade. The sale is a totally electronic event.

- *Applied Materials* designs and produces chip-making machines that enable companies like Intel to manufacture their magic little slivers of silicon. Who sells these machines to Intel? Over a hundred Applied Materials people. But not through a conventional selling effort. Engineers, researchers, designers, technical specialists, accountants, and people from dozens of other disciplines all work with Intel on a daily basis to meet Intel's needs. Sit in on a typical meeting, and it's so integrated that you can't tell who comes from Applied Materials and who's from Intel. And you certainly wouldn't see anything happening that Mr. Van Winkle would call "selling." Yet those meetings *are* the sales relationship. The good old definition of *selling*, where a seller persuades a buyer to purchase goods or services, doesn't begin to describe what's happening.

There's no doubt that something radically different is going on within sales relationships like these. But it's not simply that selling is getting more complex and sophisticated. It's not that the hard sell has become softer, that selling has a greater technology component, or that individual salespeople have been replaced by teams. These may be symptoms of change, but the causes are much more fundamental. Selling is in the early stages of a complete transformation.

WHAT'S A SALES FORCE FOR?

You can tell that the whole nature of sales is changing from the questions that top executives are starting to ask. Over the years we've run a number of chief executive forums on sales force issues. If we go back two or three years, typical CEO questions would be on topics such as compensation, training, or sales force automation—bread-and-butter concerns about how to run an existing sales force a little more effectively or efficiently. But at recent CEO forums, the questions have taken on a much more searching and fundamental tone. "Do I need a sales force at all?" mused one chairman of a technology company. Another CEO asked, "What's the difference between selling and marketing—I'm not sure that I understand the distinction clearly any more?" The head of a large communications company suggested, "Perhaps the time has come to ask the most basic question of all—what's the purpose of a sales force?"

COMMUNICATING VALUE TO CUSTOMERS

Questions like these—about the fundamental definition of *selling*—would have sounded academic or naïve just a couple of years ago. Now, coming from experienced business leaders, they are a sure sign that selling as we know it is in flux. What *is* the purpose of a sales force? That's a good question, and it takes us straight to one of the central themes of this book. The traditional purpose and role of the sales force is changing dramatically. As a starting point, here's a representative sample of how a cross section of salespeople, sales managers, and sales vice presidents see the purpose of their existing sales forces:

> "The reason for a sales force is to ensure that the customer has the right information about the advantages of your products at the right time, so that the purchasing decision is influenced in your favor." *Regional Sales Manager, Printing Equipment Company.*

> "The sales force convinces the client to buy from you rather than from a competitor by showing how your services are superior." *Senior Consultant, Systems Integration and Software Company.*

"The sales force exists to show customers that you have something worthwhile to offer that meets their needs." *Salesperson, Office Products Company.*

"The sales function is like a translator: Its job is to take your products and services and translate them into language that the customer understands." *Sales Manager, Control Systems Manufacturer.*

"The purpose of a sales force is to communicate to customers the value of your offerings." *Senior Vice President, Sales and Marketing, Large Regional Bank.*

What's the common thread here? The last of these definitions sums it up well: *The purpose of a sales force is to communicate the value of your offerings.* That's the general idea expressed in each of these fairly traditional views of selling. For years this has been the universally accepted role of the sales force. Selling has been about value communication.

While the sales function has been busy fulfilling its role as a value communicator, a great change has swept over the rest of the business world. Whether we're talking about manufacturing, engineering, product development, or even human resources, other functions in the organization have been restructuring and realigning themselves to *create* more value for customers. Activities that don't add value have been reduced or eliminated. New work methods have been introduced, such as continuous improvement, business process reengineering, Kaizen, and self-directed work teams. The effect of these innovations has been to create products and services more cheaply, more efficiently, and at higher quality. In other words, other functions in the organization have become conscious value creators in their own right. In today's enterprises it's hard for functions or even individuals to survive—and impossible for them to prosper—unless they clearly add value to the customer.

In yesterday's world it was possible to argue that by communicating product information to customers, the sales force was actually adding some value. "We're useful to doctors

because we educate them on the latest drugs," a pharmaceuticals rep told us. "We tell them about new options that haven't
gotten into the reference books. Without us, doctors would
quickly become out of date." Generations of salespeople in
many other industries have survived on the basis of similar
justification. We inform customers, they claim. We tell them
things they didn't know, we give them product information
they couldn't get anywhere else. At one time this might have
been a legitimate way to add value. But, increasingly, buyers
know as much or more about the products as do the people
selling to them. The advent of specialization in medicine, for
example, means that many doctors will have participated in
clinical trials or will be well versed in a new drug's effects well
before the drug is approved for release. In other industries
too, buyers are better informed than they used to be. In the
information age, claims to add value by giving information
sound increasingly hollow. There are so many easy and accessible forms of data about almost everything that the idea that
it requires an expensive live salesperson to communicate fac-
tual information sounds less and less plausible. Sales forces
that see their mission as value communication are living in
the past.

THE VALUE COMMUNICATION TRAP

You would expect that the one place where the idea of adding
value to the customer would be as natural as breathing
would be in sales. But, surprisingly, rather than being a
leader in the value revolution, sales has been at best a lag-
gard and at worst an active saboteur. As Michael Hammer,
author of *Reengineering the Corporation* (Harperbusiness,
1984), says, "Sales has been curiously resistant to a value-
driven process approach. No other area of the business has
proved so stubborn." What has held sales back from playing
a leading role in the drive to create customer value? One reason is that sales functions haven't seen a need to change.
They already think of themselves as their organizations' pre-

eminent value creators. They see themselves that way because, in making sales, they create tangible and measurable value for their own company. As an account executive at Xerox Printing Systems put it, "I love the sales job because I can measure my achievement in dollar terms. Last year I brought in $5.7 million in sales. I look at the division's bottom line, and I can directly see the contribution I personally made. Without me, our revenue would be down by $5.7 million." Here's someone who is clearly convinced he creates value. But his value, as measured by sales results, is to his own company, not to its customers. Customers only gain indirectly, if at all, because a salesperson sells several million dollars of product. Value creation must directly benefit the customer. Increasingly, companies are coming to realize that their survival, first and foremost, depends on their capacity to create direct and tangible customer value in every part of their enterprise.

THE NEW MARKETING MYOPIA

Another reason that many sales forces see their mission as communicating value rather than creating it is because that's precisely the mission they have been given. Top management, brought up with a traditional view of marketing and sales, is likely to see the role of the marketing function as creating the value—through product innovation or branding—and the role of the sales function as communicating to customers the value that marketing has created. This view is so widely held, and so limiting, that we've come to think of it as the new "marketing myopia," to borrow from Ted Levitt's famous *Harvard Business Review* article of the 1970s.

What makes it particularly myopic—and particularly culpable—is that anyone connected with current business thinking should know better. There's evidence all around us that limiting the sales role to value communication is just plain bad strategy. It's one of the great business truisms of our age that products and services are becoming commoditized more rapidly than ever before. It's therefore hard, if not impossible, to create and sustain differentiation in the product. Twenty years ago you could argue quite plausibly that the value you provided to customers largely rested in your products. So, if your marketing and design effort could come up with a better mousetrap, then you had successfully created sustainable value. Today, customers have many mousetraps to choose from. As far as they are concerned, your mousetrap might have some unique features, but so do 10 competing mouse-traps. The customer can substitute one of the alternative competing products for yours and feel perfectly satisfied. What this means is that the bells and whistles you've built into your mousetrap—to mangle a metaphor—no longer add value to the customer. If substitutes are readily available and if the customer sees no extra or unique benefits from your version, then all your marketing and product design efforts are wasted. You may have differentiated your product, but the differentiation doesn't create value because it doesn't matter to the customer. You've become a commodity. As markets commoditize, the amount of value that resides in the product steadily erodes.

Where Can You Create New Customer Value? If customers show decreasing preference for one product option over another, then how can suppliers differentiate themselves? If you can no longer embed sustainable value in your products, then where can you create new customer value? There's a strong argument to be made that value migrates from the product itself to how the product is acquired. This leads to the interesting idea that, as products are perceived to be interchangeable, then the customer places increased value in their preferred acquisition environment. So, in the consumer field, you might create value by providing a wider variety of ways in which a customer could choose to acquire your products. Some customers, for example, might prefer to buy from catalogs, others might enjoy Internet purchasing. Still others might have a traditional store or a specialty outlet as their preferred acquisition environment. Consumers, in other words, increasingly place value on how the product is sold to them rather than on the product itself.

The sales process itself plays an increasing role in creating customer value.

The same is true in business-to-business sales. In the place of pure product value, as we'll see in the next chapter, customers are looking for value in other areas beyond the product. How easy and convenient is the product to acquire? How can it be customized to our specific needs? What support comes with it? Can lead times and inventory requirements be cut? What else can the supplier's organization do for us beyond providing products and services? A skilled sales force can create new value in these areas. As Dennis Courtney, chief information officer of Dunlop Tire Corporation, puts it:

> The products that a supplier offers are only a small part of the equation. Generally we could get what we need from several places, so it's not unique. These suppliers who try to sell the product—who try to show us their stuff is better—are missing the point. What we're looking for goes beyond the product. We're looking for business understanding, we're looking for whether they can adapt to our special needs or whether they can advise and help us. We want their salespeople to add something worthwhile on their own account.

In other words, salespeople who only communicate the value of their products don't cut it. What Dennis Courtney, and thousands of customers like him, look for is the capacity of salespeople to create value in their own right.

In this day and age it's just not tenable to maintain a large and expensive organizational function unless it actively creates value for customers. Sales must be more than a value communicator. Fortunately, many companies are starting to question the traditional boundary between marketing and selling. As they do so, the antiquated view of the sales role as communicating the value that marketing creates is crumbling fast. But the old roles still linger with many chief executives, even though they would never permit other functions in their companies to survive without actively creating value for customers.

BEYOND THE VALUE SLOGANS

Saying that the sales force must create value, not just communicate it, is a simple and attractive idea. Creating value has become one of the business mantras of our age, and it's hard to challenge anyone who suggests that the time has finally come for sales forces to embrace a value creation approach. Like so many slogans, it makes perfect sense if you say it quickly enough. But pause to reflect, and the simple idea starts to get more complicated. What does "create value" actually mean? Ask academics or consultants, and they will tell you that, at its simplest, value is the equation:

$$\text{VALUE} = \text{BENEFITS minus COST}$$

Then they will add complicating elements. Each has a preferred definition of *benefit*; they will argue about whether "benefits" and "costs" are real, perceived, or a mixture of the two. They will debate whether cost is pure dollars or how factors such as hassle, risk, or inconvenience should be considered on the cost side of the equation. But the basic definition is useful. It suggests that there are two distinct ways for a sales function to create value. Either you can create additional benefits, or you can reduce the cost of the benefits you already provide. As we'll see in later chapters, these are two very different strategies for increasing sales value. In the first case you must have a sales force that can create new customer benefits that don't already exist in your products or services. So, typically, you might increase the sales force capacity to deliver more benefits by giving them more technical support, by improving their problem-solving capabilities, or by allowing them to spend more time working on issues that are valuable to the customer—such as customizing your products or services to better meet customer needs. These ways of increasing customer benefits almost inevitably require you to invest more in your sales force, which leads to an increase in selling costs. As we'll see in Chapter 5, the value that a sales force can create will often more than offset this increase in cost. A sales force that adds real value can justify higher prices and can also create strong competitive advantage.

But, in the second case, where the objective is to create value by reducing cost to the customer, you certainly don't want to do anything that increases your selling costs. If your sales force can't add value by increasing benefits, then the only way to create value is for your costs to come down. And the easiest way to do that is to find cheaper ways to sell. So companies using the cost reduction route for creating value have reduced or even eliminated their sales forces. As we'll see in Chapter 4, they have found less costly ways to reach their markets. Some have created a cheaper sales force, using telephone sales or part-time salespeople. Others have eliminated their sales forces altogether, moving to channel distribution, catalogs, or electronic commerce. A few, as we'll see, have found innovative and successful ways to redefine *selling* and have been able to take advantage of an environment in which the customers' requirement for bottom-line value has forced them—and their competitors—to greatly reduce sales costs.

MORE BENEFITS OR LESS COST?

We've said that there are two distinct ways for a sales force to create value—to increase benefits or to reduce cost. Strategically, which way is better? Most of us have a sneaking preference for strategies that involve creating new benefits. That way, so the argument goes, we can create a bigger pie, capture more profit, and provide so much extra value to the customer that we put the competition to shame. A sales force that adds new value somehow feels more successful than one that merely manages to slash its costs. That's a dangerous preconception. Whether it's better to create new benefits or to provide cheaper and easier acquisition depends entirely on the customer. Take the case of utility companies facing deregulation. The average utility is acutely aware that the deregulated market will be much more aggressive and that their whole organization, including their sales force, will have to create customer value in order to compete. Should they adopt a cost reduction strategy or a create new benefits strategy? Ask their major commercial customers. Some will tell you, "Kilowatt hours are a pure commodity. There's no way a utility's salespeople could add any value to us. All we want is cheap power that's hassle free—and if we can buy it over the phone or on the net, without wasting time with a salesperson, then so much the better." For them, the sales force is incapable of creating new benefits, and, if it adds a fraction of a cent to the cost of energy, they would rather give their business to a competitor. But go to other large commercial customers, and they'll say, "We want a utility that has some core competencies that we just don't have. They probably know a lot more than we do about energy management. They understand how to generate steam. They can maintain electrical equipment far better than we can ourselves. What we want is good help and advice in these areas— and we're prepared to pay well for it." Customers like these have a very different view of value, and they will cheerfully pay for the added cost of a sales force that focuses on creating new benefits. In terms of value creation strategy, it's clear that one size will not fit all. The model that works best for one type of customer may not work at all well for another.

LIMITATIONS OF ORGANIZING BY SIZE ALONE

Sales forces, of course, are already familiar with the idea that different customers must be treated differently. Historically, large customers have provided greater opportunity and total profit potential, and, as a consequence, they have justified greater selling effort and greater resources than smaller customers. Since the late 1960s most sales functions have been organized around a customer segmentation that's based on account size. So the typical sales force of today—whether it's a bank, a manufacturer, or a service provider—has, at the top end, a group of salespeople dedicated to serving global or national accounts in depth. These accounts receive a disproportionate amount of attention and resources because of their size. Next, there's a bigger group of salespeople that works with medium to large accounts. Finally, there's either a geographically based sales force that calls on small "mom-and-pop" customers, or, increasingly, there's an indirect channel and telephone sales operation to give coverage to these smaller accounts that are generally higher in margin but lower in overall profitability.

This size-based segmentation has worked well for 30 years as a structuring principle for sales force design. Unfortunately, it's becoming increasingly apparent that organizing the sales effort by customer size alone is no longer an adequate way to segment customers. Take the two types of customer in our utility example. Both would be large commercial customers. Both would qualify for the attention given to national accounts. But, while one of these customers would value national account attention with all the associated sales costs, the other would not only reject it but would see the sales overhead as a negative that reduces value rather than adds it.

Size and Profitability. A sure sign that segmentation of the sales force by customer size is no longer working as well as it once did can be seen by tracking the profitability of accounts. At one time, account size and profitability tracked so closely that they were almost interchangeable. Big accounts were invariably profitable, small accounts weren't. The obvious conclusion was to segment by customer size and to put more resources to the largest, and therefore most profitable, accounts. Recently, the correlation between size and profitability has become much less clear. The experience of a major U.S.-based component manufacturer provides a typical example. Not long ago they analyzed the profit contribution of their 10 largest accounts. In 1987, these accounts had represented 72 percent of overall profit. Ten years later, in 1997, this contribution had shrunk to less than 40 percent. Every single one of the top 10 accounts was highly profitable in 1987. By 1997, 2 of these accounts were making a loss for the company and 2 others were barely breaking even. Many other organizations have been finding that size is no longer a proxy for profitability. A supplier's largest accounts may be squeezing margins mercilessly, while some middle-sized accounts may be far more profitable than ever before. Bigger is not necessarily better. Segmenting the sales force by account size may no longer be a complete, or even an adequate, answer.

But what's the alternative? If we truly believe that sales forces must create customer value, then it's logical to ask why we continue to segment the sales effort primarily by customer size. Admittedly, small accounts can never justify a high level of sales resources. But the converse isn't necessarily true. Account size, at best, tracks only approximately with the value creation needs and expectations of buyers. While some large accounts may want and value the extra benefits that a higher level of selling resources can create, others may simply want a lower price. Adding resources to these large, price-driven customers can destroy value rather than create it. Size alone can be misleading. Why not also segment the selling effort according to the value requirements of customers? It's an idea worth exploring, not least because it starts with the customer, which is the genesis of most good business strategies. What would a value-based sales force segmentation look like? Fortunately, as we'll see, many of the pieces of the sales value jigsaw already exist. All we need to do is to assemble them into a complete strategic picture.

THE THREE TYPES OF CUSTOMERS

In value terms, customers can be segmented into three distinct types, as follows.

INTRINSIC VALUE CUSTOMERS

For these customers, value is intrinsic to the product itself. They focus largely or exclusively on the cost elements of value. They generally already understand the product well. They know how they want to use it. They see the product or service as a commodity that is readily substitutable by competitive offerings. They want a favorable cost—either in terms of price or ease of acquisition. For them, because all the value is intrinsic to the product, there's little or nothing that a sales force adds. They even resent the time they spend with salespeople. Selling is an added expense which they, as customers, must ultimately bear—and they believe they would be better off without it. Most of us recognize the typical intrinsic value customer as the traditional bottom-line purchasing agent who buys raw materials or supplies. However, as we'll see in the next chapter, the new purchasing world is dramatically changing that traditional view of the purchasing function. And intrinsic value customers aren't only in industries we normally associate with commodities. An increasing number of customers buying specialist products, or even professional services, have an intrinsic value orientation.

Extrinsic Value Customers

These customers focus largely or exclusively on the benefits or extrinsic elements of the value equation. For them, value is not intrinsic to the product itself but lies in how the product is used. Extrinsic value customers are interested in solutions and applications. The sales force can create a great deal of new value for them. They put a premium on advice and help. They expect salespeople to give them new understanding of needs and options. They will willingly invest time, effort, and cost in working with salespeople to create customized solutions. They tend to build relationships with their suppliers that go beyond the immediate transaction. Unlike the bottom-line intrinsic value customers, who see no value in time spent with salespeople, the extrinsic value customers often want more investment of selling time to ensure that a potential supplier has a thorough understanding of their business needs and issues. Extrinsic value customers frequently reject possible suppliers—even those who have good offerings that are attractively priced—if the suppliers push their products or solutions too quickly without first becoming educated in the customer's business. For extrinsic value customers, real value can clearly be created by the salesperson.

STRATEGIC VALUE CUSTOMERS

These customers demand an extraordinary level of value creation. They want more than the supplier's products or its advice. They also want to deeply leverage the supplier's core competencies. They are prepared to make radical changes in their own organization and its strategies to get the best from their relationship with their chosen strategic supplier. In a strategic value relationship, it's almost impossible to tell who's selling and who's buying. It's more a relationship between business equals who are working together to create an extraordinary level of new value that neither could create alone. The analogy of "sharing the pie" is a common one in selling. Intrinsic value customers look for larger share of a cheaper, more convenient pie. Extrinsic value customers look for a bigger pie with more benefits that both parties can share—in other words, extra value for the customer in exchange for worthwhile margins for the supplier. In contrast, the strategic value customer looks for a soup-to-nuts meal—many more things than are contained in the product or service pie. The product is clearly secondary to other forms of value the supplier can bring. Earlier we referenced a typical strategic value customer relationship, the Applied Materials association with Intel where both parties work cross functionally to jointly design the machines that manufacture the chips. Each partner shares technology and research, as well as manufacturing and design know-how. Each leverages the competencies of the other to be more successful. In effect, they have redesigned the boundaries between them to create new value.

Figure 1-1 summarizes the three fundamental strategies for creating value:

- *Intrinsic value customers,* whether large or small, don't receive value from the selling effort itself. Because they already understand the product and how it fits their needs—and because they have no special requirements for advice or customization—the greatest value for them comes from a selling strategy that involves low selling cost and easy acquisition.

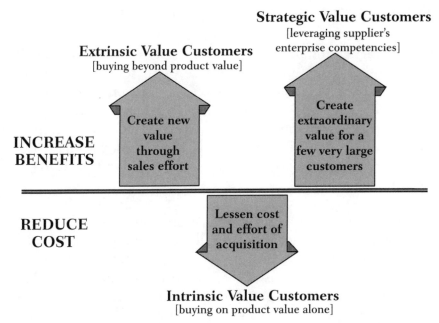

FIGURE 1-1.   Value creation strategy.

- *Extrinsic value customers* look for value from the sales effort that goes beyond the product or service. Because they require such things as advice and customization, they demand a sales force whose help and advice creates extra value, even at some additional cost. Consequently, the most effective selling strategy will be one where the sales force is trained, equipped, and compensated to create new value. Extrinsic value customers may be large or small although, as we'll see in the next chapter, there are clearly some economic limits to the feasibility of a value creation strategy for customers who are too small to justify the mutual investment of time, cost, and effort required in a value creation sale.

- *Strategic value customers,* as we'll see in Chapter 6, involve relationships that are highly selective and invariably confined to a few very large customers. So, while a supplier could configure its sales effort to meet the needs of small accounts for either an intrinsic or an extrinsic value relationship, strategic value relationships are economically practical only between large suppliers and their large customers.

WHEN SIZE SEGMENTATION FAILS

If customers fall into one of these three value buckets, how do we design a sales effort to best respond to each customer type? It's clear that a conventional segmentation based on customer size will not be enough. A very large customer, for example, could be any one of the three value types. Here's a case in point. One insurance company we work with has three major channel customers [brokers] who are each key accounts:

- *Customer A,* an aggressive regional broker, tells them, "Don't send me your salespeople, just send me your quotes [the insurance "product"]—and your quotes had better be fast and cheap because there's a dozen of your competitors out there who will get our business if they beat you on speed and price." Here's clearly an intrinsic value customer who sees all the value in the product and no added value from a sales force.

- *Customer B,* another large broker who has grown by merger and consolidation, tells them a very different story. "We need a lot of help. Every one of our offices does things its own way. We don't have a common set of procedures, and we haven't got a common information system. We'll write a lot of business with you if your people are prepared to work with each office individually and help them get their act together." Here the sales force can create real value, and its advice is welcomed. This is a typical extrinsic value customer who is prepared to look outside of the product and pay a premium for the benefits that salespeople can add.

- *Customer C* is about the same size as the other brokers but is looking for a different relationship. "What we want," they tell the insurance carrier, "is a strategic partner who will put their underwriters into our offices, who will develop cutting-edge information systems with us to turn quotes around quicker than anyone thought possible, and who can work with us to develop new and innovative risk management systems. We'd like to leverage some of your back-office know-how, and we'd be interested in having your marketing people input to our internal planning process." This is a customer who looks far beyond the product and wants a strategic value relationship, where the boundaries between carrier and broker are totally redesigned.

These three customers represent the three largest accounts of the insurance company. Yet each wants a completely different kind of relationship. A conventional size-based segmentation would treat each as a key account. They would, on the basis of their size and business volume, be allocated approximately the same amount of selling effort, and they would be sold to in a very similar way by a key account sales team. But, because their value needs are so different, a standard key account approach would clearly be inappropriate.

MATCHING THE CUSTOMER'S INVESTMENT

How well does a typical sales force handle very different customer value requirements like the three insurance customers in our example? If, like most sales functions, selling efforts are organized solely on the basis of account size, then there will be problems. A sales group dedicated to serving large account customers will generally overresource accounts that are intrinsic value buyers. As we've seen, many customers, both large and small, don't want—and won't pay for—an expensive investment of selling time. The result, shown in Figure 1-2, is that value can be wasted or destroyed by putting unnecessary sales resources into these accounts. It's uneconomic for the supplier to waste value by putting more into the sales effort than customers want or need. However, although margins suffer, few sales are lost through overresourcing the selling effort. In contrast, underresourcing often does lose sales. As Figure 1-2 shows, a customer may be prepared to invest considerable time and resources in the acquisition process. A supplier who doesn't provide an equivalent level of selling effort becomes

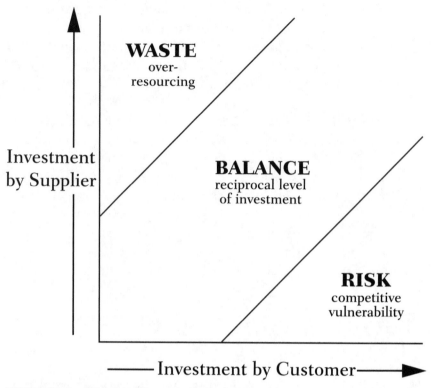

FIGURE 1-2.   Matching the customer's investment.

vulnerable. Competitors who do match or exceed the customer's investment will be likely to win the business.

Similar issues of value misalignment also happen in sales forces dedicated to serving smaller customers. The general size segmentation model assumes that smaller customers justify a smaller sales effort. Yet small-and middle-sized customers who are extrinsic value buyers will often invest in a careful acquisition process and will be prepared to pay handsomely for advice and help. Because a size-segmented sales force is generally not designed for this type of customer, there's no mechanism allowing salespeople to provide the resources required to play a value-added role, so the opportunity to create and capture value is lost. But, if the small account sales force is underinvesting in its extrinsic value customers, it is probably overinvesting in small intrinsic value customers who are looking for the cheapest way to acquire products with minimal effort. Increasingly, as we'll see in Chapter 4, these customers must be served through cheaper channels such as telephone sales or electronic commerce.

The optimum selling position, of course, is where buyer and seller are perfectly matched in terms of the investment each makes. So the intrinsic value customer, who sees all the value in the product and not in the sales force, will generally prefer an acquisition process that, is simple, cheap, and hassle free, requiring very little investment of time or effort. The extrinsic value customer will generally expect the opposite. As Burleigh Hutchins, Chairman of Zymark says, "A segment of your customers—both large and small—are buying your advice more than your product. They need you to invest in understanding their business and they'll make the investment required to educate you. If you short-change them you're in trouble. They want to spend time with you. You'd better be prepared to do it, or a competitor will give them the kind of hand-holding they need. Doesn't matter if you've a better product. You can't afford to be too busy to spend the time it takes." The importance of a reciprocal level of investment is especially clear with strategic value customers. To create extraordinary value on a strategic level requires a very high level of investment by both parties. It's not at all uncommon for a supplier to have selling costs well into the seven figures for the initial sale at this strategic level. That's a sizeable investment. The customer, too, may be spending an equivalent amount. If only one party is willing to make this kind of investment, then, as we'll see in Chapter 6, the relationship is probably doomed.

SEGMENTING THE SALES EFFORT BY VALUE

Intrinsic, extrinsic, and strategic value customers each require a different amount of sales investment in terms of time, effort, and cost. But there's a lot more to it than that. Each type

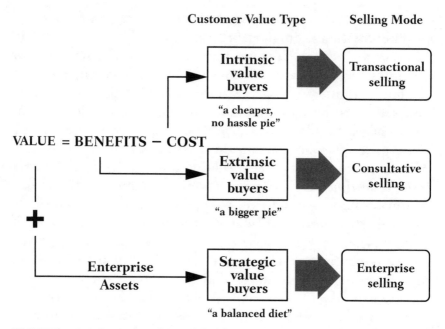

FIGURE 1-3.   Customer value and the three selling modes.

requires a different sales strategy and a fundamentally different set of selling skills.

As Figure 1-3 shows, for each customer value type, there is
a corresponding mode of selling that best fits the customer's
value creation needs. We've tried to use familiar terms for
these three selling modes. But beware—the problem of using
terms everyone knows is that most readers already have pre-
conceptions about what these terms mean. Each of these
three modes of selling has different and distinct characteristics that may not quite fit the existing meaning you presently
give to these labels. Although the terms *transactional selling*
and *consultative selling* have been around for 20 years, we're
using them here with a special meaning to refer to the bundle
of skills and strategies that are emerging as sales forces focus
their efforts to meet the demands of the three customer value
types. We will be devoting a whole chapter to each selling
mode, but, for starters, here's a brief description of each one.

- *Transactional selling* is the set of skills, strategies, and sales processes that most effectively matches the needs of intrinsic value buyers who treat suppliers as a commodity and are mainly or exclusively interested in price and convenience. From the customer's point of view, in the transactional sale there are no additional benefits that the seller can bring to the party. So, for example, Wal-Mart will deal with smaller suppliers but will refuse to meet on a regular basis with their salespeople. As a Wal-Mart spokesperson put it, "We'd rather their [sales force] salaries and commissions were taken off the price. Why should we pay for something that takes up our time without providing anything in return?" The issues in transactional selling are about cost reduction—how to strip cost out of the sales process and to make the transaction risk and hassle free for the customer.

  As we'll see in the next chapter, sweeping changes in the purchasing world are bringing an increasing number of selling organizations face to face for the first time with the harsh realities of transactional selling. It's no longer just traditional industrial commodity suppliers that sell transactionally. Professional service providers, such as lawyers, accountants, consultants, and doctors—people who had never dreamed of their services as commodities bought "by the yard"—are finding that a growing percentage of their clients want to purchase transactionally. For most sales organizations, transactional selling is a debilitating rearguard action trying desperately and unsuccessfully to preserve shrinking margins and to resist the increasingly aggressive demands of intrinsic value customers. But not for all. As we'll see in Chapter 4, some sales forces are adopting strategies that not only let them survive in a transactional environment but let them actively innovate and prosper.

- *Consultative selling* is the set of skills strategies and processes that works most effectively with customers who are extrinsic value buyers. These customers demand, and are willing to pay for, a sales effort that creates new value and provides additional benefits outside of the product.

Consultative selling rests on salespeople who become close to the customer and who have an intimate grasp of the customer's business issues. As we'll see in Chapter 5, selling consultatively involves a mutual investment of time and effort by both seller and customer. Listening and gaining business understanding are more important selling skills than persuasion; creativity is more important than product knowledge. In the consultative sale the role of the sales force is to create value in three primary ways:

- To help customers understand their problems, issues, and opportunities in a new or different way
- To help customers arrive at new or better solutions to their problems than they would have discovered on their own
- To act as the customer's advocate inside the supplier organization, ensuring the timely allocation of resources to deliver customized or unique solutions that meet the customer's special needs

Because these are demanding skills, good consultative salespeople are hard to find. Organizations that want to develop an improved consultative selling capability can easily become hostage to highly paid "rock-star" sales performers. For this reason, as we'll see in later chapters, effective consultative sales efforts increasingly use diagnostic tools, sales processes, and information systems to allow ordinary mortals to perform well in the increasingly sophisticated consultative selling role.

- *Enterprise selling* is the set of skills, strategies, and processes that work most effectively with strategically important customers who demand an extraordinary level of value creation from a key supplier. In enterprise selling, both the product and the sales force are secondary. The primary function of the enterprise sale is to leverage any and all corporate assets of the supplier in order to contribute to the customer's strategic success. No single salesperson, or even a sales team, can set up or maintain an enterprise relationship. Invariably, these sales are initiated at a very high level in each organization. They are deeply tied to the customer's strategic direction, and they are usually implemented by cross-functional teams on each side of the relationship. A good way to think about enterprise selling is to see it as the redesign and continuous improvement of the boundary between supplier and customer. Frequently hundreds of people from each side are involved in such a relationship, and it's difficult, if not impossible, to tell where selling begins and ends. In Chapter 6 we'll look closely at how successful enterprise relationships are set up. Because enterprise selling is an expensive process and has to be very selective, we'll also look at the preconditions that will tell you whether an enterprise sales effort is likely to succeed.

Figure 1-4 shows how the three modes of selling link to the idea of a reciprocal commitment of resources from suppliers and customers:

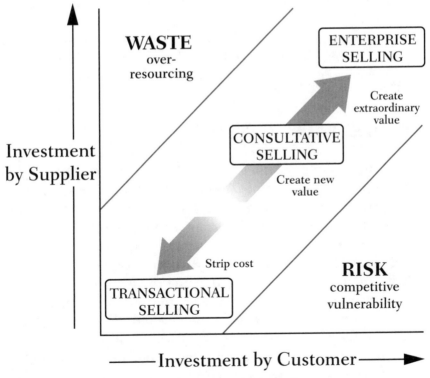

FIGURE 1-4.   Investment to add value to the selling effort.

- *Transactional selling* **reduces** resources allocated to selling because customers don't value or want to pay for the sales effort. So transactional selling creates its value by stripping cost and making acquisition easy, with neither party making much investment in the process of buying or selling.

- *Consultative selling* **adds** resources to the selling effort, matching the customer's willingness to invest time and trouble in the acquisition process. Consultative selling creates new value through the ability of the sales force to advise, customize, and bring expertise beyond the product. The customer, in turn, invests time in educating the supplier during the sales process. So both parties put more resources into the buying and selling effort.

- *Enterprise selling* **adds** even more resources to the selling process. Both supplier and customer make major investment to redesign their relationship to create a powerful collaboration for creating a high level of new value.

A mismatch of resources will, as Figure 1-4 indicates, cause waste in cases where the seller overinvests and risk in cases where the seller invests insufficiently.

MAKING FATAL MISTAKES

Since the days of Julius Caesar, dividing the world up into three parts has been a convenient way to think about complex problems. But is there any real advantage to splitting the sales world into the three parts of transactional, consultative, and enterprise structures? Don't most sales organizations seem to survive on the basis of simply dividing customers by size? What's the great advantage of dividing them according to their value creation needs? We believe that any sales force that wants to survive has reached a point where it has no alternative. Unless your value creation effort is closely coupled to your customers' value creation needs, your selling will fail. A few examples will show what we mean:

- A *manufacturer of packaging materials* was in a marketplace where more than 90 percent of customers were intrinsic value buyers who bought transactionally. Because the manufacturer's costs were slightly higher than competitors', they were losing business. They decided that the best way to halt this decline was to upgrade their sales force. Instead of "sales reps," they created "packaging consultants" who were charged with the task of adding value to their products through providing customers with help and advice. The direct investment in retooling their salespeople, including retraining and recruiting, together with the development of a new marketing strategy and support collateral, was in excess of $10 million. But the operating cost of the new sales force was even more frightening. The average cost of each sales call was $890. The average sales cost to acquire a new account was $112,000—far more than the average profitability over the life of the account. Predictably, the strategy was a disaster. Customers didn't need and didn't want help or advice. For them, all the value was intrinsic to the product. They needed packaging material, pure and simple—that's all they were prepared to pay for. They bought transactionally, but the manufacturer had created a high-cost consultative strategy. The company was soon taken over, at a fire-sale price, by a major competitor who stripped sales cost and created a transactional selling effort that matched the customer's value needs.

- A *small consulting company* developed a number of new products to improve the productivity of its clients. Being a consulting firm, they didn't have a dedicated sales force. Instead, their consultants worked closely with their clients to define needs and create customized solutions. They had, in other words, a classic consultative sale. Seeing an opportunity to grow their market based on the new products, the company brought in a chief executive who had previously worked in the packaged-software business. The new chief executive was horrified at the length of the selling cycle and at the use of expensive consultants in the business development process. He removed the existing consultants from the direct selling role. In their place, he created a telephone selling capability and recruited commission-based salespeople who were managed with ruthless cost efficiency. He worked tirelessly to increase coverage. Salespeople were instructed to "make the sale and move on" and were ordered not to spend unnecessary time understanding customers and their business needs. Under his management, the number of new customer contacts quadrupled, while the cost per contact fell by more than half. He had successfully created a high-coverage, low-cost transactional sales force. Unfortunately, the company's clients—especially those that were most profitable—were extrinsic value buyers who bought consultatively. They were willing to pay well for the customized solutions and the understanding of their business that the company had provided in the past. Under the new regime, many of them jumped ship and went to competitors that offered a value-creating sales force. The company began to lose business and soon decided to lose its chief executive instead. By returning to a higher-cost value creation model that matched their clients' value expectations, they were able to recover some of their previous profitable position.

- A *manufacturer of containers* had a long-term relationship with a major food company. For many years they had supplied not only containers but also specially adapted machinery and container design advice to their customer's needs. The relationship had been a good and happy one on both sides. One day their customer asked whether they would be interested in a very different kind of relationship. It would involve outsourcing some of the food company's production and joining in some risk-sharing codevelopment of radically new packaging approaches. The sales team lacked the authority to respond to such a revolutionary proposal, but they took it back to their top management. "We're not equipped to run their lines," said the CEO. "We're not a production company, and this codevelopment idea sounds mighty risky. But they are a valued customer, so let's offer them lots of extra design support and more engineering help." To their surprise, the customer declined the help and informed them that they were switching to a new supplier. The president and executive team of this new supplier had worked for six months at a high level within the food company to create new risk-sharing strategies, and they had agreed to take on full management of the food company's production lines and to codevelop a range of innovative food-packaging concepts to be created jointly by an R&D team with membership from each company. The customer had wanted a strategic value relationship. The existing supplier was unable to offer this within the constraints of their consultative selling effort. When a new supplier appeared on the scene who understood how to initiate a high-level enterprise sale, a 30-year relationship was irretrievably broken. The packaging company recently announced a significant downturn in its results and a major restructuring.

Cases like these—and hundreds of others like them—show that it's fatal to adopt one value-selling mode if your customers want another. No amount of selling skill, no amount of clever strategies, and no well-crafted value propositions can bridge the gap unless there is a basic alignment of the supplier with the value creation requirements of the customer. A sales force can't fundamentally transform customers who have decided to purchase transactionally into ones who purchase consultatively. At best, effective selling can slightly shift the balance, but it's uphill work. In an age when customers not only demand *more* value than ever before but are also increasingly clear about the *kind* of value they are looking for, value alignment with the customer is essential.

Whether we're talking of large business customers, small business customers, or even individual consumers, there have been dramatic changes in their value expectations. Understanding these changes is the first step to rethinking what it takes to build an effective value-creating sales force. In the next chapter we'll look at the new purchasing world and how purchasing decisions are being shaped by this changing awareness of value.

THE NEW PURCHASING WORLD

How Value Is Reshaping Purchasing Decisions

A few years ago we were working with a group of senior executives from a cross section of industries and we tried a little experiment—a word association test. "What word comes into your head when you hear the term *marketing?* we asked. Typical replies included, "dynamic," "trend setting," "strategic," and "powerful." We then asked the same executives for their reactions to the word *purchasing*. Among the responses were "boring," "routine," "safe," "mechanistic," "play by the rules," and "back room." Not the most dynamic and sparkling image for a function that spends more of the average corporation's money than all the other functions put together. Unfortunately, this colorless reputation has generally been well deserved. It wasn't so very long ago that being sentenced to read purchasing journals might have fallen into the category of cruel and unusual punishment. Purchasing lectures at business schools were hardly the best attended; few executives were excited about the prospect of a long assignment in the department, and there was little chance of purchasing issues reaching the agenda of senior management.

Times have changed. There has been a dramatic shift of thinking in this area over the last several years. Few senior executives would use terms like "routine" or "boring" today. This shift has elevated purchasing to real strategic importance in most corporations. It has raised some new and significant insights into the relationships between buyers and sellers, and it is leading to innovative ways of selecting and working with suppliers. Purchasing is literally altering the way the world does business. The new trends in purchasing are powerful enough to transform every aspect of selling. In response, leading companies are redesigning their sales efforts and rethinking the very purpose of their sales forces. Purchasing is becoming an exciting and dynamic force for change. Even the deadly pages of purchasing journals have taken on a new excitement and flair.

We're not suggesting that you load up on purchasing journals for your next vacation's reading list, but if you haven't given purchasing much thought lately, a quick look through the literature might turn up some surprises. You'll see case studies attacking the old vendor-customer relationships that have been a comfortable foundation of traditional purchasing since the dawn of institutional time. You'll find innovative articles about new theories of purchasing. You'll find sophisticated acquisition models and many other interesting and thought-provoking ideas. You'll find a new colorful language too. Writers warn about the hidden costs and disadvantages of "purchasing promiscuity," saying that we're in an era of "safe purchasing" and "supplier monogamy." The purchasing world buzzes with talk of "strategic purchasing," partnering relationships, and supply chain management issues. Poke around major corporations today, and you'll find signs of a sea change in thinking about the role and importance of managing the cost, quality, and delivery aspects of acquisition. Purchasing and supply chain issues are high on the agenda of most senior management teams. Up-and-coming young executives are leading this charge. Inevitably, legions of consultants are wandering the corporate corridors, helping to redirect a long-neglected function and starting to make a real difference to the bottom line. Purchasing has changed—and selling will never be the same again.

This new energy in purchasing has created unprecedented changes in business-to-business sales. Dramatic shifts in buyer-seller relationships are the norm rather than the exception. It's an exciting time for purchasing, but, from a sales perspective, the predominant emotions are more likely to be confusion and fear rather than excitement. Salespeople will tell you uneasily about the loss of thousands of selling opportunities. Five years ago, Xerox Corporation had 18,000 suppliers—now they have fewer than 500. Ford has taken its supplier base from 75,000 down to 5000. In case after case, and in every industry, companies have drastically cut down the number of suppliers they will deal with, ruthlessly eliminating legions of companies that don't make the cut. A corporation that had relationships with 30 banks two years ago now deals with 7 and is looking to consolidate down to 3. The average *Fortune* 500 company has reduced its supplier base by half and projects a further 25 to 35 percent cut in the next two years. The effect on suppliers has been devastating. The magazine distribution business is a typical example. A couple of years ago, retailers began to cut down on the number of distributors they used. Wal-Mart, for example, reduced their magazine suppliers from 280 down to 3. Other retailers went through a similar consolidation. As a result, in an 18-month period, the magazine business fell from over 300 distributors down to less than 50. Many of these disappearing companies and sales relationships were long established. In every industry, salespeople will tell you stories of what has happened to safe, solid, seemingly unshakable relationships that had been in place for decades. Suddenly, without warning, these comfortable annuities have been discarded in favor of open-for-bid contracts. Existing relationships have become vulnerable and—with the reduction in suppliers—new opportunities are increasingly hard to find.

THE CONFUSING CUSTOMER

Customer decision-making roles are changing too. Pharmaceutical salespeople who once only had to worry about selling the prescribing physician on the superiority of their drug will now tell you of the gauntlet of review boards they face at insurers, hospitals, HMOs, and pharmacy benefit management companies. Getting a drug on approved lists today requires sophisticated selling of pharmaeconomics as much as it requires convincing doctors of the drug's superior effects in disease management. "It's not clear who the customer is anymore," says Jack Robinson, sales consultant and former Xerox sales manager. "Yesterday I sold to a decision maker who could say yes or no. Today, I may be selling to a wide range of people inside the customer organization, including committees and user groups. But it doesn't stop there. I may also have to sell to consultants whose job is to advise on acquisition strategy, or even to competitors who have been given a role in deciding which other suppliers will interface with their equipment."

So, even for those companies who survive the waves of supplier reduction, life isn't exactly easy street where the winners divide up a bigger share of the purchasing largesse. Not only is the sale itself getting more complex but salespeople will also tell you of the constant treadmill of seemingly endless demands for greater and greater price concessions, and of ever higher service standards, all just to keep the business. Legions of salespeople and sales managers are finding themselves ill equipped to succeed in this new purchasing world they find themselves in, or even to understand it. They complain bitterly about the contradictions they're facing and their inability to cope with them. "Sure, there's a lot of talk about partnering," they'll tell you, "but the next week that same customer that went on and on about partnership, is beating the hell out of you for price." Or others will say, "First there's a big push on cost reduction— driving everyone nuts to find any way possible to save every last cent. Then they turn around and demand faster delivery, more technical support, and more quality enhancements. Where will it end? What the heck do they really want?"

VALUE: THE COMMON FACTOR IN A CONFUSING WORLD

These are fair questions to ask, even if they arise out of the frustration that salespeople have felt as they tried to adapt to the new purchasing rules. So what *is* really going on? We think that there is a relatively simple answer. What customers fundamentally want is "value." But like all simple answers, while it may be accurate, it needs a lot more explanation, which we'll try to provide in this chapter. Inevitably, as we explore the idea of purchasing value, it will get much more complicated because the way buyers are perceiving value today is indeed shifting and evolving.

In both business and consumer sales, customers are taking a harder and harder look at their spending, and they are much more willing to consider different options and to undertake significant effort to get better value. These changes seem to be happening regardless of economic class at the consumer level and regardless of company size, industry, or financial condition at the business level. As we saw in the last chapter, there are three distinct types of business customers:

- *Intrinsic value customers* who see value only in the product and, as a result, define value as the cheapest, easiest way to obtain the supply of product that they need
- *Extrinsic value customers* who see real value beyond the product and who define value in terms of advice, problem solving, customization, or the capacity to meet special and unique needs
- *Strategic value customers* who look for an extraordinary level of value from a deep strategic relationship with a few chosen suppliers

These different value orientations have a profound effect on the kind of relationship business customers expect from their suppliers.

What is driving this shift in value orientation? We believe there are two sets of factors worth exploring. On the one hand, there are a number of major environmental shifts—globalization, financial restructuring, and the explosion of information availability—that have had a massive impact on the business decision-making environment and have reshaped both company and consumer attitudes toward cost and value.

The second factor, in addition to these environmental shifts, is the rise of new purchasing concepts, particularly in business purchasing. Some very powerful new ideas are emerging about how purchasers should approach buying decisions. These ideas are transforming the relationships between buyers and sellers and have taken us far beyond older notions of "balance of power" and "negotiating skill." In the rest of this chapter we'll explore both of these factors that are driving customer buying behavior. We'll identify the major trends underway and the implications for sellers, and we'll lay the foundation for the selling strategies that are beginning to emerge in response to these new purchasing behaviors.

NEW REALITIES SHAPING THE BUYING ENVIRONMENT

In a conversation a few years back, a friend of ours who had spent her career at AT&T observed that deregulation and the subsequent restructuring and downsizing that ensued had a really dramatic, if not outright traumatic, impact on most of the people involved. The onset of competition, after a generation in a protected position, not to mention the subsequent waves of downsizing and cost cutting needed to reach competitive levels, forever changed people's view of the world and their own sense of job security. The more we talked about it, though, the more we realized that while AT&T's transition had been more severe than most, it was not really that atypical. Although most companies haven't been impacted by deregulation, they have been impacted by other discontinuities in the past two decades, with similar result. Globalization, for example, has fundamentally increased the level of competition of scores of industries, redefined quality or "value" standards, and forced a massive reduction in costs to stay in the game. Look at the automotive market. In 1958, the "Big 3" collectively held 89 percent of the market and defined the rules of competition in the United States. Each of the Big 3 merely had to remain competitive with the other two in styling, quality, and cost dimensions to maintain their position. Globalization of the industry, and the onslaught of Japanese and European competitors, totally shattered that world. By the 1990s, the Big 3 accounted for only 63 percent of the U.S. market; the North American (United States and Canada) share of the world's total motor vehicle production had fallen almost in half, from 56 percent in 1960 to 29 percent in 1990. The global offerings, which hit the market at lower price points or with higher quality or more features, forced American auto manufacturers to make dramatic changes to their operations and take out massive amounts of cost to become competitive. The impact was dramatic. All three companies responded successfully to the new competitive realities, but not without tremendous change. Between 1980 and 1990 alone, the Big 3 auto makers in the United States would shut down more than one-third of their U.S. assembly plants, undertake massive productivity and quality programs, eliminate more than 300,000 blue-collar jobs and nearly 50,000 white-collar jobs in order to be competitive. The industries that supported automotive are estimated to have lost an additional 200,000 jobs. There was little, if anything, that remained untouched, and certainly no one who worked in the industry could ignore the massive restructuring and the focus on downsizing and cost reduction. A similar story could be told in steel, in electronics, in textiles, and in other industries whose way of doing business was forever changed by globalization.

In other cases financial restructuring, rather than globalization or deregulation, led to the intensified focus on cost and value, but the end result was the same. The rise of "junk bonds" fueled a wave of leveraged buyouts, mergers, and acquisitions to previously unimaginable levels. Older notions about debt capacity were replaced by a more aggressive breed of financiers who looked to free-cash flows rather than debt-to-equity ratios as their guideposts. We don't intend to argue the merits or the limitations of this new thinking—others are far better qualified to judge that. What we are most interested in is the impact on buyers, their attitudes and behaviors. One thing is certain: With massive debt payments due, the focus of business managers in these newly restructured companies quickly turned to generating the cash required to meet the looming burden of debt. And that led inevitably to a greater scrutiny on costs and expenses. Efficiency became the order of the day, by necessity. Company after company moved to squeeze as much cash as possible out of their operations and costs. "Downsizing," the closing of inefficient and redundant facilities and the elimination of excess people, became commonplace in these industries as well. In a very short time, millions were facing job transitions, reassignment, out-placement, or simple unemployment.

There is little question that American business, and eventually European business too, became tougher, leaner, and more competitive as a result. But in the process the drive for efficiency fundamentally changed the way people faced buying decisions. In the workplace, there was much greater sensitivity to the cost and value of incoming materials and supplies. It was clear that costs had to come down. While pressuring suppliers wasn't a pleasant prospect, it was certainly preferable to forcing further rounds of internal layoffs and other downsizing activities. And on the consumer front, the wave of downsizings and layoffs fundamentally changed individuals' notion of job security, as restructuring hit people at all levels, tenures, and industries. Even people not directly involved were well aware of the impact on friends, neighbors, relatives, or coworkers. Just as the depression of the 1930s shaped a generation's perceptions, so this wave of job uncertainty seems to have helped to shape recent consumer purchasing behavior. Despite the record length of the U.S. economic expansion, low levels of unemployment, and record levels of consumer confidence, consumers still appear to be extremely cautious and careful with spending decisions. This caution isn't just on big-ticket items but extends to simple everyday purchases as well. Across a broad range of consumer goods, manufacturers are finding much greater price sensitivity and greater resistance to even modest price hikes. In conjunction with the greater competitiveness resulting from globalization and deregulation, this greater consumer price-value sensitivity virtually precludes manufacturers from passing along cost increases to the customer. In turn, this further reinforces the already intensive focus and pressure on cost control, and thus continues this cycle.

These changes are transforming both business and consumer markets—each in a distinctive way. Let's first look at how these new buying realities have affected consumer attitudes and buying behavior.

HOW CONSUMER IDEAS OF VALUE ARE CHANGING

Consumer purchases are getting more complex and confusing. Brand loyalty has continued to decline, with consumers becoming increasingly fickle and almost eager to abandon the tried and true and experiment with alternatives. That also goes for their choices of where to buy as well as what to buy. Consider this: Through the 1970s, consumers satisfied virtually all of their grocery needs at supermarkets. Today, despite all of the increased demands on their time, the average consumer will satisfy only 66 percent of their grocery needs there. Once a month, they will go out of their way and drive a considerable distance to do a stock-up trip to the club store and load up on many items in bulk, with related bulk-quantity savings. They will make this additional shopping trip for items they used to buy in supermarkets—but now they buy virtually exclusively at the club store—because the savings potential is greater than the value of "one-stop shopping." The same consumers, so price conscious in the club store, will stop by specialty stores on the way home from work to buy prepared items for tonight's dinner at a substantial premium, but one that saves them the time of cooking a meal "from scratch." They'll spend a part of their Sunday clipping coupons, but they still spend an increasing portion of the food budget eating out. And even then, they are very likely to use convenience stores for fill-in items at much higher prices, when convenience and a quick purchase are worth the higher premium.

Consumer behavior has become more complex—they are increasingly seeking value, but *value* no longer means just "low price"—they are making tradeoffs of price for true convenience but taking a harder and harder look at just what those tradeoffs are and what they really cost.

Other consumer purchases also reflect changing buyer behavior. For bigger expenditures, such as automobiles, appliances, or financial services, consumers will spend considerably more time than ever researching their alternatives before shopping at an increasingly broad set of providers. It wasn't so long ago that typical home buyers would limit their search for a mortgage to their bank and maybe one or two others in town. Today, it's much more typical for mortgagees to research mortgage rates through financial advice publications, mortgage brokers, and even the Internet. And it's not just the top quartile of sophisticated consumers who are changing. Take the case of Green Tree Financial Corp., a company that grew rich lending mortgage money to working-class borrowers for mobile homes. They assumed that their borrowers would continue with the traditional working-class disregard for high interest rates. Until very recently, this seemed a safe enough bet. Blue-collar consumers were often grateful to get any loan. They expected to pay top interest rates and were unlikely to think about refinancing their high-interest borrowings. Based on the assumption that this unsophisticated buying behavior would continue, Green Tree thought its loan portfolio safe. Early in 1998, however, they were forced to take a $390 million pretax charge due to an unexpected surge in refinancing among their blue-collar customers. And Green Tree wasn't alone. Profits of competitors, such as Aames Financial Corporation have also been hit. Credit card companies too are feeling the pinch as traditionally passive and acquiescent customers have suddenly woken up and started to search for the best sources of value.

IMPACT OF PROLIFERATING INFORMATION SOURCES AND RETAILING FORMATS

In addition to the shift in consumer attitudes to value, easy access to buying information has helped inform their purchasing decisions, while the proliferation of retail formats has created a new range of supply options. Today, customers are much better informed than ever before and, quite simply, smarter about buying choices. Take a look at consumer purchases of big-ticket items such as autos or appliances. A generation ago, there was limited availability of objective, third-party information for these purchases, and consumers had to rely on the advice of more experienced friends or relatives. Alternatively, they could try to get the information they needed from available salespeople or sales promotional material. Getting fully informed in any product category was difficult, if not impossible. Most people simply used their instincts as much as anything, or relied on reputation or brand name.

Today, there is a wealth of information available to consumers. They appear much more willing to do their homework and research their intended purchases. They are much better armed with hard facts and less vulnerable to softer, less tangible elements like "reputation" or "image." Third-party sources, such as *Consumer Reports* or J D Powers, conduct tests and surveys on all sorts of products and services. Sources like these help buyers narrow their choices and understand the value tradeoffs that are at stake. By their nature, these survey companies are analytical and fact oriented. They remove some of the emotional content of buyer decisions. They focus buyers increasingly on the harder, more quantifiable aspects that support "best-buy" or "best-value" conclusions. The proliferation of special-interest magazines like *PC World* or *BYTE* in the computer world, or *Road and Track* in the automotive world, also provide sources of product information and assist in buyer decision making. And, of course, there is the Internet, with its virtually limitless source of information, that consumers are only just beginning to tap.

For sellers, inevitably, this new information age is forcing a greater focus on the measurable performance of their products and services. But, perhaps more importantly, it is also forcing a reassessment of the traditional thinking about sales and its role in providing customers with such information. With so little control over the information sources that today's customers are using, manufacturer's historic obsession with the messages their salespeople deliver appears increasingly redundant and even futile. Traditional sales approaches often seem more and more ineffective and out of touch. The idea that a sales force can exist solely to communicate product value—the proverbial "talking brochure"—is no longer supportable when customers already have all the information they need to make a confident decision. As we'll see, the winners in this emerging market have fundamentally changed their approach and have rethought their overall sales strategies to develop new ways to deal effectively with today's smarter customers.

NEW RETAIL OPTIONS CHANGING BEHAVIOR

While access to more, "unbiased" information has helped consumers get smarter about many purchasing decisions, retailing options have also increased. Space expansion and the explosion of different retail formats have greatly aided consumers in their search for value, increasing their alternatives and providing easy access to them. Retail space, in virtually all categories, whether food, general merchandise, or specialty stores, has expanded exponentially. In the United States in 1970, there was 7 square feet of retail space for each person—man, woman, or child. By 1996, that number had tripled to 21 square feet per person. It's not just more new stores for traditional retailers, although this has certainly been a part of the growth. It is also, and perhaps more importantly, an increase in the different *types* of stores. Expansion has increased the breadth of value alternatives available to consumers in a number of ways.

A good example is the "category killer" store. These are large retail formats focused on a specific category, like Home Depot in the do-it-yourself/home improvement category, or Staples and Office Depot in the office supplies category. These large retail spaces, dedicated to only one type of good, typically carry more than twice the selection of traditional retailers, provide knowledgeable sales staff, and have economics that permit pricing that is often 20 percent lower than others. This value formula of better selection, service, *and* price has been extraordinarily effective, and these category killers—as the name implies—now dominate the market for sales in their areas.

Club stores offer a slightly different formula, but they also give consumers a value choice. Here the assortment is more limited than traditional retail outlets. There are no small sizes. In fact, there is very little here that isn't in the "jumbo industrial" size, that might represent a year's supply for a small family. But these bulk buys are offered at an attractive discount of 20 to 30 percent compared with more normal sizes from traditional retail outlets. There are a few other "give-ups" as well. Not only are sizes limited but so are brands. You might or you might not find your favorite. Further, you can't count on specific items being there—items that were there last time might not be there this time. And you have to do a fair amount of work yourself. There generally is no one to bag your purchases—or even bags for that matter—you have to load your items into discarded cardboard cases and take them out to your car yourself. But, despite all the give-ups, the dollar savings are considerable and their success over the last decade testifies to the attractiveness of the tradeoffs to the new value-conscious shopper.

THE RESURGENCE OF CATALOG BUYING

In addition to the proliferation of storefront options, nonstore-front retail formats, like catalog sales and the Internet, are also having an impact on shoppers and shopping behavior. Granted, catalog sales are a pretty old format—the first Sears catalog was published in 1888—but catalog sales have undergone such a resurgence and expansion that they again represent a widely used channel for a broad range of consumer purchases. Over the past decade or so, catalog sales in the United States have grown from $30 billion to $90 billion and now represent 4 percent of all consumer retail purchases. This resurgence has been fueled by changes in the catalog format that have increased value for customers—it wasn't just that catalogs started carrying a broader range of merchandise. The Sears catalog at one time offered all of the pieces required to construct a house, in one package delivered to your building site. Part of the new value is in the greater speed and reliability of delivery that UPS and Federal Express have added to the catalog offering. There is also value in the ease of 1-800 numbers and a credit card to initiate a transaction. Easy return policies lower risk and add further value, while the expanding variety of specialty catalog companies has greatly expanded the quality and quantity of offerings. What's more, consumers find enormous value in the convenience of the catalog purchase and, in many instances, are willing to pay a bit more to save time and hassle or to obtain access to different merchandise. This resurgence of catalog sales has created a vehicle for reaching tens of millions of consumers that has offered them a greatly expanded set of products and choices.

THE RISE OF ELECTRONIC COMMERCE

The Internet itself is another nonstorefront format that is beginning to have an impact on consumers, although this format is so new and incipient that the excitement lies in its potential rather than the results to date. To be sure, if you were to judge from a financial perspective alone, so far there is little to cheer about. Even some of the most talked about successes, like *amazon.com*, (the Internet bookstore) have yet to show a worthwhile profit, and penetration of this new "e-commerce" (electronic commerce) is still minuscule by virtually any consumer marketing standard. Further, most consumer marketers continue to view the Internet as an advertising vehicle rather than as a serious channel contender. While there is a case to be made for each of these perspectives, over time penetration and profitability of e-commerce will see great gains, and the Internet will play a much more significant role in consumer buying behavior from a transaction, rather than an advertising, perspective.

The Internet, or e-commerce, has a number of characteristics that play very well to the continuing and growing importance for consumers to be better informed about purchasing decisions. For consumers and businesses alike, the Internet greatly expands both the selection of available goods and services and the range of available suppliers. The result is to further facilitate the consumer thrust to find better value in terms of more benefits for the dollar or less cost for the same benefits. *Amazon.com,* the Internet bookstore we referred to earlier, is a great example. It boasts a selection of 2.5 million books, many times more than one could hope to find at a retail site, even in a warehouse-sized location. Further, the electronic format makes it relatively easy to search through the selection, find specific volumes you're interested in, and access information about content, reviews, or comments of other readers. In addition, the format offers a discounted price from typical retail bookstores. As consumers get more comfortable with computers, this format promises some clear advantages to satisfy the growing consumer push for more information, more choice, and less cost.

IMPLICATIONS OF CHANGES IN CONSUMER ENVIRONMENT

Clearly the electronic bookstore format will not be for everyone. Many consumers are not too interested in specific content or review information, and they prefer to browse through bookstore shelves with the ability to leaf through the book and get a sense of the writing. Others may be more interested in getting the book immediately, rather than waiting several days for delivery. They will choose alternative, more traditional formats. And that's the key dilemma for manufacturers and suppliers. The Internet, catalog sales, club stores—all of the newer retail formats are additions to the retail landscape, not replacements. For consumers this means expanded choices and better value potential. But, as we'll see in Chapter 8, for manufacturers, this means horrendous increases in complexity and conflict. They can no longer focus on just one type of channel, without cutting themselves off from large parts of market potential. And it's not just having more stores to deal with—it is more types of stores, each with its own "value formula" and needs. For sellers to succeed in this emerging market, they will must learn how to adapt to these multiple models and how to manage the conflicts that will inevitably arise.

Increasing price sensitivity also puts pressure on suppliers to really understand consumer tradeoffs. To succeed they must transfer investment and effort into areas that really count to customers in value terms. To fund this investment in value creation, they must work ruthlessly to contain their cost in areas that their customers don't value. With better-informed consumers, manufacturers can no longer rely primarily on soft differentiators such as image or nonspecific claims of better quality. Instead, successful players will focus on developing measurable hard differentiators that provide objective advantages over competing products. Above all, the increased sophistication of customers means that it's no longer enough for the sales force to simply communicate product value. Smarter consumers demand more than a talking brochure (see Figure 2-1).

ENVIRONMENTAL SHIFTS	IMPLICATIONS FOR SELLERS
Increasing price sensitivity	• Must understand true value levers • Must put even greater focus on cost containment
Smarter, better-informed consumers	• Must improve measurable comparison features • Must avoid excessive reliance on image and softer differentiators that are becoming less effective. • Must recognize that value communication is no longer enough
New channels emerging	• Must use multiple channels for broad market coverage • Must manage channel conflict

FIGURE 2-1.   How these changes will affect selling.

CHANGES IN BUSINESS BUYING

Business buying behavior has experienced an even more dramatic shift. Deregulation, globalization, and financial restructuring, the same events that drove much of the change in consumer behavior, have had a similar impact on changing business purchasing attitudes and behaviors. And, for businesses just as for consumers, advances in information technology have helped buyers to be better armed with facts to make smarter buying decisions For smaller businesses, new retail formats have probably made the biggest difference. Club stores, for example, were initially targeted mainly to the small-business customer, and many of the offerings in this channel are commercial rather than residential. Those large rolls of plastic wrap for example, are more suitable for restaurants unless you have an extraordinarily large family—and it's hard to imagine any family needing spices in the sizes carried at the club store. In fact, nearly half (46 percent) of sales in the club store channel are sold to small-business customers for business use, at prices that are quite attractive relative to the wholesalers and distributors that have traditionally served this market

For larger businesses, the greatest impact has unquestionably come from the new thinking and new perspectives that are transforming the purchasing function. Three fundamental purchasing concepts—the lifetime cost of ownership, supplier reduction, and supplier segmentation—have revolutionized business purchasing and have created a new reality for sellers to deal with.

LIFETIME COST OF OWNERSHIP

It wasn't so long ago that a purchasing department's effectiveness was judged by how much it could limit annual expenditures—its ability to beat down suppliers' prices and get goods for the lowest possible amount. Indeed, as cost reduction efforts intensified to get companies more competitive with global or other domestic firms, purchasers' attention was primarily focused on this "first cost." But an increasing skepticism arose about whether the lowest-price deal actually lowered the total cost. There was an emerging and interesting notion that what counted was the "lifetime" cost of ownership, and not the initial cost. As consumers, of course, we all implicitly understand the concept—most of us have been burned by the false economy of buying a "no-name" appliance for 20 percent less than a well-known brand, only to find that the no-name item breaks down or needs to be replaced twice as frequently as the better-recognized brand. And, of course, purchasing agents have long considered product quality in weighing buying decisions.

What is new here is the level of sophistication that has arisen in considering lifetime costs and the impact of better information systems that allow purchasing departments to capture that information. Sure, even the most myopic purchasing department recognizes that how long something lasts is a key element in its lifetime cost—but it's only one of many factors. Some equipment, for example, incurs higher maintenance and repair costs than others, and this certainly has an impact on the cost of ownership. Anyone who has bought an exotic car is liable to find that a simple service and oil change is an exorbitant extra they may not have bargained on and that each new tire costs a king's ransom. In addition to maintenance and repair, some business equipment may require less operator time or perhaps need less skilled, and hence less costly, operators. This, too, counts in the total cost picture. There are also more subtle, or hidden, elements that affect the total cost equation. Each defective item a manufacturer delivers obviously increases the cost of each usable item—but it can also impact cost in other ways. A defective part, once assembled into the product, can cause the entire product to fail. This either leads to the additional cost of disassembly and replacement or, in some cases, to the scrapping of the entire product. Further, replacing defective parts eats up valuable manufacturing capacity and assets, increasing the time and cost it takes to produce net useable products. Hidden costs like these are found in dozens of other ways: Erratic shipments cause excess safety stock, low-yielding ingredients cause more of the product or related materials to be used, large order-quantity requirements cause additional storage charges, and on and on. Of course, the situation varies across product categories, but in some cases purchasers have found that as little as 25 percent of the total cost of ownership was represented in its first cost, and they rightly concluded that they were focusing too much attention on the tip of the iceberg, and too little on the bulk of cost.

This shift in focus from first cost to total cost is both a blessing and a curse for sellers. On the blessing side, this shift provides increasing ways for sellers to differentiate their offering and to move beyond the confrontational game of negotiating price. It also provides a bit of a barrier to cheap imitation products. The curse is that many sellers are not used to selling from this perspective, and it really is a different type of sale. The more sophisticated and informed that buyers become, the less likely they are to be impressed with unsupported assertions, slick presentations, or unsupported claims of superior quality. They need, and are demanding, more quantifiable evidence of superior value over a product's lifetime, placing enormous pressure on salespeople without strong analytic skills or tools. And sophisticated purchasing presents an even greater challenge to those who still cling to the notion that the buying process is emotional rather than rational and that the most important success factors in selling are personal chemistry and a good relationship.

THE COST OF PURCHASING PROMISCUITY

Purchasers are also challenging the notion that if a little competition among suppliers is good, then more must be better, and lots more must be great. Certainly, there are risks associated with exclusive reliance on a single supplier, not the least of which are potentially excessive prices and substandard products or service. While there are metrics to guard against these risks, it is easy to understand why organizations would not want to put all of their eggs in one basket. Most of us feel a bit safer in negotiations if we have some alternatives, and we generally believe bidding situations will help get us a better deal. The idea of the competitive bid has been mainstream thinking in business purchasing for over a century. Requests for Proposals, or RFPs, inviting suppliers to submit competitive bids, have long been standard operating procedure for most companies acquiring major items or projects. Even in smaller purchases, the RFP process is alive and well. It has the advantage of fairness, it encourages competition, and it keeps vendors honest. Yet the competitive RFP process, that has been so central to purchasing for so long, is now under attack. And, curiously, that attack is coming not from suppliers but from the very purchasing departments who, on the surface at least, would seem to have the most to gain from a system of competitive bidding.

Leading thinkers in the purchasing field are increasingly challenging the conventional notions of competitive bidding, pointing out the hidden, and often excessive costs created by such systems. There's growing evidence to support the argument that the costs of maintaining all of these vendors far exceed any possible savings from the added competition. First of all, there's the cost of qualifying each of these suppliers, which by itself can be considerable. In addition, there is the cost of getting each supplier informed about the buyer's needs, which usually requires access to operations and discussions with others in the company. Of course, purchasing departments can limit this access, or they can try to simply specify all of the requirements up front. But neither of these options is attractive. Specifying every purchasing need is time-consuming and costly. And the more you limit a supplier's understanding of your situation, the less likely it is that the supplier will be able to really meet your needs. On top of that there is simply the enormous time it takes for purchasing agents to meet with and handle all of these suppliers; one large department store chain determined that more than half of its purchasing costs were driven by suppliers who provided less than 20 percent of total purchases. Add it up, and it's a heck of a lot of cost for the organization to take on. Even worse, it increases with each added extra supplier.

There's also cost from the seller's side that no one seems to notice. Those hours of purchasers' time eat up comparable hours of sellers' time, and there are substantial hidden costs in the seller's organization as well. There are technical or operations people who must get involved in the response to the RFP to see which products are most suitable or what customization is possible. There is marketing and senior management time to determine pricing, and on and on. As one executive remarked to us, "These 'beauty contests' take a whole lot of resources from everybody, and you know you're going to wind up paying for that somehow." In some major sales the expense of the bidding process is frightening. When a public company puts its audit out to bid, for example, the competing accounting firms commonly spend well over a million dollars between them in bidding cost for a piece of business that is unlikely to generate a million dollars in profit over its lifetime. In the end nobody wins from this kind of inefficient and costly acquisition process. When all is said and done, it's the customer who pays the final bill, and sophisticated purchasing executives are all too well aware that costly bid cycles are no longer in their interests in a world driven by value.

THE MOVEMENT TOWARD SUPPLIER REDUCTION

Another factor that is pushing purchasers toward a reduction of suppliers is the recognition that in trying to manage hordes of suppliers and focusing so much on squeezing out another nickel of price, many are missing the opportunity for "continuous-improvement" programs that can take dollars of unnecessary cost out of the overall system. Much progress has been made in the operations area over the past decade or so from the recognition that there is always further opportunity to improve a process and that cost reduction is an ongoing rather than a one-time event. To stay competitive, organizations have to develop the mindset of continuous improvement—that tomorrow has to be a bit better than today and that the more you learn about an operation, the more ways you'll find to improve it. So why not bring suppliers into the act? Working closely with selected suppliers opens up a lot more improvement options. What's more, the time that often gets spent in bringing many suppliers up to speed can more effectively be spent working with just a few of them to find ways to continuously improve things. What's more, with few suppliers, there's more commitment from them. This leads to greater familiarity with the customer's business that will likely yield better ideas and a greater willingness by both parties to make investments to facilitate improvements.

This line of reasoning is taking hold at an increasing number of companies who are taking their supplier bases down from yesterday's list that numbered in the thousands to today's that numbers in the hundreds. But this, too, has both good news and bad news for sellers. For the winners there's more business to be had and the clear intention for extended-term agreements and commitments that should help in long-term planning for the business. And with fewer competitors involved, plus a reduction in bidding battles, there is an opportunity to reduce much of the wasted time and effort spent today in preparing for beauty contests. But it's not an altogether rosy picture for sellers. The stakes have been raised considerably—more business if you win, but if you're one of the losers, you lose it all. Equally serious for the losing suppliers, you won't be able to come back in to make up for it by winning the next bidding contest in a few months' time. There may not be a next time. The customer is likely to be working over the long term with the chosen supplier to improve the process. As a result, particularly if the customer is an extrinsic value buyer who looks to the supplier for support and advice outside the product itself, the business will probably not be put out to bid.

It isn't a bed of roses for the winners either. Winning one of the limited or exclusive spots is a ticket to play, not the end of the game. Purchasers fully expect that they will see continuous improvement and cost savings from these selected suppliers and that their cost of managing suppliers will decline. After all, that's the basis for making a reduction of suppliers in the first place. Once a supplier has won such a position, it isn't the time to exhale and relax—it's only the beginning of a long hard road earning the right to retain the business. Further, it isn't a license to steal. One executive related the story to us of a sole-source relationship that blew apart when the purchaser realized they were being taken advantage of. It had all the apparent elements of a continuous-improvement partnership, a representative of the supplier was resident at the purchaser's site. There was a closely integrated relationship in which the supplier became very knowledgeable about the customer's business. However, in testing for market prices, the buyer discovered they were paying more than 30 percent over market. As you might guess, this is no longer a sole-source arrangement. The story underscores an important lesson in the new world of customer value. Winning the battle to be the sole or preferred supplier used to be akin to winning an easy future. Now it's just the first step on an arduous road to find ways to continually create more value and to prove that you should be kept in this privileged relationship.

SEGMENTING SUPPLIERS

While these changes we've talked about have had a dramatic impact on sellers, probably none can compare with the impact that purchasing's use of supplier segmentation is causing. The notion of segmentation will not be news for many readers—marketers have long recognized that different groups have different needs and accordingly should be treated differently. What is new, however, is that purchasers have picked up the concept from marketing and are using it themselves to rethink their purchasing approach across different product categories, often to the seller's disadvantage.

One of the new models being widely adopted, that many companies have found useful in segmenting their suppliers, looks at two fundamental characteristics that practitioners believe should shape purchasers decisions. These are:

1. *Substitutability and/or availability of comparable products.* This dimension assesses how easily the customer could obtain an alternative supply, both in terms of cost and ease of substitution.

2. *Strategic importance of the supplier's product.* This dimension assesses the product's relative importance either strategically or in terms of cost.

The basic underpinnings of the model are that purchasers should be concerned primarily with products that are mission critical or those that represent the largest portion of cost for the company. They should worry less about the products that really don't matter all that much to the ultimate cost or strategic position. Second, the model suggests that purchasers should take a different posture toward those suppliers who have unique capability or product offerings than they would toward suppliers whose products could be easily replaced by alternatives. Putting these two dimensions together results in the four-box matrix, shown in Figure 2-2, revealing buying guidelines that have significant implications for selling strategy.

A purchasing function using this matrix would place products and suppliers along the horizontal dimension according to how unique their capabilities or offerings were. So very standardized products that many suppliers could produce, with little differentiation between them, would fall to the far left. Products or capabilities that no one else could duplicate would fall to the far right. The vertical dimension describes the strategic or cost importance of the product or service, with those that are essential to competitive position, or represent major portions of cost, falling into the upper half. Less important products would fall lower in the matrix. Arraying suppliers' products in this manner defines four different segments

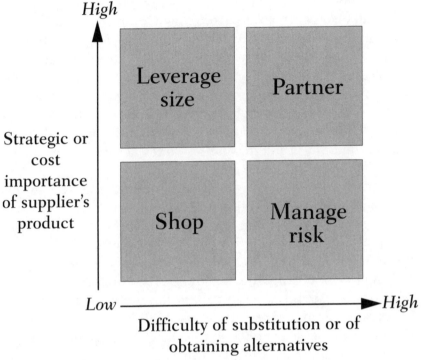

FIGURE 2-2.   Supplier segmentation matrix.

that call for four different ways of dealing with them: shop, leverage, manage risk, or partner.

THE SHOP QUADRANT

The lower left, or shop, quadrant covers items that are readily available, easily substitutable, and neither strategically important nor a large part of the cost structure. Office supplies would normally fall in this quadrant. So would standardized, low-cost parts, basic ingredients, or the thousands of other products that at least several suppliers could offer. Characteristically, products in this quadrant individually don't cost much, even though collectively they probably will add up to a fair bit of money. "Shopping" makes good sense for this category of products. It's worth it to look around for a favorable price, and take the best deal of the moment—but not to waste a whole lot of purchasing time, energy, or money chasing small change. It isn't worth trying to "game the market" for these items, figuring out when to stock up and when to wait on your buy—it's unlikely that anyone's gone out of business because they failed to stock up on office supplies when prices were low. Increasingly, purchasing departments are squeezing suppliers in this quadrant, ending long-established relationships in favor of lower-cost alternatives and substantially cutting the amount of purchasing resources devoted to managing relationships in this category.

Not surprisingly, sellers who have found themselves in this quadrant have not adapted well to the new realities. After years of ongoing business and streams of repeat orders without questioning prices, prime customers have suddenly ceased the automatic reorder cycle and have turned to new, lower-cost suppliers. Fearing they had relied too much in the past on relationship selling, losing sellers have rushed to embrace other sales approaches, often drawn like moths to a flame toward trendy concepts like partnering in a desperate attempt to regain a tight, comfortable selling relationship. Unfortunately, few find much success or comfort in this new path. As we'll discuss in subsequent chapters, partnering has more than its share of land mines and pitfalls, but, beyond that, suppliers in this quadrant will find very few purchasers receptive to the notion of a partnership relationship with them. As Glenn Ramsdell, a consultant specialized in supply chain management noted, "Why would any rational purchaser want to develop a partnership arrangement with a paper clip manufacturer or other vendors with a-dime-a-dozen goods." Why indeed?

Finding themselves trapped in this quadrant is a threatening situation for sellers to be in. Their customers are intrinsic value buyers. All that matters is cheap and easy acquisition of the product. The buyer doesn't want a relationship, doesn't want to invest time and effort in the seller or the product, and is constantly looking for cheaper or more convenient alternatives. It's happening to more and more suppliers every day. Few know how to cope with buyers who will no longer invest the time to see them and who are, frankly, uninterested in their products. Many are searching for new selling strategies that can succeed in this quadrant. Some have found ways to survive, or even prosper, in this brutal shop-it segment. Their success isn't dependent on sales techniques or the latest selling fad. The winners, as we'll see in Chapter 4, have developed innovative sales approaches that have adapted to the new buyer perspectives.

THE LEVERAGE QUADRANT

Products and services that fall in the upper left quadrant have greater importance to purchasers. They are items that represent a major part of the cost structure or are important strategically. But while they are more important, the buyer is still in a strong negotiating position because the items are readily substitutable, with several possible suppliers. Major ingredients would fall in this quadrant. So would major equipment purchases, or high-volume product packaging, say. In some ways the buyer's approach here is not that dissimilar from the shopping quadrant. Price matters. These are also purchases that individually or in aggregate will make a real difference to the bottom line and the long-term success of the business. Consequently, it's worth significant time and attention to get a good deal, or to try to time purchases to take advantage of favorable market conditions. For purchasers, leverage is a good concept to keep in mind for items in this quadrant because here purchasers do have leverage over suppliers competing for their business. Items in this quadrant, while important, are readily substitutable and have at least a few qualified vendors who can meet the purchaser's needs. As a result, purchasers are able to make use of their negotiating position.

This doesn't mean that purchasers should switch back and forth among suppliers. Unlike goods in the shopping quadrant, these items do make a difference to the operation, and there is likely to be additional value possible from longer-term relationships, especially those built around continuous-improvement notions and metrics. But smart purchasers will be increasingly reluctant to give this business away without really being sure that the suppliers getting this business will, in fact, deliver the best-value package now, and in the future. The economics of this quadrant have been a principal driver of the trend toward supplier consolidation. Offering higher volume to fewer suppliers is an easy way for a purchasing department to begin executing a leverage strategy. Often, although not always, buyers in this quadrant will be purchasing transactionally, motivated by the value intrinsic to the product, and will place little importance on the capacity of salespeople—or the supplier organization—to create new value outside of the product.

For sellers, this, too, is a difficult arena to play in. Like those in the shopping quadrant, many who see old established relationships eroding are driven to the same futile attempts at partnership or relationship building. But smart purchasers are unlikely to be swayed. Part of the buyer's advantage in this quadrant is the ability to play suppliers off against each other and to have them compete away some of the surplus they would ordinarily pocket. Few purchasers are going to be interested in deeper relationships with the supplier unless the price is right. Successful suppliers are those who recognize that buyers in this quadrant are likely to be intrinsic value purchasers who will be sharpest in terms of price-value assessments and who will pay the most attention to quantifiable value.

THE MANAGE-RISK QUADRANT

On the right-hand side of the matrix are the manage-risk and partner quadrants. At first blush, both seem more attractive for sellers. It's certainly true that in these quadrants the landscape shifts in the seller's favor and the seller's negotiating position strengthens. However, both of these quadrants are areas where sellers can all too easily get into trouble. In the manage-risk quadrant, purchasers recognize that they have more limited bargaining power, but these items aren't mission critical or they are not that important a part of the cost picture. As a result, they don't warrant a great deal of time and attention, either. Items that might fall here are such things as specialty chemicals or specialized equipment that are not at the heart of the company's production. Because of the limited number of substitutes or suppliers who can provide these items, purchasers are prepared to invest more time and effort in acquiring them. Unlike the shopping quadrant, purchasers are prepared to invest at least some time meeting and talking with potential suppliers. And they may welcome extrinsic sources of value such as advice, customization, and special services that a sales force can provide. For a purchaser, the uniqueness of a product that falls in this quadrant means that they are unlikely to find easy substitutes. But no one wants to be gouged either. Purchasers are likely to be somewhat less price sensitive in this area, at least within limits, but as the manage-risk title suggests, smarter purchasers might time purchases for favorable market conditions or take a quick look at possible substitutes just to be sure they don't overspend unnecessarily.

For sellers this is a more favorable position and clearly more comfortable than previous quadrants. A degree of differentiation, or limited competition, is certainly a position most suppliers would choose if they could. But this quadrant isn't risk free either. Although purchasers are less price sensitive here, they know that with fewer available suppliers, they are more vulnerable and buyers will be nervous about being exploited. Smarter sellers will take a careful look at the relative value they are providing, and make sure that their pricing and service don't get out of line with competitive offerings. This is a favorable position for sellers, allowing consultative selling, and successful players will try to stay on this side of the matrix. They will attempt to maintain the uniqueness of their offering and will try to stay under the "radar screen" so that buyers don't find it worth the effort to actively seek an alternative supplier.

THE PARTNER QUADRANT

This last quadrant is the position most sellers *think* they want to be in. The goods and services in this quadrant are mission critical, that is, they are central to the success of the purchaser for either strategic or cost reasons. What's more, the seller has a unique offering that is not easily substitutable. High-end computer chips would likely fit into this quadrant, as would specialized parts that represent the bulk of a product's cost or perhaps a unique set of financial or information technology products or services. These are items that make a fundamental difference to the purchaser, and, because of the limited number of possible suppliers, buyers will be willing, even eager, to form partnering relationships with relevant suppliers.

Given the trends going on in purchasing, and the cost squeezes and uncertainties these trends are creating for suppliers, it's no wonder that sellers in this position find a partnering proposal from a customer almost irresistible. Many suppliers will leap to enter into some kind of partnering arrangement hoping that it will lead to a safe and easy long-term relationship. Partnership certainly makes sense from the buyer's perspective in this quadrant. Customers actively seek out mission-critical suppliers to entice with promises of partnership. It's hard for a seller to resist—this may be the one time, if at all, that a seller has a serious chance of establishing a partnering relationship with a key customer. However, from the seller's perspective, partnering is not necessarily a good idea. This path, as we'll see, has its own set of difficulties, and is littered with more failures than successes. Strategically, it's not always clear that it is in the seller's best interest to even try this route. From the buyer's perspective, a partnership relationship makes sense—it helps reduce their risk, and may lower their cost—but perhaps at the seller's expense. What could be a very good deal for the buyer sometimes proves to be a rather bad deal for the seller. This is the quadrant of greatest advantage and leverage for the seller, providing a unique opportunity to capture a good bit of market position and profit. In addition to the difficulty of managing a partnering relationship, such a sales approach often limits flexibility in dealing with other customers and may simply represent an unnecessary yet costly transfer of value from the seller to the buyer. Sellers should tread carefully, even in this most advantaged of situations, to ensure that they are capturing a fair enough share of the value for themselves. They should certainly be wary of rushing headlong toward a partnering arrangement that is clearly in the customer's interest but, once entered into, may limit their options and restrict their opportunities to capture value.

Strategic value buyers, who look for an extraordinary level of new value creation from their relationships with a few chosen suppliers, will certainly be placing their potential partners into this quadrant. In Chapter 6, we'll look closely at the enterprise sale, where every asset and competence of the supplier is potentially leveraged to achieve a customer's strategic goals. These enterprise sales fall into the partnering quadrant. They are potentially the most rewarding and the most dangerous of supplier-customer relationships. They offer the most opportunity to create customer value, yet they are by far the most costly to set up and maintain—and the most devastating when they go wrong.

WHAT DOES THE NEW SELLING LOOK LIKE?

As we've seen in this chapter, customers are changing. And these changes are deep and fundamental. They affect every level of purchasing from the individual consumer faced with more acquisition options to the giant corporation segmenting its suppliers. The common thread throughout these changes is a new awareness of value. Customers, at every level, have changed and, as a result, selling can never be the same again. The increasing sophistication of customers in their search for value poses significant threats to sellers trying to use traditional selling strategies to compete in the new value-driven marketplace. All around us is evidence that traditional thinking about selling is simply not cutting it. But what does the new selling look like? How are successful organizations redesigning their sales forces to compete successfully in these new value driven marketplaces? In subsequent chapters we'll explore some of the emerging approaches to selling strategy that may prove essential to success in this new buyer's world.

RESPONDING TO THE NEW BUYING REALITY

THE THREE EMERGING SELLING MODES

The old saying that "selling is selling" reflects a broadly accepted notion that there is a set of sales basics that applies, more or less, to all selling situations. The believers in conventional sales wisdom will tell you that there are fundamental characteristics that define successful salespeople. Excellent sales forces, they say, consist of smart, aggressive, outgoing personalities, with strong self-confidence, who can smoothly develop needs, present product benefits, and who have good customer-handling skills. And the same conventional wisdom is equally clear about the symptoms of poor sales forces—salespeople who are just order takers, who don't know how to sell benefits, or who don't know the product well enough to sell against competitors. Corporations spend millions trying to build generalized selection profiles of the "ideal" salesperson on the assumption that there are a successful set of competencies, personality dimensions, and skills that span the entire spectrum of selling situations. But how well does this one-size-fits-all view of selling hold up in a world driven by customer value? Is there a single set of strategies and skills that can handle the diverse value requirements of customers who, as we've seen, are becoming ever more focused in the kind of value that they demand?

The evidence suggests that the one-size-fits-all view of selling has been outdated for some time, and, in the new era of customer value, it has become hopelessly obsolete. Repeatedly, objective studies of successful salespeople, such as the pioneering Huthwaite studies reported in *SPIN® Selling* [McGraw-Hill, 1988] and *Major Account Sales Strategy* [McGraw-Hill, 1989] show that different types of sales require very different—and sometimes even contradictory—skills and strategies for success. But the selling-is-selling notion is deeply ingrained. Just ask most executives to describe the characteristics of a successful salesperson. They won't look at you quizzically and tell you that they can't answer that question without understanding the sales situation or the customer type. Instead, they will cheerfully give you a list of success characteristics that runs roughly along the lines of the conventional wisdom and reverts unconsciously to an outdated view of the world. On a more sophisticated level, talk to those who are earnestly trying to improve sales force performance, and you are likely to find a relentless search for benchmarks, for the one best-practice model that will solve their sales problems. Unfortunately, these searches are proving to be increasingly frustrating and futile. We're entering an era where no single model will suffice. We are going to need a number of very different selling models to deal with the broad range of buying behavior we met in the previous chapter.

CREATING VALUE ACROSS THE BUYING PROCESS

The only single "truth" that seems to be holding for all sales forces is that they will have to create value for customers if they are to be successful. Just communicating the value inherent in their products and services isn't enough. All sales forces that hope to prosper, or even survive, in the new world must create real value for customers to justify their existence. But, as we've seen, there are different ways for sales to create value and, depending on the value orientation of the customer, some of these ways will be much more effective than others. A strategic value customer in an enterprise relationship, for example, is likely to demand an extraordinary level of cross-functional value creation from a supplier, and the role of sales will be just one component of a very complex value creation process. Customers buying transactionally may view salespeople as an unnecessary cost and will often see sales calls as value drains that take up time, add to the price, and provide little or nothing useful in return. These customers will perceive value only in those salespeople who can make acquisition as cheap, efficient, and trouble free as possible. In contrast, the extrinsic value customer who wants advice, help, and problem-solving capability from salespeople may very well see salespeople as far more valuable than the products they represent. In short, different customers demand different approaches to value creation. The key to success will be figuring out which selling approach will best fit the customer and then creating the most value. One starting point for thinking about the different ways that sales forces can create value for customers is to look at the different points in the buying process where a sales force can potentially add value.

Figure 3-1 shows a typical buying process [or sequence of acquisition steps] that purchasers go through in both business-to-business and large consumer acquisitions.

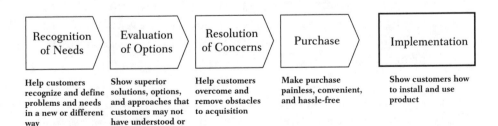

FIGURE 3-1. Adding value to a typical buying process.

- *Recognition of Needs.*   Acquisition starts with the customer's recognition that something is imperfect, incomplete, or missing. Completely satisfied customers, by definition, don't need anything, so there's no reason for
  acquisition. Needs arise when customers no longer feel satisfied with the existing situation and become receptive to
  the idea of change or purchase. Salespeople can add value
  to this stage of the buying process if they can help customers see that they have problems that should be solved.
  For customers, the issue in this step of the buying process
  is deciding whether they have a problem big enough to justify the effort and cost of a solution. By helping define
  problems, or by assisting customers in understanding the
  severity or consequences of problems, salespeople can create real value.

- *Evaluation of Options.*   Once customers have decided that
  they have a need that requires action, the issue is not
  whether to purchase but *how* to purchase. Customers must
  choose from competing solutions. Sometimes this choice
  will be between competitors—does product A meet the need
  better than product B? Sometimes the choice is between
  alternative solutions provided by one supplier—is the super-
  deluxe version a better value than the standard product?
  Salespeople can add value to this stage of the buying
  process if they can help customers make better choices.
  They can create value here in a number of ways. They
  might, for example, show customers new and better options
  that they hadn't previously considered. They might customize the product or service so that it more closely fits the
  customer's decision criteria. They might help the customer
  in the choice process itself by introducing new criteria into
  the decision that will let the customer make a more
  informed choice.

- *Resolution of Concerns.*   In simple sales, it's usually the
  case that once a customer has decided to buy and has chosen from the competing options, the decision to purchase
  automatically follows. In more complex sales that's rarely

the case. The customer is likely to have issues and concerns that must be resolved before moving ahead. "How do we know the system will perform the way you claim?" "What if my boss doesn't approve?" "We've worked with your competitor for several years, and we'll have to find a way to break that relationship before we can bring you in." Issues like these frequently delay or derail major acquisition decisions. Salespeople can add value to this stage of the buying process if they can counsel customers and help them problem solve their way around these obstacles to acquisition.

- *Purchase.*   Once any remaining obstacles and concerns have been overcome, the customer is ready to move ahead with the acquisition. Salespeople can add value to this stage by ensuring that the purchase is painless. In many cases salespeople can create value by simplifying the process for customers, saving them administrative hassle, personnel, and other cost. Salespeople often play a valuable—and value-creating—role as "customer advocate," negotiating within their own organizations to get emergency shipments expedited or securing supply of in times of shortages. Part of the value may simply be a sense of security for the customers—the notion that they can trust the sales individual to make things happen or to solve any order-fulfillment or distribution issues that might arise. In addition, selling organizations sometimes add value by developing innovative payment options for customers that do a better job of meeting their financing needs.

- *Implementation.*   With many products and with most services, the customer has to implement the purchased item. Salespeople can create significant value here by showing customers the most effective way to use the product or by providing training, implementation advice, and support.

Of course, there are lots of variations to this simple buying process, such as different cycle lengths, different rigor and approaches to identifying possible suppliers, and different degrees of formality in the evaluation procedures. But, whatever specific form the buying model takes, the idea of breaking the buying process down into stages is a useful one because, as we shall see, it helps to pinpoint where sales forces can create value.

THE THREE EMERGING SELLING MODES

Although there may be a theoretical ability to add value across the whole buying process, in practice value exists only to the extent that the customer perceives and wants it. So, for example, while it's possible to add considerable value in the recognition of needs stage by helping customers understand their problems and issues, some customers will be perfectly clear about their problems with no help from outside suppliers. For these customers there is no new value to create in this stage. For others, in contrast, a fresh insight into their problems might be the most useful and important value contribution in the whole buying process. The same is true at the evaluation of options stage. The experience of one of our friends provides a typical example. He is a certified public accountant and a financial planner. Recently he purchased a new home and began the search for his best mortgage option. One lender he contacted said they couldn't give him information over the phone but they did have several innovative products that could be shaped to meet his needs and that he should come in personally so that they could understand his financial situation. With mixed feelings, he scheduled an appointment, and he spent an hour at this institution, sharing his financial statements and other information about the purchase. It was a pretty painful hour for all parties. He didn't learn anything new or gain any new insights about his needs or choices—if anything, he was educating the two reps he met with. The "innovative" products they talked about weren't at all applicable to his situation, and their products that did fit had rates that were among the highest in the market. There was no value created in this selling process; in fact, value was destroyed by wasting our friend's time as well as that of the two financial institution sales reps that met with him. In contrast, the mortgage company that got the business posted their rates on the Internet, conducted the sale conveniently and efficiently, almost entirely by computer, fax, and phone, making the entire process easy. These two selling approaches illustrate two different selling modes. The first financial institution tried consultative selling, which could have been very effective with a less-experienced purchaser who would value advice and be prepared to pay a premium for financial counseling. The second institution used transactional selling. While this worked well with a CPA who just wanted an easy transaction with good rates, this transactional approach might not have created value for someone new to the mortgage field who was seeking consultative help.

Transactional and consultative selling, as in this example, have very different value propositions. There is also a third type of sale applicable primarily in certain large business-to-business sales and which we have called *enterprise selling,* where extraordinary value is created through complex redesign of the total relationship between supplier and customer. None of these selling approaches is inherently "better" than the others—but each is most effective in a specific set of sales conditions. We briefly introduced these ideas in the opening chapter, and, later in the book, we'll devote a whole chapter to each type of selling. Let's now further explore each of these selling modes and begin to develop an understanding of when to use each one.

TRANSACTIONAL SALES

In a transactional sale, purchasers already have a full understanding of their needs and also know a lot about the products or services they intend to purchase. They are intrinsic value buyers—in other words, they look for value in the product itself. Customers may purchase transactionally because they are very sophisticated buyers who have a clear understanding of their needs and of the product they intend to acquire—like our friend, the financial planner shopping for a mortgage. Or transactional purchasing may be the result of a fairly simple and very well understood product category. Commodities, or standardized products, for example, generally fit this kind of sale. There is little real difference between offerings, and even a relatively uninformed and unsophisticated buyer understands the product and how it can be used. In situations like these, there is very little opportunity for sellers to create value by developing customer needs or expounding on product features. In a true transactional sale, buyers already know the fit between their needs and the available product options. Customers can find value from new insight into their problems, or new information about products, but that very rarely happens in the transactional sale. Salespeople are more likely to tell customers what they already know. So, in transactional sales, buyers are not looking for information or advice from salespeople. Their concerns revolve much more around the acquisition stage—around getting what they want at a good price with as little hassle as possible. As Figure 3-2 shows, there is little or no opportunity for the seller to add value during the recognition of needs or the evaluation of options stage of the acquisition process.

There are usually a number of potential suppliers in a transactional sale, and this, coupled with well-informed buyers, makes this type of sale highly competitive, somewhat confrontational, and very cost-price sensitive. Successful sellers in

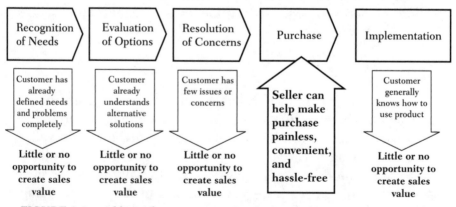

FIGURE 3-2. Adding value to a transactional sale.

transactional situations will focus on facilitating the purchase, streamlining the process to eliminate any unnecessary costs, and providing a good deal to an informed, savvy buyer. Success is difficult in the transactional sale and many companies are struggling to stay afloat as customers press them ever harder and margins decline. As we saw in the last chapter, business customers are increasingly likely to be segmenting transactional suppliers into categories where they will strategically leverage and pressure for better and better deals. Many suppliers have worked to add value to their products and services so that they can escape from the tyranny of the transactional sale. Few, alas, have succeeded. Their added value efforts have either been cosmetic or quickly commoditized by their competitors. A few have discovered innovative ways to prosper in a transactional environment. The next chapter will deal with examples of different strategies that are being employed in this very difficult selling mode.

CONSULTATIVE SALES

Consultative selling situations are fundamentally different from transactional sales in several important respects. In consultative sales, buyers don't enter the buying process knowing enough to make a sound buying decision—either because they have an incomplete understanding of the product or because they may not have fully defined their problems, needs, and issues. The selling organization can create value by raising awareness of some of these hidden factors, adding insight to customer problems, and developing unique, innovative solutions. Some situations are innately consultative because the product or service choices are sufficiently complex or different from one another so that customers require a fair amount of information in understanding these differences, and interpreting what the differences can mean to them. Complex financial products would be one example, specialized production equipment another. Other situations are consultative because the offerings change very quickly and customers need help and information to stay current. Many high-tech offerings would fall into this category. Sometimes sales are consultative because of buyer qualifications. A buyer who is unfamiliar with the product category—either a first-time buyer or someone who makes this kind of purchase infrequently—would benefit from consultative selling approaches. For example, most home buyers would see a consultative approach for making their mortgage decisions as creating a great deal of value, but some sophisticated buyers would view the consultative element as a waste of time.

While a successful transactional sale requires focusing mostly around the transaction, research studies of consultative sales shows that successful consultative salespeople focus most of their attention on the early stages of the acquisition cycle, in particular, the recognition of needs stage. This is the point where sellers can create the most value by helping customers gain new insight into their problems and discover new solutions that will give superior value. However, as Figure 3-3 shows, consultative selling can also add value at other points of the cycle. An effective salesperson will help the buyer to resolve concerns and find ways around obstacles. In the implementation stage, effective sellers will help customers through installation and will accelerate the learning curve by training customers and helping them get up to speed with the new product or service.

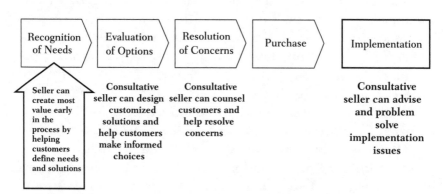

FIGURE 3-3.   Adding value to a consultative sale.

ENTERPRISE SALES

The third sales mode, the enterprise sale, is primarily appropriate for very large and strategic business-to-business sales, and even then, in only a limited set of circumstances. In contrast to transactional and consultative sales, which basically seek to leverage the product or service offerings, in enterprise sales, product and service offerings may be of secondary or incidental importance. In enterprise relationships, it's the total assets and capabilities of the seller's enterprise that are being leveraged.

Enterprise selling requires that the strategic interests of customer and supplier are aligned and that there is opportunity for significant value creation across a number of functions. My R&D capability may be able to help solve some of your toughest product development problems. Joint investments in manufacturing equipment may create mutually beneficial operating capability, or integrating our inventory management approaches might create value by saving costs for both of us. The key to successful enterprise relationships, as we'll see in Chapter 6, is that value creation potential is built by leveraging all of the supplier's assets and resources. By definition, then, these sales require the leveraging of cross-functional capabilities. Because of this, it's often "function-to-function" interactions (for example, R&D group from one company working directly with the R&D group of the other company) rather than the selling to decision makers and influencers that characterizes transactional or consultative sales. There is also the possibility of going even further than one's own assets—the more innovative companies will look for ways to leverage the assets of unrelated third parties. These "web" types of arrangements recognize that there may be other players with unique capability to create value for a customer, and initiating or facilitating arrangements to bring that third-party value to bear on a customer's problems is another way that the enterprise seller can help create value.

The customer process for initiating an enterprise sale is very different from transactional or consultative acquisition.

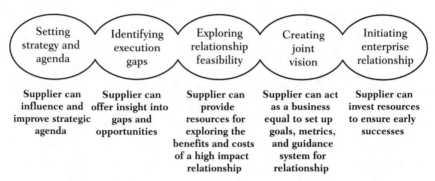

FIGURE 3-4.   Adding value to an enterprise sale.

As Figure 3-4 shows, the acquisition process starts at a high strategic level and progresses through a series of exploratory steps where the two parties act not as supplier and customer but as business equals. As the discussions progress, both parties invest resources in creating a shared vision and an action plan for achieving an extraordinary level of value creation. These enterprise relationships must be very selective. There are a very limited number of situations in which they make sense. First of all, there must be the opportunity for substantial mutual benefit and mutual alignment of strategic interest to make the relationship even feasible. It would be foolish for a supplier to offer full use of their assets to anyone and everyone, a path that would inevitably lead quickly to financial ruin. The high cost and risk involved means that enterprise selling is clearly going to be offered only to those customers who are extremely important. The same is true on the buyer's side. Customers should be interested in this type of selling arrangement only if a supplier is also extremely important to them. Being able to create value here will require close understanding of each other's strategies, at a depth that should be shared only with someone who is an important player and who can bring great benefit. This type of sale also requires common perspective and values of the senior management of both companies. Creating value at the cross-functional boundaries implies change in both companies and also requires multiple cross-functional linkages. Enterprise sales are difficult enough to establish and maintain with fully committed management teams—the odds of succeeding by simply working in each functional area independently are close to zero.

VALUE CREATION OPPORTUNITY

Each type of sale, whether transactional, consultative, or enterprise, has potential to create customer value. But, as we've seen, the value levers are different for each class of sale. Figure 3-5 summarizes the value creation opportunities for each type.

SALES VALUE LEVERS	TRANSACTIONAL SALES	CONSULTATIVE SALES	ENTERPRISE SALES
Deliver "new news" about product or application.	—	*	✓
Provide insight into customer problems, issues, and needs.	—	*	*
Act as customer advocate, advisor, and customizer.	—	*	✓
Facilitate acquisition transaction.	*	✓	—
Lower acquisition costs.	*	—	—
Help customer reduce or hedge acquisition risk.	*	—	—
Leverage cross-functional capability.	—	✓	*
Create solutions for customers leveraging full assets of company.	—	✓	*
Creatively leverage the assets of third parties.	✓	✓	*

* = high value creation opportunity.
✓ = moderate value creation opportunity.

FIGURE 3-5.   Value creation opportunities in each type of sale.

As Figure 3-5 shows, a value lever can be effective for more than one type of selling. So, for example, consultative salespeople can add enormous value by acting as the customers' advocates inside their own organizations to ensure that customer orders are expedited and their special needs are met. In the enterprise sale, the salesperson can also act as the customer's advocate but, because there may be a hundred or more other people from the supplier organization working on a daily basis inside the customer's organization, the value-added contribution of a single salesperson—or even a sales team—is inevitably limited. Figure 3-6 shows a comparison of some of the success factors for each type of selling.

A closer look at some of these factors shows how different the three types of selling are in terms of customer issues and selling strategy. For example:

- *Getting in the Door.*   A prerequisite for success in the traditional transactional sale has always been access to the decision maker. Generations of salespeople have been taught how to "get around the screen" and obtain the all-important face-to-face meeting with the person who makes the decision. Other customer staff involved in the decision have been seen as an inconvenience and an impediment to be avoided. Sales managers still ask their people, "Why talk to the monkey when you can talk to the organ grinder?" Judging by the fact that organ grinders with begging monkeys seem to have become largely extinct toward the end of the nineteenth century, it's fair to assume that this advice has been around for some time. In the transactional sale, with limited resources and with customers who know what they want, it's probably still sound counsel—access to the decision maker is a prerequisite for success. In the consultative sale, however, access to the decision maker can be a snare and a delusion. More important is access to the people who have the deepest and most thorough understanding of the problems that the product or service can solve. Decision makers are frequently remote from day-to-day difficulties, and, for consultative salespeople to create value,

	Transactional	Consultative	Enterprise
Product or service characteristics	• Well understood • Readily substitutable • Standard items	• Differentiated • Customizable • Hidden capabilities	• High strategic and/or cost importance • Limited substitutability
Key buyer concerns and decision criteria	• Price • Availability risk • Ease of acquisition	• Importance of problem • Solution fit • Price-performance tradeoffs	• Platform fit • Values fit • Sustainability • Sufficient value for effort
Time horizon	• Event	• Purchasing stream	• Strategic plan
Nature of relationship	• Cost-based • Buyer-seller • Confrontational	• Benefits-based • Client-adviser • Cooperative	• Trust-based • Business equals • Insider • Both parties change fundamentally
Prerequisites for success	• Access to decision maker	• Access to influencers	• Access to strategy
Nature of sale	• Doing the deal	• Problem solving	• Agenda setting • Boundaries blur—unclear who is selling and who is buying

FIGURE 3-6. Comparison of sales models.

they must work through decision influencers and specialists who have the best understanding of the issues. Getting in the door means getting access to the customer's problems. The prerequisite for the enterprise sale isn't the immediate problem; it's the underlying strategy. Without access to customer strategy on a fairly deep level, the enterprise relationship is unlikely to add the very high level of value required to justify its high cost.

- *Nature of the Relationship.* In the transactional sale the relationship is characteristically between a buyer and a seller who sit on opposite sides of the table negotiating about prices and terms. The buyer, generally, has the power—and uses it. In the consultative sale, the relationship is between a client and an advisor who both sit on the client's side of the table. It's not quite a relationship between equals, but it's rarely as confrontational as the transactional sale. In the enterprise sale the relationship *is* between business equals at all levels of the two organizations. Top executives from both companies meet to share and discuss strategic issues. Customer functions works with supplier functions. Specialists work with specialists. Watch a mixed meeting of people from both organizations, and it's hard to tell who is supplier and who is customer. In the enterprise relationship the supplier has truly become an "insider" who is an integral part of the customer's business.

- *Key Buyer Concerns.* Transactional buyers tend to be concerned with factors intrinsic to the product or service, such as price, terms, and ease of acquisition. Consultative buyers, on the other hand, look for value outside of the product or service. Their key issues focus on the severity of the problem to be solved and the relative benefits of alternative solutions. The enterprise buyer, as we'll see in Chapter 6, has much more strategic concerns. Do the values of the two organizations fit? Does the potential partner provide a powerful enough underlying platform of capability? Can the relationship sustain itself in its quest to generate an extraordinary level of value?

In the next three chapters we'll look more closely at the differences between each selling mode, and we'll see how successful sales forces are using each type of selling to create value for their customers and competitive advantage for themselves.

WHAT ABOUT RELATIONSHIP SELLING?

Whenever we discuss these three emerging selling models, someone will invariably ask about the role of personal relationships in selling. What is the value of relationships with buyers? Aren't they important in every type of sale? Of course they are—very important. Several years ago, a group of European sales and marketing executives were discussing sales issues and a Scandinavian sales VP remarked, "You know, I personally have never bought anything from someone I didn't like." There were nods of agreement from the others and a general consensus that his experience seemed to hold for all of them. Then another executive raised an interesting question: "Yes, but has anyone bought goods that were clearly inferior, or a bad deal, simply because you liked the salesperson?" In the lively discussion that followed, a key insight into the value of relationships emerged—the idea of the "zone of indifference" shown in Figure 3-7. Of course relationships are important—and if your offer is roughly equivalent to competitors—in the "zone of indifference"—then the sale will likely go to the salesperson the buyer likes best. But, if there is a big difference between offerings, then although buyers may wish their favorite salesperson had a better offer, they will nevertheless give the sale to the competitor with the superior offering.

	ZONE OF INDIFFERENCE	
Inferior price/ performance	Price/ performance parity	Superior price/ performance

FIGURE 3-7.   The zone of indifference.

The nature of relationships, as well as their relative importance, varies a great deal among transactional, consultative, and enterprise sales. In the transactional sale, where product or service offerings have little real difference and competitiveness normally drives prices into a narrow range, there are usually several alternative competitors within the "indifference zone" and a salesperson's relationship alone can make the difference. And, given the nature of the sale, personality, social interaction, and helpfulness in making things happen can be the basis of the relationship.

In the consultative sale, however, the impact of relationships on the sale becomes more complex. Here products and services are different—or differentiable—and there's opportunity to create substantial value by helping the buyer recognize hidden opportunities. If the alternative offerings are in the zone of indifference in terms of the value they provide, then the salesperson's relationship can swing the balance here as well. But first you have to get to this indifference zone. In the consultative sale, just being likable isn't going to cut it—the sale depends on the ability to uncover hidden needs, or the ability to create custom solutions. A good personal relationship may open the door, but, once inside that door, it's the value-creating business relationship that makes the sale. Without the competence to create new business value, the social interaction aspects of a relationship will have little or no impact.

In the enterprise sale, things become even more complex. Again, relationships are important, but they can't be just salespeople's relationships; they need to be enterprise-wide. These sales are cross functional in nature, and the relationships between functional counterparts have enormous importance—whether it's R&D to R&D group, shipping to receiving, or billing to payments. Because much of the value creation happens between supplier and customer functions, it's here that sound working relationships must be in place. Like the consultative sale, these relationships have more to do with professional competence than with personal pleasantry. They rest on the ability of each of these functional relationships to identify hidden needs and solve new problems at the interface between buying and selling organizations. The enterprise sale also needs sound relationships at senior management levels— the place where the functional groups report. It is impossible to create a successful enterprise sale between two organizations unless the senior management at both companies are fully on board. And that type of commitment is going to happen only where senior executives trust each other, recognize common values, and have mutual interests.

THE CHANGING MEANING OF *TRUST*

Trust is an essential ingredient in every sale, from routine transactional selling all the way to deep enterprise relationships. But the meaning of *trust* changes with the type of sale. Some aspects of trust seem to be common to all sales. For example, research has long shown that customers are more likely to trust sellers when:

- *They Interact Frequently,* and salespeople who meet buyers more often are rated by their customers as more trustworthy than those salespeople who have less frequent contact.
- *They Show Consistency,* in that the salesperson's behavior is predictable and not subject to swings or other inconsistencies. This includes, at the macrolevel, a consistent customer relationship strategy without "hot and cold" elements and, at the microlevel, consistency between verbal and nonverbal behavior.

However, as Figure 3-8 shows, *trust* means something very different in each of the three selling modes.

- *Trust in Transactional Sales* primarily means trust in the product and its ability to perform. Trust in the salesperson is somewhat less important. If the product has price performance superiority, transactional buyers will frequently say, "I think the salesperson is sleazy, but I buy because it's the product I'm acquiring, not the salesperson." At the other

	TRANSACTIONAL SALES	CONSULTATIVE SALES	ENTERPRISE SALES
Trust what?	Trust the product	Trust the person	Trust the institution
To do what?	To provide me with reliable, effort-less, and cheap supply	To understand and solve my problems	To share my business future
Based on?	Product performance and personal relationship	Individual expertise, track record, and problem-solving ability	Institutional values and core competencies

FIGURE 3-8. What *trust* means.

end of the spectrum, transactional buyers will choose not to buy from a salesperson they do trust if the seller's product is more expensive or performs less well. However, where there's product parity, in the zone of indifference, then frequency and consistency of interaction may establish a level of trust that makes a winning difference.

- *Trust in Consultative Sales* shifts from the product to the people who sell and deliver it. "I trust this supplier" means that I can have confidence that the supplier's people have the expertise and ability to understand and solve my problems. Unlike the transactional sale, consultative customers don't easily separate the product from the person selling it. So mistrust of the seller usually translates into mistrust of the total offering.

- *Trust in Enterprise Sales* means that the customer trusts the institution. This is a wider definition of trust than simple confidence in the salesperson. At an enterprise level the customer must trust the whole supplier organization, its people, and its competencies. The customer is comfortable with the values of the supplier and feels confident in sharing strategy and putting key elements of the customer's business future into the supplier's hands.

WHICH SELLING MODEL IS BEST?

There are significant differences among each of the three selling models (transactional, consultative, and enterprise), but they can't be thought of as a hierarchy—consultative selling is indeed different from transactional selling, but it is not inherently a better or preferable selling model. One of the most frequent strategic mistakes made by sales forces is the attempt to "move up" from transactional selling to consultative, or from consultative to enterprise. It's a natural enough mistake. After all, everyone wants to create customer value, and consultative selling creates more value than transactional selling, while enterprise selling creates the most value of all. Moving up the value ladder seems a smart strategy.

It is a common, and even understandable, mistake but one that can lead to value destruction. In a transactional sales situation, there is inevitably a great deal of price pressure, and, naturally, many sales forces grasp at consultative selling as a way to avoid having to cut prices to compete. Unfortunately, this is often a double whammy, as moving to consultative selling will unquestionably add cost but may add no benefit and hence destroy value. If there is no "new news" to give to the buyer and no capacity to solve new problems, a consultative approach will produce no benefit and will actually hurt your competitive position. You'd be much better off to face up to the transactional sales situation and begin to adopt strategies that can help you survive—even thrive—in a transactional mode. Instead of trying to find ways to add benefits, you might find ways to adapt to the price sensitivity by stripping costs—using lower-cost channels and selling models. You might even focus on profiting from the transaction itself. These strategies, which will be discussed further in the next chapter, will provide much better odds of success than the strategy of trying to pretend that consultative efforts will help a transactional buyer.

The problem is even more severe when companies try to move into the enterprise sale. Again, it's an understandable temptation. Enterprise sales, often under the name of "partnering" or "strategic alliances," seem like dream arrangements for a seller. They lock in a key customer, move away from the constant day-to-day price haggling, and can open up enormous new opportunities. There is no question, if the situation is right, that there is something extraordinarily compelling about the enterprise sale. But when the prerequisites aren't met or when they are handled in the wrong way, that "dream customer" becomes the seller's worst nightmare. Most of the time, sellers have unrealistic expectations of an enterprise relationship, sometimes assuming that it removes the necessity to continually create value for the customer. In fact, this relationship simply opens up new opportunities and different ways to create value. "Careful what you wish for" is a saying well worth keeping in mind as you assess whether you should enter an enterprise relationship—"wishes come true, not free." The enterprise relationship is a ticket to play, not an excuse for failure to perform, and in fact it will raise performance expectations considerably.

Recently, a partner at a professional services firm talked about his own experiences with a long-standing enterprise relationship that had gone awry. After many years of a solid relationship, he and the customer had "stepped up the game"—greatly expanding the range of services and level of involvement with the customer. There was a trust-based understanding, and most of the new services were agreed to without competitive bids or even competitive discussions. From the service provider's perspective, things were, as the partner put it, "going great." They had more business than ever from the customer, they had developed many more relationships with the new divisions they were serving, and the absence of competitive bids had taken off much of the pressure. Yes, things seemed to be "going great" from the supplier's perspective, until a couple of years had gone by and the customer sat down to discuss their belief that they weren't being served well—that all they'd seen from this expanded relationship was bigger bills. Where were the new ideas and insights that were supposed to come from working across all of the divisions? Where was the value from these enterprise-wide capabilities? Where were the new international opportunities that might be identified? And, with the expanded business, were the best people still being assigned? The work was no better than it had been from the prior supplier. Worst of all—the customer still believed that there would be value in an expanded partnerlike relationship, but they began to think they had chosen the wrong partner.

A nightmare indeed. Here was the case of a corporate customer whose executives had been reasonably happy in a consultative situation. But now that they had been wooed into an enterprise relationship, they expected results of a different order. They expected to see real value from the higher level of involvement, and it was the raised expectations that were now the source of great dissatisfaction. And it wasn't at all clear that these expectations could be met, or met profitably. Quite frankly, the supplier often wishes that the relationship had never left the consultative mode, but it's now difficult or impossible to go back. The lesson is clear—choose carefully before you leap, and be sure you understand the differences and requirements of each of the selling models.

MATCHING SELLING MODE TO CUSTOMER TYPE

Each of the three selling modes creates greatest value when used to sell to the corresponding customer type. So, for example, consultative selling creates most value for extrinsic value customers, and transactional selling for intrinsic value customers. But that doesn't mean that each mode of selling can be used only with its corresponding customer type. Figure 3-9 shows diagrammatically the return on sales investment for each type of sale.

- *Transactional Selling* brings the best return with intrinsic value customers who buy on the basis of product and ease of acquisition. Successful transactional selling strategy is about ruthlessly creating an efficient selling effort. This

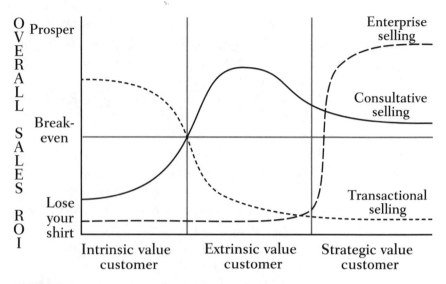

FIGURE 3-9.   Return on selling investment by customer type.

makes it a good match for intrinsic value customers who see all the value in the product and little or no value in the sales effort. However, it's a less good strategy for extrinsic value customers who are likely to want knowledgeable salespeople who will invest time playing a more advisory role. Consequently, adopting a transactional selling mode with extrinsic customers is likely to fail—and will certainly fail with strategic customers.

- *Consultative Selling* brings the best return on selling effort from extrinsic value customers who need the advice, insight, and help that consultative salespeople provide. Consultative salespeople can still make sales to transactional buyers but usually at a higher cost which, because it is ultimately reflected in the product price, gives the product a less attractive value proposition. Similarly, consultative salespeople can successfully make sales to strategic value customers, but, because they can't leverage enterprise resources, they are not an ideal match for the high value demands of the strategic customer.

- *Enterprise Selling* requires special and extensive organizational commitment, making it an inappropriate selling mode except with very large strategic value customers. As Figure 3-9 shows, adopting the costly infrastructure of an enterprise sale is a sure way to lose your shirt with intrinsic or extrinsic value customers.

INVESTMENT IN VALUE CREATION

One of the most important differences between each of the selling models is the level and nature of investment required to create customer value. Transactional sales, in general, require the lowest level of ongoing investment, and the investments should be aimed primarily at lowering cost, or facilitating acquisition. The commoditylike nature of these sales, with a number of alternative suppliers, savvy buyers, and heavy emphasis on price, really limits margin potential. Value creation in the transactional sale is driven by reducing cost to serve, rather than by adding new benefits. Technology investments can play a big role in the transactional sale, but that role is generally one of improving efficiencies. So effective use of technology automates tasks to reduce cost and people requirements, eases acquisition, or shifts tasks to lower-cost resources. As we'll see in the next chapter, successful transactional players will limit salespeople's time investments and, further, seek to use the lowest-cost sales resources that can do the job.

Consultative sales, however, require and can afford a higher level of investment because value is created primarily by increasing customer benefits rather than by reducing the cost to serve. Companies in consultative selling situations need to invest in developing a rich understanding of the customer's needs and problems because this allows them to develop higher value-creating solutions for these customers. The ability to create differentiated solutions and, in the process, to deliver more real benefits to customers provides the opportunity for higher margins. In turn, better margins allow the supplier to afford the cost of investing higher levels of resources.

Technology's role in the consultative sale is also different from the transactional sale. Its focus needs to be much less concerned with the efficiency of the sale and more concerned with supporting effectiveness and helping customers understand their needs or how product offerings can be shaped to better meet them. For example, Bombardier, which sells aircraft to corporations and individuals, has CD-ROM-based computer programs that let buyers configure their aircraft and perform a virtual walk through the plane to get a better understanding of their choices. The program also calculates operating costs and performance across different city pairs and/or routes to further aid customers in evaluating alternatives. In other sales, computer modeling is used to simulate a customer's economics and help them gain insight into the financial implications of their purchase.

In the enterprise sale, the investment level is the greatest. By definition, the enterprise sale is all about leveraging the full assets of the company to create value, and the investments go well beyond the sales force. People resources get fairly intensive as different cross-functional teams are formed, and relationships spread to include multiple locations or divisions. This is true even at senior levels, and one of the often-overlooked investments is the senior management time from both parties that is essential to make these types of relationships work. Physical assets may also be involved—in an enterprise relationship, it is common to fund joint ventures—manufacturing facilities, warehouses, and so on, that benefit both parties. Further, considerable IT investments are often required to more effectively and efficiently link the information systems of these strategically aligned companies.

MATCHING SELLING STRATEGIES TO BUYING STRATEGIES

As we discussed in the last chapter, an increasing number of buyers are adopting different strategies for different categories of goods, for example, shopping around for relatively standard-ized goods while seeking long-term commitments and partner-ing arrangements for unique and strategically important goods. Much of this new purchasing thinking is being formal-ized with *strategic buying programs*—that is, structured processes that categorize each purchase and set up acquisition rules based on category placement. In other cases, the process is not as formal, but, instinctively, buyers are moving to this type of supplier segmentation.

Successful sellers have begun to reply to this new buyer behavior by adapting their selling strategy to respond to the new buying strategies. Figure 3-10 shows one of the buying models we discussed in the previous chapter that divided purchases along two dimensions—the availability of substitutes and the relative importance of the purchase. Each of the four categories had different acquisition strategies—shop for those items with

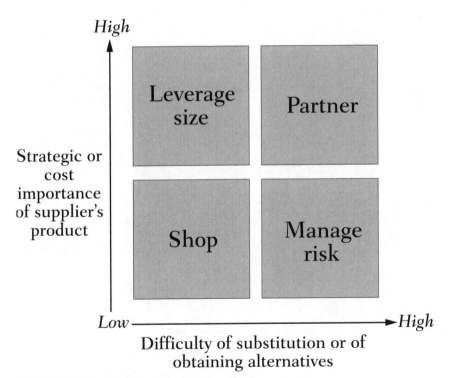

FIGURE 3-10. Supplier segmentation matrix.

many suppliers and relatively low importance; invest more time and leverage to those purchases with higher importance; manage risk for those items that don't have many substitutes but are less strategically important, and finally, develop partnering relationships for those items that are of great importance but have few supplier alternatives. Each of these buying strategies calls for a somewhat different selling strategy in order to be effective. Figure 3-11 shows how the three selling modes broadly map to the supplier segmentation matrix.

The shopping quadrant is clearly a transactional sale, and the seller's best strategy is to focus on creating value in the acquisition stages of the buying process and to adapt to the highly competitive, price-sensitive nature of this sale. As items become more differentiable, and more important to the purchaser (the manage-risk and leverage quadrants of Figure 3-10), sellers should adopt consultative selling approaches. They

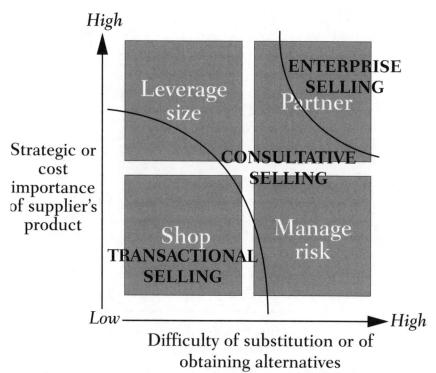

FIGURE 3-11.   Supplier segmentation matrix.

should, in other words, focus value creation early in the buying process, by helping customers identify hidden needs, and by developing customized solutions to customers' problems. Finally, in the partnering quadrant, sellers need to make some very difficult choices. For some small subset of customers, enterprise selling will be the best approach. For others, however, the best strategy will be to remain in a consultative selling mode, taking advantage of the unusual "seller-advantaged" position, reinvesting profits to sustain product or service uniqueness.

BREAKING OUT OF THE BUYING QUADRANTS

The strategies that we've described presuppose that suppliers are able and willing to adapt to the buying quadrant in which they have been placed by their customers and that they will configure their efforts to create the best possible fit with the value demands of that quadrant. There's an entirely different set of strategies for those who decide that they don't want to play in their existing quadrant. A transactional sales force caught in the shop quadrant, for example, might be tempted to try to move into a more advantaged quadrant, such as manage risk. How feasible is such a move? In theory it sounds attractive. And there's no shortage of writers and sales gurus who will tell you to "sell your way out of the commodity market by positioning yourself as unique and better" or to "build customer relationships that make you strategically important to your buyer's business." It's nice work if you can get it. Unfortunately, if buyers have accurately placed you fairly and squarely in a low strategic importance or readily substitutable quadrant, then the most that a salesperson can do is to create small shifts in perception. These shifts are rarely sufficient to move you into a different quadrant. "OK," your buyer will say, "you've shown me that your paper clips perform better than your competitors'—and you've even convinced me that paper clips are more useful to my business than I had imagined. But, as far as I'm concerned, they *are* still paper clips, and I will still `shop' for them."

It's a different matter if you've been placed in a quadrant because of a buyer's misperception. Fifteen years ago, an industrial pump manufacturer told us this story:

> Most buyers see pumps as a pure commodity. So we often find that our pumps, which are specialist products and more expensive, don't even get considered because purchasing agents have just been told to "go out and buy 25 pumps." But our pumps have some unique design features—for example, some can operate in extreme temperature ranges, others are the quietest on the market, while still others have outstanding reliability that makes them ideal for inaccessible places. Once we get face to face we can show that our product range is truly unique. Then we're no longer a commodity—our salespeople have turned the purchasing agent round through 180 degrees.

In those days, when value communication was enough to influence buying behavior, it was clearly possible just to correct the misperception and to sell your way to a differentiated position. However, although the folklore of selling relies heavily on tales of this kind, the cold reality is that the opportunity to create such a large shift in buyer perception today is becoming quite rare. For one thing, products are increasingly commoditized. Perhaps it was true 15 years ago that the pump supplier's products were genuinely unique. Today it's likely that there are six other manufacturers offering equally quiet or equally versatile pumps. For another thing, as we saw in the last chapter, buyers now have more access than ever before to information about suppliers' products. Chances are that today's purchasing agent would have already learned the information from a five-minute visit to the supplier's Web site. The face-to-face sales call that shifts the supplier into a new value quadrant merely by communicating product value has become a thing of the past.

Yet it *is* possible to shift from one value quadrant to another. To make such a shift requires two things: first, customers who are prepared to buy from you in the new quadrant and second, as we'll see in Chapter 9, a realignment of the supplier's whole business chain to meet the changed value needs of the new quadrant. Let's take an example. Suppose that a supplier is presently in the partner quadrant but decides that the manage-risk quadrant is more attractive. This isn't as improbable as it sounds—in the "partner" quadrant the close partnering relationship with one customer may make it impossible to sell to others in the same industry, or a few customers may be having too great an influence on the supplier's R&D direction. To become a successful player in the manage-risk quadrant will require a different kind of sales effort. For one thing, the supplier will almost certainly need more salespeople because it's likely that it will take many more people to achieve the same sales volume generated by a few very large partnering accounts. The sales force will have to become consultative and good at creating unique value that customers will find hard to substitute—for example, by customizing or configuring special solutions for manage-risk quadrant customers. But the rest of the business chain must change too. The R&D effort must do an excellent job of creating products with real differentiation—otherwise the supplier will become easy to substitute and will soon be forced out of the new quadrant. To remain competitive in the quadrant, manufacturing must learn to handle multiple demands for special and customized orders. In short, every function in the business chain must be aligned to the value creation demands of the quadrant.

It's no easy task to move from one mode of value creation to another. And it's certainly naïve to imagine that such a move can be made solely through clever market positioning or talented individual selling. Building a consistent value orientation is essential to success. As we've already seen, the approaches that work in transactional, consultative, or enterprise selling are very different. In the next three chapters we will explore each of these selling modes in more depth, and we'll look at examples of the strategies that successful sales forces are using to create customer value in each type of sale.

THE NEW TRANSACTIONAL SELLING

FROM FAT AND HAPPY TO LEAN AND MEAN

Bracing themselves for competition in a deregulated environment, Peco Energy, Pennsylvania's largest utility, was
negotiating a price cut with its regulators. After months of
grueling negotiations, Peco thought they had a deal. In
exchange for a 10 percent price reduction, Peco's market
arrangement would be extended for several years. A few days
before final approval, the chairman of Peco looked out of his
office window in Philadelphia to see a small plane circling his
building dragging a banner reading "Enron Choice Plan Saves
20 percent." Enron, the giant energy company with upward of
$20 billion in assets, was moving in and declaring a price war
on the local utility. It must have been an unpleasant moment.
Gone were the gentlemanly and civilized relationships that
characterized the way utilities had always dealt with each
other. In their place was ruthless price competition, lean and
unquestionably mean.
No wonder sales and marketing executives for electric utilities
have become increasingly nervous about the impending deregulation of their markets. In anticipation of the inevitable
squeeze, many of them have invested months of work, searching for ways to counter the approaching price pressures by differentiating and adding capabilities to their offerings. Most of

them have made little progress, and after dozens of discussions with customers they have come to the sobering conclusion that after deregulation they will likely be competing in the very difficult arena of "commodity" products. Their customers see little or no difference in their product (electric power) versus that of their competitors. Price is clearly the dominant factor, and their customers are looking forward with great anticipation to deregulation to increase the number of vendors and to allow them to play one supplier off against another, shopping for the best deals. Yes, service is important, but in truth—as well as in customers' perception—service levels aren't all that different, and most of the ideas for "special services" that sales and marketing strategists have come up with will cost more to implement than customers are willing to pay.

Utilities are facing the range of issues that are characteristic of the transactional sale. Their core product is perceived to be a commodity. A kilowatthour from Peco is no different from any other kilowatthour. Unlike many consumer goods, it's hard to brand it or give it a distinctive name. That which we call a "kilowatthour" by any other name would still smell remarkably like 1000 watts in 60 minutes. This commodity element is an important component of transactional sales. But there are other, equally important, elements. Transactional sales are sales that favor the buyer. Selling occurs in situations in which the product or service is readily available, there are multiple possible sources, and there is relatively little difference among suppliers' offerings. Buying a gallon of gasoline, for example, would clearly be a transactional sale in most circumstances. It could readily be purchased from any one of many gas stations, and few consumers would perceive noticeable differences among brands except for price. However, for one of the authors living in a remote jungle village in Borneo, the same gallon of gas took on a different buying perspective when the nearest alternative gas station was a two-day journey down river. The gas may have been a commodity, but lack of alternative sources meant going through an elaborate and time-consuming ritual for wheedling a gallon from the wretched old curmudgeon who controlled the one pump for a hundred miles in any direction. Transactional buying rests on the availability of other supply options. Where alternative sources are available, the buying strategy for this type of purchase is clearly to shop for the best deal and to leverage size and bargaining power to squeeze out the best price or terms.

WHEN THERE'S NO VALUE TO CREATE

This is obviously a difficult position for sellers to find themselves in. Not only are they, as sellers, in a weak bargaining position but also they have very few value-creating levers available to them. As we saw in Chapter 3, sellers have a number of ways to add value in the selling process; they can provide information about their product or service that customers don't know about, or provide insight into new applications for their products that create real benefits for customers. They can help customize products or services to better fit customers' needs, they can reduce risk for customers, and finally, they can facilitate the transaction itself. In the transactional sale, however, most of these value-adding paths are blind alleys, and the only real value-adding lever available to the seller is facilitation of the transaction—reducing the cost, risk, or difficulty of acquiring a well-defined and well-understood product or service.

TRANSACTIONAL SALES NEEDN'T BE SMALL

Are transactional sales simply small sales, or are they sales to smaller customers? Hardly. Transactional sales cover the full range of customer and sale size, and they know no industry or geographic boundaries. The battle between Peco and Enron is a transactional sale where there are tens of millions of dollars at stake. Many suppliers selling to *Fortune* 500–sized companies have transactional sales contracts valued at hundreds of thousands, if not millions, of dollars. Most office supplies are purchased in transactional sales, as is an increasing amount of office equipment. At the other end of the scale from huge business-to-business transactional sales come small individual consumer purchases. Some of these might be classified as simple commodity purchases—a carton of paper clips, a dozen eggs, or a box of matches. But even noncommodity items— packaged goods such as soap, cereal, or coffee—are transactional sales at the retail store level.

At first sight this sounds odd. After all, manufacturers put great resource and energy into developing branded and differentiated consumer products. For the shopper, Coke and Pepsi are very distinct, thanks to almost superhuman efforts by each company to position their version of colored water differently. But, while a branded product may not be a commodity, at the retail level it is nevertheless facing a transactional sale. This is so even though many decisions are made right at the point of purchase. What makes the sale transactional is that the only things affecting the sale at the retail location are price and availability. Other factors that shape a consumer's choice, such as product design and/or formulation, brand reputation, or image, have all been established long before this moment of truth, and the "salesperson" (retailer) has no control or influence on them. The customer enters the store with a defined selection set, and the only things that will really affect the specific sale is whether the product is available (or convenient to find) and what its price is. Even if salespeople were available to interact with customers while they made their selections, it's unlikely they would have much success in changing the choice. The sale the packaged goods manufacturer makes to the retailer—to get them to carry the product in their store or to give it more shelf space or favorable merchandising support—may be a consultative or an enterprise sale involving more than price and availability. But the sale to the consumer—the end user—is most certainly a transactional one.

Even big-ticket consumer purchases are increasingly likely to be transactional. For example, look at automobile sales. Today, consumers enter dealerships with their minds pretty well made up. They have read the recommendations of *Consumer*

Reports, talked to friends and others, and have a generally firm sense of a car's features. They are not looking for a salesperson who can help them understand their needs better or unravel the mystery of what's under the hood. They're simply looking for a way to complete the transaction—to get a good price on the car they've already decided to buy. Lamentable for sellers as it may be, transactional sales are becoming a larger part of the selling landscape, and the odds are that most sellers will see more of their business becoming transactional.

COMMODITIZATION AND THE PACE OF CHANGE

There are a number of factors that are likely to continue the growth of transactional sales into the foreseeable future. Globalization and deregulation will continue to increase the number of suppliers, with relatively undifferentiated products across a broad number of industries. As a result, customer choice will continue to grow. While this increase of choice is a welcome boon for consumers, suppliers are unlikely to do much celebrating as greater choice results in tougher, more price based buying. Technological advances are also pushing more sales into the transactional category. It is becoming harder and harder to maintain true product differences. Technology increases innovation potential, but it also greatly shortens the time it takes to copy a competitor's product. Ten years ago, it was common for complex innovative products to have as much as a two-year lead time before competitors were able to bring "me-too" versions to the market. Today it's not uncommon for the look-alike versions to be out in the marketplace in a matter of weeks.

TRANSACTIONAL BUYING PRESSURE

There are also pressures from buyers that relentlessly push sales toward the transactional mode. Over the past decade, the era of downsizing, reengineering and cost benchmarking has fundamentally changed purchasing thinking and behavior and has increased the focus on cost-expense management. On the business side, company after company has undergone strategic purchasing initiatives, recasting countless vendors into the transactional shop and leverage categories that we encountered in the last chapter. There has also been increasing demand for "common standards," "open architectures," and specifications that multiple suppliers can meet. This has resulted in opportunities for substituting cheaper products, diminishing differentiation potential, and pushing price to the forefront of purchasing negotiations. In industry after industry, sellers have watched long-standing, "safe" customer relationships evaporate as a new buying order has emerged. They have also seen new decision makers enter the arena, buying committees or even outside, third-party buying groups whose sole purpose is to commoditize the sale and drive down prices even further.

A similar trend is visible among consumers. It is not just car manufacturers that are facing customers who are smarter and a great deal better informed than ever before. Consumers are much more aware of the choices they have, and they are increasingly likely to get their information from impartial sources. As a result, a larger percentage of their purchases are becoming transactional, where price and availability are the only sales factors that hold sway.

Even suppliers that have complex and differentiated offerings or services face transactional sales pressure from a segment of their customer base. These suppliers are finding that, although their salespeople have potential to add great value, some of their customers don't need or want that assistance and have become transactional buyers. Stock brokerage is a good example of this phenomenon. Traditionally, this market has been one where there was a great deal of opportunity for differentiating offerings. Salespeople were able to add value by helping buyers understand their financial goals and risk profile and by providing advice about a complex set of product options. This had long been thought of as a typical consultative sale, and to many consumers it still is. However, there are a growing number of consumers for whom stock trading is a purely transactional buy. They are not seeking help or advice—they're simply looking for a simple and low-cost way to trade their stock positions—and the traditional selling models really don't fit. They see no benefit to the advice and other services that full-service brokers offer. As a consequence, they are unwilling to pay the related high prices when all they want is a simple trade executed. To meet the needs of this transactionally oriented group, discount brokers have arisen, and full-service brokers have been forced to rethink their approach or risk losing a substantial piece of their customer base. These trends are unlikely to reverse, and, in fact, they are more likely to accelerate. Most buyers—consumers or businesses—have changed the way they approach purchases for many of the products and services they buy. As a result, virtually every company is going to face transactional sales for part, if not all, of their product line and/or customer base.

SURVIVING THE TRANSACTIONAL SALE

"All right," you may be saying. "I believe that we are going to be facing an increasing number of transactional sales—but how the heck do we come out of this with some skin left?" It's not an unreasonable concern. Those whose markets have gone through a shift to transaction-based sales have usually seen their profits severely battered. Most have struggled to survive, and many have gone under. But a few have done much better than merely survive, and in this chapter we'll explore some of the strategies that successful players are using to cope—and even thrive—in this type of selling environment.

How should transactional sales be approached? The most typical reaction salespeople and executives have when they're facing a transactional sales situation is to try to find a way to escape it. "Let's differentiate our offering," they'll say, "make ourselves different from the others so we won't be shopped." Or in a similar vein, some will say, "We need to pursue value-added services—add special extras that will justify our premium prices for standard products." We can't fault these thoughts or the instincts that prompt them. Indeed, "flee or fight" are the most basic of nature's survival instincts, especially since "stay and fight" in this case is often a painful and bloody experience. For the seller, the transactional sale is clearly the most disadvantaged. The buyer is in the driver's seat with many choices and readily substitutable products, and for most sellers who stay and fight the outcome is usually declining volume and share, and even more rapidly declining prices, margins, profits, and stock market value. So the desire to get out of this trap by adding value and differentiating is quite defensible, even if it's depressingly difficult to achieve.

But the added-value route is just one of the options available. There are basically four different strategies you can take in a transactional sales situation, and all of them should be well explored before choosing which to pursue. These four options are:

1. *Create new value.* Find a way to create a truly distinctive offering, either by product innovation or by developing truly distinctive services that are of real and measurable value to customers and, in so doing, escape a transactional sale.

2. *Adapt.* Reengineer your sales approach to succeed in transactional selling by relentlessly stripping out sales and related costs.

3. *"Make the market."* Find ways to profit from the transaction itself, either in addition to or in place of the profit you make from the products you sell.

4. *Exit.* If you can't figure out a way to succeed in this type of sale, then seriously consider disengaging from this transactional segment of the market, this transactional product, or this transactional customer type.

In the remainder of this chapter, we'll explore each of these options and look at companies who have succeeded by following the four approaches outlined here.

STRATEGY 1: CREATE NEW VALUE

The most seductive option for the seller in a transactional situation is to pursue a value-added selling strategy, trying to add special services that will reduce competitive intensity and capture either a price or volume premium. This is a worthwhile objective; if successful, it can create a more protected and profitable position than most organizations can sustain within the purely transactional sale. Take, for example, American Express, which has done a masterful job of building a differentiated position and creating real value in its charge card business, which could easily have devolved into a purely transactional sale. Starting with a focus on the business traveler, they developed a number of true value-added elements and services that resulted not only in distinctiveness but in real preference and loyalty. They began not by looking at the typical features of the charge card but by looking at the characteristic problems their target customers encountered. They then invented ways for the card to help avoid or solve those problems. Arrive at a hotel late and find that your room has been given away? They added a late-arrival guarantee feature to the card so that if you used an American Express card to reserve your room, you were guaranteed a room no matter how late you arrived. Lose your wallet while you're out of town or out of the country? They developed the ability to replace your card within 24 hours no matter where you happened to be on the face of the earth. Worried about rental car insurance? Use your American Express card, and you're automatically insured. Frequent Flyer miles important to you? A membership miles program lets you accrue points for your spending on the card and lets you use them on a range of airlines and other service establishments or merchants. These are just some of the unique benefits that American Express developed for its card users. Over the years, American Express has been able to develop a series of true value-adding features or services that have let it differentiate and justify premium pricing and have kept it largely out of the transactional sales arena.

Another approach to creating differentiated value is to create targeted pricing options. The airlines, for example, by developing special "saver" packages, with certain restrictions like nonrefundable booking and Saturday night stays, have created a good value for price-sensitive leisure travelers, without having to reduce prices for business travelers. Similarly, the long-distance telephone carriers have created different saving plans for transactional price buyers that may offer better value to certain segments without across-the-board price reductions and certainly makes it more difficult to directly compare one phone company with another.

Developing differentiated value is a very good strategy if you can do it—the trouble is, it's a very difficult strategy to execute and you will find many more failures than successes along this path. It's relatively easy to identify things that could benefit customers and that they would like—but that alone doesn't create value. You create value only if the benefits to the customer are greater than your cost to provide those services—and there's the rub. Most ideas people come up with in "value-added selling strategies" seldom create real value. At best they shift value from the seller to the buyer. For example, if you extend payment terms for customers, letting them make payments in 60 or 90 days instead of the more typical 30 days, you will be providing value to them by reducing their working capital needs. But this action, while attractive to the customer, won't create any new value. The savings in working capital that the customer will see will be funded by the added expense you will incur in *your* working capital. There is no more value created with that kind of action than by those that simply lower prices. Yes, lower prices provide value to customers by lowering their costs, but they reduce value to sellers because of the resulting lower margins and profits. These are value-shifting strategies that take value from the seller and give it to the buyer. It may be necessary to take some of these actions, but they are hardly creating value and can't be the basis of competing over the long term. As one marketing executive from a major bank told us, "We've provided value by taking our margins and giving them to our customers. The question is, now that our margins are eroded to nothing, what else have we left to give?"

In many cases, attempting to add value can simply add cost—not just shifting value but actively destroying it. For example, adding extra salespeople and technical service reps is a common response of companies who find themselves sliding into the transactional abyss. Their margins are falling, and their customer base is shrinking. What can they do? At first sight, beefing up their sales and service effort seems an obvious solution. More salespeople will let us reverse our falling market share, they reason. And increased service support will keep our existing customers. This strategy, although superficially attractive, can work only in those cases where the increased numbers allow new customer value to be created. Unfortunately, that's rarely the case. All too often, the new salespeople are ineffective because, like their colleagues in the existing sales force, there is no value for them to create. They make costly calls on customers to communicate product features and benefits that the buyer is already well aware of. They add no new value—they simply waste customers' time. In doing so, they further destroy existing value by raising the seller's cost base.

A similar value problem exists in the area of customer support. Many companies have attempted to add more technical service reps, hoping that they can provide special service or information to buyers. Once started down this costly road, they find that there is little the technician can do either to enhance the buyer's operation or to influence the sale. As a result, they find themselves in an even more disadvantaged position, with a higher cost structure but no greater customer satisfaction or preference. To be fair, in most cases, it isn't readily apparent in advance whether true value is being created or destroyed. In most transactional sales there are some benefits that the customer receives from special-services programs. Customers often respond favorably to them. But while these added-value programs may do some good, they often don't justify the cost of provision and are simply slowly eroding a seller's competitive position.

We're not against value-added approaches to avoiding transactional selling. On the contrary, if the potential exists to create real new customer value at a viable cost, then there's no better way out of the transactional selling dilemma. Our concern is that we've become skeptical about the success potential of value creation strategies after seeing so many well-intentioned and apparently smart efforts in this direction go awry. What you need to be sure of before committing to this path, is that serious and rigorous homework has been done and that there is *real* value creation potential. You must be sure that you can quantify the dollars and cents benefits that customers will get and be able to show that these exceed the costs you will incur. You also need to be sure that you can keep the innovation going along this path to stay ahead of competitors. There may be a first-mover advantage, but it dissipates quickly. If the value creation ideas are easily copied and there are no new ones to replace them, you will once again be in the transactional dilemma—only with a higher cost burden and greater profitability problems.

STRATEGY 2: ADAPT BY STRIPPING COSTS

For the majority of sales organizations, creating uniqueness to escape transactional sales is neither feasible nor economically viable, and they resort to the default strategy of stay and fight. Unfortunately, most of these companies continue to sell in the same way they always have, trying harder perhaps, but using the same fundamental approaches of the past. Working on a sell-harder strategy, they change incentive systems to increase sales motivation, hoping that just charging up the sales force will let them reverse declining sales and profits. They also adjust the cost base a bit—cutting the travel and entertainment budget, stretching territories, or increasing the span of control. These actions sometimes help a little in the short term, but inevitably sales, prices, and profits return to the downward spiral as the supplier continues to transfer value to customers in the transaction, just to stay in the game.

The trouble with these actions is that they do not go far enough to fundamentally change the competitive sales position. Transactional buying is by its very nature cold and heartless, with price its dominant decision factor. The most likely key to creating value for customers here is not by adding additional benefits to justify higher prices but by lowering the cost of acquisition. Hence, to be able to compete effectively in this arena, you need a bare-bones cost structure so you can meet price demands—or exceed them—without destroying your profitability. You simply can't afford to carry excess cost. Customers are rarely willing to pay more simply because a seller's cost structure is high, and this is doubly true in the transactional sale. So your objective in preparing for transactional sales is to eliminate any cost item you can. "If a sales activity can't be cost justified in terms of providing customer value, then eliminate it" is probably the best mantra we've heard for managing transactional sales. If there is a lower-cost way to perform a sales activity, then that's the way you have to do it. And if the sales activity under the lowest-cost method still can't be justified by real benefits to the customer, (real benefits that the customer should be *willing to pay for*), then eliminate the activity and lower the sales cost. As in most things, however, this is easier said than done. Few of us are really prepared to reorient our thinking and to take the kinds of draconian actions that are essential to succeeding in this kind of selling. This isn't fine-tuning; this is real cost deconstruction. For those with determination, there are a three ways to go about it:

1. Eliminate the sales function.
2. Move to lower-cost channels.
3. Drastically reduce the cost of the current sales force.

Let's look at each of these options in turn.

Eliminate the Sales Function.   The best option, heretical as it may seem, is to find a way to eliminate the sales function totally. Getting as close as possible to zero cost is the objective here, and if you could pull it off, this would be the nearest you could come to eliminating sales costs. And why not? If you're truly in a transactional sale, it's an attractive option. Let's remind ourselves of one of the elements that define a transactional sale. The product is perceived as a commodity, and the customer understands its capabilities so well that salespeople don't bring new insights into how the product can help the customer. In other words, not only can't salespeople create customer value, they can't even add much in terms of communicating value either. So what value does a sales force bring? Customers don't require (or want) a lot of new information about the product, or help in assessing their needs. The typical ways salespeople can add value are not at play, so the smartest sales organizations will stop trying to force a sales approach that doesn't work here. They will eliminate the sales force and be able to share the savings with happier customers.

Think about automobile sales, for instance. Surveys of car buyers consistently show that most people would rather sit in a dentist's chair and have their teeth drilled than go through the current sales process of buying a new car. And with good reason. The most burning questions on their mind concern availability of the model and features they want and the price they'll have to pay. But to get that information, they'll most likely spend the better part of a day, enduring a car sales ritual that includes listening to a "talking brochure" of performance features and comparisons, a series of inane closing techniques, and seemingly endless delays while the salesperson disappears for extended periods to get approval for "special pricing." Customers clearly don't enjoy it, and there isn't much in it for the dealership either. Most car buyers today have done their homework before walking into a car showroom and know almost as much about a dealer's invoice price as the dealer's salespeople do. They're not readily fooled by the ritual dance, and quite honestly there isn't that much profit margin left to be concerned with. In 1997, the typical dealer sold a new automobile at a few hundred dollars over invoice. In today's marketplace, a dealer makes money on service and resale of used cars, not new cars. At most, the new-car sale is simply a way to get access to service business and used-car inventory. So why not simplify the new-car sales process? Eliminate salespeople and their expense, set low fixed prices on the vehicles, and save customers the time and hassle and pain of what should be a simple transaction. Saturn's done it, with great response—and Car Max and Auto Nation are applying the thinking to used-car sales. An automated kiosk provides information about what's available, and a set price means that no one has to go through an unproductive sales process. This approach responds to the two biggest customer needs in a transactional sale: creating customer value by lowering cost and by facilitating acquisition. In addition, the elimination of salespeople permits a competitively advantaged cost structure. Car Max has twice the sales productivity of the average dealer and turns inventory at roughly five times the dealer's rate (10 to 14 days versus 60 days for the average dealer). In just four years Car Max has grown from startup to $1 billion in revenue.

For many organizations caught in the ever-tighter grip of transactional selling, the thought of getting rid of the sales force is an attractive idea but an idea that comes with one huge danger. "What about relationships?" people ask. "Even transactional sales depend on relationships. If we didn't have a sales rep visiting the customer, then we'd lose the relationship and lose the business." How justified is this fear? There's clear evidence that relationships are, and always have been, an important factor in sales. It's possible to argue that relationships become even more important in commodity sales because, when there's no differentiation in the product, then the relationship becomes the differentiator. How much business would be put at risk without a salesperson to maintain the customer relationship? The answer, unfortunately, is that nobody knows. There's a dearth of hard research in this area. But we suspect that the nature and importance of customer relationships is in the process of radical change. Twenty years ago we carried out a study of commodity buyers in Exxon Chemicals. They were asked to rate the relative importance of 10 factors in their chemical purchasing decisions, including relationship with the sales rep, price, and consistency of supply. The top-rated factor was relationship with the sales rep with price coming in third. Ten years later, a similar study put price as the number 1 factor and relationship with the sales rep relationship in second place.

Today, we suspect, price is likely to be even more important compared with relationships. Buyers in the new purchasing organizations are busy people, increasingly measured on performance and value. They are prepared to invest time with those salespeople who create true value, but, at the other end of the scale, they don't want to waste time with salespeople who have nothing to add. As Bill Budney, Vice President of Distribution Services for Public Service Electric and Gas put it, "In the new purchasing, you've got to invest your time where it counts. Time spent with a vendor who doesn't have anything to say is time wasted." If the customer's choice is between a cheaper product and a face-to-face relationship, it's our view that the cheaper product will increasingly win. Yes, losing the relationship may be a big risk from stripping salespeople. But an even greater risk may be keeping the relationship but, because of your inevitably higher costs, losing the business to a competitor who has ruthlessly stripped away every element of the sales force that customers are not prepared to pay for.

Move to Lower-Cost Channels.   Sometimes the draconian elimination of sales isn't a realistic option. When you can't eliminate sales activities, then the focus in a transactional sales environment should shift to finding lower-cost alternatives, and new channels can often provide dramatic reductions in selling cost, especially as the needs for consultative services decline. The personal computer market is an excellent illustration of the alternative channel opportunities that are created as the marketplace shifts toward the transaction mode. Twenty years ago, if you wanted a personal computer, your choices were pretty limited—you could buy an IBM or you could buy a Mac, and your options of where and how to buy them were limited to exclusive dealers. These dealers added value using fairly traditional sales functions, providing new information about products and applications to still relatively unsophisticated buyers. It was a somewhat expensive selling process but justifiable in terms of the amount of help customers needed during the sale. Economically, it was feasible because of the limited set of competitive offerings that reduced pricing pressures. Through the eighties, personal computer sales moved further and further into the transactional quadrant. Buyers became increasingly knowledgeable and sophisticated, relying less and less on salespeople for product or application knowledge. In addition, "clones" were introduced, and the number of competitors rapidly multiplied, opening up choices for buyers. As a result, the importance of price and availability quickly passed that of "information" or technical assistance in the buying decision. By 1982, IBM and Apple had given up the notion of trying to maintain "exclusive" sales distribution channels and had opened sales up to other dealers and retailers.

Through the eighties, as buyers became even more knowledgeable, there was diminishing value being created by the sales function. In fact, for the sophisticated buyers in the market, it could readily be argued that value was actually being destroyed. *Sophisticated* buyers knew what they wanted, and they needed none of the "technical" or other sales assistance being provided by traditional selling channels. They more often than not knew more about the products and applications than salespeople could hope to keep up with. A sign of the shift of expertise to the customer was the joke that became popular in the mid-eighties that asked, "What's the difference between the people who sell computers and people who sell used cars?" The answer was, "The people who sell used cars *know* they're lying." There could be no greater evidence of the value-destroying capacity of salespeople than that punch line. For this increasingly sophisticated group of buyers, the high-cost sales and distribution approach made less and less sense.

Michael Dell was among the first to see the enormous opportunity that was opening to provide sophisticated buyers with the kind of transactional sale they were looking for. Dell developed a direct sales channel for computer equipment. At last, buyers who really knew what they wanted could simply use the telephone to call Dell and order the computer feature and functionality they desired. Dell could afford to quote a more than competitive price, and they could give the customer exactly what he or she wanted because the costs of the direct channel were roughly 15 percent lower than the indirect channel. Michael Dell had recognized the imperative in the transactional sale to strip cost, but he also had the insight to see that customer knowledge implicit in this kind of sale could be used to advantage. The customer could take on the sales activity of "customizing" the product to his or her individual needs. The only sales function that had to be performed by Dell was efficient order taking, and that could be accomplished at a fraction of the cost of traditional sales. This new channel would provide additional cost advantages to Dell that further enhanced their ability to compete in a marketplace driven by price. The direct telesales channel eliminated the need for large inventories deployed to field or retail locations. Equipment could be assembled "as ordered," reducing inventory carrying cost as well as the risk of product obsolescence. This allowed Dell to actually cut the cost of providing equipment "exactly" as customers wanted, at a price normally associated with a "standard" item having just a few feature choices. The direct-by-telephone-sales channel would enable Dell to become the fourth-largest PC manufacturer and supplier with nearly 10 percent of the market by 1997.

The long-distance telephone market provides another example of channel choices that dramatically reduce the cost of reaching transactional customers. In the 1980s the breakup of AT&T opened up the long-distance telephone market to competition and initiated the intense battle to capture the market position of primary long-distance provider. It was quickly apparent that these would be transactional sales. Sprint did attempt to get some mileage out of its all-optic-cable network, with sound quality that enabled the sound of a pin dropping to be heard across the country, but consumers seemed little swayed by that distinction. Competition quickly devolved to price, a key characteristic of the transactional sale. Almost all programs and communications revolved around savings, usually pegged to AT&T as the majority player and product standard. From the outset it was clear that efficient sales would be a key element of the competitive battle, for while there were many billions of dollars at stake, each "sale" was relatively small. All competitors learned a great deal about transactional selling during the ensuing years and honed their skills, but none as effectively as MCI. MCI quickly realized that the key to the transactional sale would be leveraging the perceived low price to transactional buyers and minimizing the cost of reaching that buyer. They employed aggressive tele-sales and lower-price plans for the transactional segment, almost doubling their share in three years from 4.5 percent in 1984 to 8.8 percent by 1987.

The cost of telesales, while low compared with face-to-face interactions, was still considerable, especially as the "take rate" declined. All the low-hanging fruit had been collected, and by the early nineties, the need for still lower cost approaches and channels was increasingly evident. MCI then began their "Family and Friends" campaign, which not only created an interesting new value for customers (saving on their most frequent calls) but also introduced a more indirect channel for increasing acquisitions. MCI was able to leverage its own customer base as a channel to customers' relatives, at very low cost and great effectiveness, taking their share up to 18 percent by 1993. At that point, Telco entered the fray, using the mails instead of telesales channels, and launched their "Dial and Save" program with remarkable success. The transactional offer was by now well understood. People had gained experience with alternative long-distance providers and perceived little, if any, difference. Price had become an even greater part of the decision, and the direct-mail approach offered a much lower cost way to reach consumers with an offer. The company mailed stickers with their access code printed on them to potential customers advising them to put them on their telephones. Using these access codes before dialing the long-distance number would save the customer 25 percent over AT&T's nondiscounted rate. The customer saw it as value created, and the acquisition costs for Telco were sub-stantially lower than others. Estimates suggest that the aver-age cost of each telesales contact runs somewhere between $7 to $12, while the cost of a contact through the mails is only

$1.50. Of course, there is very high slippage from the number of mail pieces sent to those actually read—research indicates that nearly 60 percent of people toss direct-mail pieces before they've read them—but the cost differences in a sale like this one more than offset it. Others quickly followed with similar plans, and in just four years, these "dial-around' companies chipped off $700 million or 1 percent from the roughly $70 billion U.S. long-distance market.

MCI also began to leverage direct mail, but it was quite clever in finding ways to connect the transactional offer with other mail pieces customers were likely to open. Leveraging the popularity of frequent-flyer programs, they developed joint programs with the airlines, offering frequent-flyer points to sweeten the offer The joint mailings prominently displayed the airline frequent-flyer program to get their mail message opened and read and, hopefully, acted upon. These joint programs also enabled MCI to place the offer in airline magazines at even lower cost than direct mail permitted, further lowering their overall sales cost. The success of this type of approach is well worth noting and copying, if possible. The cost of a direct-mail-based program was less than half that of the telesales approach, representing hundreds of millions of dollars in savings that could be used to enhance profits or to share with customers.

Drastically Reduce the Cost of the Current Sales Force. Another area that a number of companies have found fruitful is to take a much harder look at the customer base and rethink the amount of time and sales expense devoted to each customer or territory. We all know the "80/20 rule"—that 80 percent of sales potential is located in only 20 percent of customers—but few have acted aggressively enough to really benefit from this insight. Most sales forces spend a little more time and resources with larger customers, pulling back some from smaller accounts. However, most of the actions taken are fine-tuning adjustments. In the transactional sale fine-tuning isn't going to cut it, and a more drastic perspective is called for. One sales executive facing a transactional market put it this way: "Rigorously using the 80/20 rule showed us that we simply couldn't afford to call on more than half of our customers. The 80/20 rule used twice suggested that half of our customers would account for less than 5 percent of our sales—we checked it and found that to be true. When we looked at it that way, we realized that we were really losing money on these accounts—half of our sales expense was chasing this 5 percent of potential. We finally faced up to reality, stopped calling on these customers, cut our sales expense in half, and dramatically improved our profit picture."

Still another avenue that can yield substantial savings is to rethink how salespeople are spending their time, and take action against *unproductive* activities. No one disputes that a lot of time is wasted on unproductive activities, but most sales managers are at a loss as to how to identify and eliminate these sources of waste. One way that we have found to be successful is to divide activities into those that drive near-term customer revenue and those that don't, even though they may be necessary. Hence, time spent directly with customers, developing proposals, or customized presentations would fall into the revenue-producing set. On the other hand, time spent writing administrative reports, attending sales meetings, traveling, and waiting or firefighting are not. The typical sales force finds that only 20 to 30 percent of their time is spent on revenue-producing areas, while the most tightly managed sales forces get closer to 40 to 50 percent. It doesn't get any better than that, but the range by itself is a huge gap. Consider it this way—a sales force operating at a 40 percent level has twice the firepower of one operating at 20 percent, with the same amount of people. Or from another perspective, you can have the same selling capacity with half the number of people and expense. Once people look at the facts, they are usually quite resourceful in finding ways to whittle away unproductive drains on their time. Do we really need a weekly sales meeting? And does it need to be as long as it is? One very creative company took all the chairs out of meeting rooms, and banished donuts and coffee from sales meetings, resulting in a 30 percent reduction in the number of meetings, with the average length of meetings cut in half. Do we really need to travel as much as we do? Could we get better at scheduling our sales calls and think about combining calls on nearby accounts, especially when travel is eating up one out of every five hours? Do we really need to fill out these administrative reports? Are they really worth the 10 percent of sales expense that they are currently costing us? Couldn't we do without call reports? And so on.

Even if you can't eliminate activities, there are other ways to reduce their cost. One is to simply shift them to lower-cost employees. Use administrative assistants to handle much of the firefighting and administrative tasks. Or try to replace some direct, face-to-face time with telephone contact, mailings, or electronic connections. It's a dangerous thing to do in a consultative sale because telephone and other indirect methods are seldom as effective as face-to-face encounters, but in a transactional sale, you're concerned with efficiency rather than effectiveness. As a result, you can more easily afford some loss of effectiveness than you can afford excess cost. Finally, you might consider making greater use of part-time resources. Part-timers can often improve sales capacity utilization while lowering selling costs by as much as 40 percent.

We recognize that all these ideas won't work for every sales force, but the smarter players faced with transactional sales will make use of as many efficiency levers as feasible and greatly improve their odds of success as a result.

STRATEGY 3: MAKE THE MARKET

Beyond cost cutting to adapt to the rigors of transactional selling, there is another, very different approach some companies are taking that is well worth exploring. Instead of looking at transactional selling as a way to move products, they are looking at the transaction itself as a source of profit. This third approach to transactional selling—making your money from managing the transaction rather than the product—represents some very fresh and innovative thinking, and the results for a couple of the early pioneers along this path are quite impressive. This approach is especially interesting for transactions that have a great deal of volatility in price and/or supply and availability. In the remainder of this chapter we'll describe a few of these companies and how they've gone down this new and very exciting path.

AMR SABRE System. Probably the best known of approaches that profit from the transaction itself is the SABRE system, developed by AMR, the parent organization of American Airlines. Most people don't think of a reservation system as a transactional selling innovation, and, frankly, AMR didn't think of it in those terms when the system was first established. But it is a great illustration of how to make money from managing the transaction. It's an approach that has handsomely rewarded AMR, even if the primary benefits were unintended. Airlines compete in a very difficult industry. Deregulation in the United States opened the way for increased competition, and it ended set pricing between destination points. In the wake of deregulation, the industry as a whole has seen a lot of very innovative marketing such as frequent-flyer programs, special meals and amenities, or cabin reconfigurations. There's no question that these efforts have had an impact on customer preference and loyalty, particularly among frequent travelers. But for many airline seat purchases, if not most, the primary sale determinants are the availability and convenience of flights and the price of the seat. The buying process is spent mostly in gathering facts about the flight options and the corresponding fares. To be sure, the process has become more complicated with the broad range of restricted fares and discounts that have been introduced to improve yield, but decisions still revolve around availability and price—the main drivers of a transactional sale.

Initially, AMR developed the SABRE system to give its flights a sales advantage. It was designed to have available American flights appear first in the list of options users would find. Whether that really would work to American's advantage or not became a moot point; regulators found it to be "unfair," and AMR was forced to remove that feature from the system. At the time, most pundits thought that the SABRE system had lost most of its value for AMR—that if you couldn't place your offering in a favorable position, it was simply a transaction device that would offer no competitive advantage or real profit potential. History has proved the pundits wrong—or, at least, only partly right. It *was* simply a transaction device, but in the transactional sale, such a device has enormous value and profit potential. It was aimed at the only two things that really count in this kind of sale: availability-convenience and price. As a result, it did an excellent job of facilitating the selling-buying process. Travel agents could quickly and easily see what the options were, have the customer decide which he or she wanted, and then complete the transaction automatically. Using the system, they could manage the complexity of multiple fare codes and restrictions or blackout dates and could even be kept current with scheduling, equipment, and capacity-availability changes. No, it didn't provide American Airline flights with a competitive sales advantage, but it did allow AMR to profit from the ticket sale itself—not only of American Airline flights but of all flights. This profit potential was considerable. In 1996 the profit to AMR from the SABRE system was 51 percent of total profits—this transaction vehicle exceeded the profit contribution of the airline itself.

Transactional Sales through the Internet.   Emerging technology clearly played a key role in the success of the SABRE reservation system. Technology is also enabling a transaction-based sales through the Internet across a broad range of industries. In consultative sales of the kind we'll meet in the next chapter, salespeople create value by understanding problems their customers are having and figuring out creative ways to solve them. Among the ways they do this is by identifying unusual applications for their products that can be especially cost effective, by having their product modified so that it fits a customer operations a bit better, or by helping a customer learn how to use their product or service more efficiently or effectively. The processes of these types of sales situations are hard to envision conducted on the Internet because consultative sales benefit a great deal from a salesperson's intimate knowledge of a customer's specific operations, knowledge that would be hard to match or replace electronically. But a transactional sale is not one of these situations. By definition, true transactional buyers already have a good and valid understanding of their needs and wants There isn't much any salesperson or sales process is going to do to open up new insights or new creative applications. And for good reason. The things that are important to a transactional buyer, like the ability to shop for the best-priced deal, and the ease or convenience of making the buy, play to the Internet's strength. Of all sales situations, transactional ones appear most suited to the Internet and offer significant opportunity for profit from managing the transaction itself. Let's take a look at some of the early moves to do so.

One example of profiting from the transaction is a company appropriately named "Fast Parts," which provides a "spot market" for basic, commodity electronics components such as transistors or DRAMs. Fast Parts is purely an intermediary. It gets these standard parts from the numerous electronic components manufacturers and delivers them to its subscribers. Fast Parts has no other relationship with either the manufacturers or the buyers. The parts are delivered to customers two to four days after they have been ordered and paid for, and Fast Parts collects an 8 percent commission on the sale. From the buyer's perspective, it is a quick, easy, and relatively low cost purchase. Fast Parts, as a neutral intermediary with access to a number of suppliers, can assure fair, market-driven prices. Buyers achieve the benefits of reviewing a number of different suppliers, without the normal hassle and expense of comparison shopping. Moreover, quick order fulfillment is virtually guaranteed. There are also benefits from the seller's (manufacturer's) perspective. They get the ability to compete for business that might not otherwise be available to them, and they get this broad coverage at very low relative sales cost. The sales cost is totally variable, and there is no sales infrastructure or sales management to be concerned with. Using the Internet instead of a sales force lets Fast Parts create clear benefits to both buyers and sellers without the sales interaction cost of traditional approaches.

FreeMarkets OnLine is another innovative venture that is attempting to profit by offering market-making services for business-to-business transactions over the Internet. Its focus is on industrial components and parts—items like metal castings or plastic injection molded parts. It conducts online, real-time competitive-bidding events to get the best terms for customers. The bidding works as follows: Buyers determine their needs, and FreeMarkets works closely with them to develop a detailed RFQ—a Request for Quotation—that outlines specifications, order quantities, and other crucial elements. FreeMarkets OnLine identifies potential suppliers, screening them to be sure that they can meet the buyers' requirements, and then invites them to join the bidding for this business. Then they hold an online-bidding event for these transactional purchases. Like Fast Parts, FreeMarkets enables buyers to efficiently and effectively shop a number of possible suppliers and to drive down the prices they will have pay by open-market competition. The electronic transactions lower the cost of the buying-selling process for both parties and again create real value. The average savings for buyers using FreeMarkets OnLine have averaged 15 percent. As you might expect, market results have been very impressive: The company, founded in 1995 in Pittsburgh, brokered just two years later over $100 million in goods, and it is growing at a rate of 350 percent per year. In the first quarter of 1998, it had already conducted as much business as it did in all of 1997.

Enron Gas Services.   We met Enron, the energy company whose plane was buzzing Peco headquarters, at the start of this chapter. The history of how Enron learned to be successful in the transactional sale is an interesting example of how to profit from a seemingly disadvantaged commodity position by rethinking how to profit from the transaction. Enron Gas Services is perhaps the most successful exponent of this type of sales approach. Enron has used a rather sophisticated strategy and has taken great advantage of the opportunities inherent in deregulating environments. They have achieved this by capitalizing on the subsequent price and availability risk.

Enron in the late 1980s was the nation's largest integrated gas company. It was among the largest gas producers, operated the largest pipeline system, and was a broad gas marketer. In 1988, however, it initiated a strategy creating and capturing value in the gas market sales transaction, using a strategy of offering financial services to offset the price and supply volatility risk. A full description of the actions Enron took in this market is well beyond the scope of this book, but in very simple terms, Enron increased the use of long-term, fixed-price contracts, through which they could play a role and profit from the transaction. They used a wide range of financial products, many of them extremely sophisticated financial derivatives, to meet various producer, user, and investor needs (for example, options, natural gas swaps, caps, floors, collars, and firm forwards). It was not just about "pushing more Enron gas" with creative financing options; rather, it was creating a set of financial risk management products that could be used to improve gas market transactions and to profit from the unusual volatility in market prices and supply availability. This strategy enabled them to play in a much greater portion of the market than they could have achieved on their own, and, because they could profit from the transactions of others as well as their own, they dramatically increased Enron's profit potential.

Enron was creating real value for participants, and they enjoyed enormous market and financial success as a result. By 1992, the Enron Gas Services unit that directed this program had become the largest marketer of natural gas in North America, contributing $122 million EBIT to Enron, more than four times its 1990 earnings. Two years later, EBIT had grown to $225 million, and the unit was renamed "Enron Capital and Trade Resources" (ECT) to better reflect the nature of the business..

Strategies that focus on profit from the transaction itself are available to a much broader set of players than some of the value creation or cost stripping strategies that we've outlined. You don't have to be one of the participants in the market to make money from a transactional environment. FreeMarkets OnLine, for example, is neither a manufacturer nor a user of the parts it deals in. It facilitates the transaction as a third party. So does Fast Parts. Even the Enron Gas Services approach could have been pulled off by someone out of the industry. Because of this, while all of the transactional approaches we've outlined merit consideration, this one should be looked at especially carefully. There may be very little time before someone else views the opportunity in your industry and acts on it, leaving you the loser.

STRATEGY 4: EXIT THE MARKET

All of the approaches we've reviewed in this chapter have relied on innovation for their success although this innovation has taken many different forms. For American Express it was a fresh way to solve business travelers' problems. For Dell it was the use of new, lower-cost channels to strip out unnecessary activities or costs. Many of these innovators took great advantage of emerging technologies, such as the SABRE system and the Internet-based processes. And, of course, every one of them created real value for customers and, in doing so, created opportunities for themselves to capture a share of that value that they had created.

This chapter has covered a wide range of options for competing for transactional sales, and it has provided a number of examples of people who had managed to succeed and thrive in this difficult environment. Nonetheless, the truth is, this is the most difficult and seller disadvantaged of all sales modes, and many companies will be unable—or unwilling—to take the set of actions that would be required for success. Difficult as it may be, when that is the case, the best option is to exit this part of the market rather than trying to muddle through, waiting for the situation to improve. Transactional markets don't improve. If anything, they become tougher and tougher for competitors, as buyer demands continue to place pressure on sellers and innovative competitors continue to raise the bar for what it takes to compete in the market. The smartest players will take a careful assessment of their options but cut their losses by refocusing their resources on areas and sales situations in which they have a better chance of success.

THE NEW CONSULTATIVE SELLING

FROM ROCK STARS TO INSTITUTIONAL VALUE

In the good old Henry Ford days, when you could have any color as long as it was black, suppliers held all the power, and their products tended to be designed more for the convenience of the manufacturers than for the needs of the customers. Consumers were generally undemanding and, by today's standards, amazingly compliant. Manufacturers pushed their products with only a token interest in understanding customer requirements. Generations of salespeople were trained to recite product advantages, to close hard and often, and to batter reluctant customers into submission through pressure and persistence. Even in sophisticated business-to-business sales, until the late 1970s most corporations taught salespeople that their role was simply to thrust products forcefully at potential customers. An influential sales book of the time, *Compelling Selling* by Philip Lund, advised readers to concentrate exclusively on the product, not to let the customer talk more than absolutely necessary but instead to "close whenever possible, even if you're miles from the order." Transactional selling, of a generally manipulative and pushy sort, was the norm. At a time when the focus was on the product and not the customer, value wasn't a noticeable part of the selling lexicon.

A profound change began during the mid 1970s, when a number of major multinational corporations started to become uneasy about how they were teaching their people to sell. IBM, for example, worried that a new generation of computers might demand a less product-centered approach from their salespeople. The chief scientist of IBM, speaking at a World Trade conference in Paris in 1975, was asked about the new machines and whether they would have to be sold differently. He replied that the IBM sales force knew how to sell hardware, but the new machines would create different situations. He went on to define the new generation of systems products by saying that "the hardware is irrelevant—it's only the solution that counts." He concluded: "I don't think that IBM, or anyone else, really knows how to sell solutions." He was prophetically right. During the next 10 years the shift from the product sale to the solutions sale turned out to be a radical and difficult transition for IBM, and for most other technology companies.

At around the same time, Xerox Corporation was coming to a similar conclusion about the need to change, but they arrived at that conclusion from a very different angle. The plain paper copier patent protection that had made their products unique and had given them a virtual monopoly was due to expire. During its years of exclusivity, Xerox had built an unenviable reputation for dictating terms to its customers. Now, with competing plain paper alternatives becoming available, they realized that they could no longer afford a sales force that was oblivious to customer needs. Xerox began to sponsor research to develop new selling models that would let them move away from their hard-sell reputation. They were looking for a customer-centered sales approach. Although they were initially motivated by a negative customer image and the fear of new competition, it so happened that, like IBM, they were also about to introduce a generation of complex new products that required something beyond transactional selling. They knew a change would be necessary, even though they weren't sure what that change would look like.

BY THE MID-SEVENTIES, THE WORLD WAS CHANGING

It wasn't only technology companies that were feeling the winds of change. Similar stories could be told about many other corporations at the time. Their products were becoming more complex, their customers less accepting of pushy or arrogant selling. Competition, was increasing, and, as a result, customers were given choices that allowed them to select suppliers who offered the most value. The world was changing, and the change would have dramatic consequences for sales. Power had begun to move from the supplier to the customer. Even the most staid and traditional institutions began to feel the pinch. Banks that had, for generations, been lofty dispensers of loans only to the most creditworthy customers suddenly found that their best customers had other sources of funds. The old saying that a banker was someone who would lend you an umbrella unless it was raining became less true when so many alternative forms of funding were becoming available. Commercial banks began a long struggle to transform themselves from credit managers to advisers and, in the process, came face to face with the nasty realization that they would have to learn how to sell. Even worse, their product—money—was becoming a commodity, and they would have to add significant value if they hoped to retain some portion of their comfortable margins.

For the first time the concept of value started to become a meaningful force across the whole spectrum of business-to-business selling, from professional services to capital goods. As customer choices increased, both as a result of competition and because products and services were increasingly customized, understanding the customer became an ever more important element of successful selling. New customer-centered selling models were developed, such as the SPIN® model that resulted from the Huthwaite research into high-level selling. These new models started with the customer's needs rather than the supplier's products. The combination of an increasing customer demand for value coupled with emerging models of how to sell differently in a value-dependent marketplace was an inevitable stimulus for change. Sales forces—particularly those in the business-to-business sales—began a slow process of transformation. This shift toward adopting more sophisticated sales models went under many names, among them "relationship selling," "customer-focused selling," "nonmanipulative selling," and "solution selling." We prefer the term "consultative selling" because it captures both the problem-solving element and the idea of selling as a helping relationship.

THE THREE PILLARS OF CONSULTATIVE SELLING

In terms of value creation, consultative selling models represent a significant advance over the older transactional models. In the most basic transactional sale the seller's contribution to value is often limited to providing product information and processing orders. Consultative selling allows a sales force to add unique customer value in three distinct areas:

1. Consultative salespeople can help customers understand their problems, issues, and opportunities in a new or different way.
2. Consultative salespeople can show customers new or better solutions to their problems.
3. Consultative salespeople can act as advocates for their customers within the supplier organization.

These are the three pillars of consultative selling—the three ways in which the sales function adds value directly to customers. Other parts of the supplier organization also add value in each of these three areas, but it's rare for any other function to equal the value creation capability that a good consultative sales force provides. So, for example, marketing and advertising play some role in helping customers understand their needs by alerting customers to the fact that opportunity exists or that solutions are available to problems. But their contribution can't approach the depth and power of a consultative sales force. Only the sales function does an effective job of uncovering and developing problems and opportunities that customers didn't even know they had. Similarly, several groups in the supplier organization, including technical support, product development, and product management can play a role in the second pillar—showing customers new or better solutions to their problems. The unique value-creating contribution of the sales force lies in their capacity to link solutions and supplier resources to the specific needs they have uncovered and to differentiate their solutions from competing alternatives. When it comes to the third pillar, acting as the customer's advocate within the supplier organization, again, other parts of the organization, such as customer support, have an important part to play. But a consultative sales force with an in-depth understanding of buyers' business and changing needs, is in the best position to represent the customer.

Together, these three pillars allow salespeople to create unique value for their customers that other functions in the supplier organization can't provide in the same depth or to the same degree. A sign that this value is a real result of consultative selling and not just derived from product superiority or well-massaged marketing efforts can be seen by reading the customer files of any organization that does a reasonably good job of selling consultatively. There you'll find unsolicited letters of thanks from grateful customers that specifically refer to the value that salespeople have created. An extract from a sample letter in our own files would be typical: "Ken Webb helped us understand the size and scope of the issues we were facing and helped us plan a more effective response. Without his insights we would not be where we are today. . . .We're thankful for the way Ken has worked to understand us better than we understand ourselves." Letters of this sort are a simple measure of the success of any consultative selling effort. If you don't have the equivalent in your own files, chances are that you're not selling consultatively.

WHEN CONSULTATIVE SELLING WORKS BEST

Consultative selling, as we saw in Chapter 3, is the preferred selling mode when one or more of these fundamental conditions are present:

- The product or service can be differentiated from competing alternatives.
- The product or service can be adapted or customized to the needs of the customer.
- The customer is not completely clear about how the product or service provides solutions or adds value.
- The delivery, installation, or use of the product or service requires coordinated support from the selling organization.
- The product or service has benefits that justify the relatively high cost of consultative selling.

When these conditions are present, it means that the salesperson can create value in the three ways we described—namely, by uncovering new needs, offering superior solutions, or acting as the customer's advocate. It's generally true that the more complex the product or service, the more possible it is to add value through consultative selling.

WHY SO DIFFICULT?

Consultative selling doesn't come easily to most sales forces. Anyone who has worked to help develop consultative selling capability will readily testify that it's not simple to transform a sales force accustomed to the transactional task of communicating value into one that can succeed in the consultative world of creating value. Many companies are still struggling to instill basic consultative competence in their salespeople. Why does the shift from transactional selling to consultative selling prove so hard? On the face of it, the change doesn't seem particularly profound or difficult. And it's not that salespeople themselves have resisted the idea. In fact, most salespeople trapped in a commoditized transactional environment will tell you that they want to sell more consultatively. "If only the company would let me spend more time with each customer," they say. "If only I were allowed to build real relationships." Very few salespeople challenge the idea of getting closer to the customer or of selling based on customer needs. So, if salespeople want to sell consultatively, and if it's also the way many customers want to be treated, then why has it proved so hard to create effective consultative sales forces?

One piece of the answer lies in that most treacherous of words *selling*. We use *selling* to cover everything from a 10-cent transaction to a sophisticated relationship where sellers know more than their customers about some parts of their buyers' businesses. At one extreme, we even use the word *selling* for the massive enterprise sale where a hundred people may be involved with a single customer for many years. Consultative selling, on the face of it, doesn't sound that different from transactional selling. The old saying "selling is selling" reflects a widely held view that it really doesn't make any difference what you sell or how you sell it—the underlying skills are basically the same. It's easy to see why people might believe this. Whether we're talking about a transactional or a consultative sale, there are a misleading number of things in common. Both have interactions with customers, both involve products or services, the objective of both is to cause customers to buy, and so on. These apparent similarities have lulled many people into seriously underestimating the magnitude of the differences. Consultative selling is so different from transactional selling that it really is misleading to use the term *selling* to describe both. It's like saying that the Concorde and a bicycle are both modes of "transportation."

WHAT'S DIFFERENT ABOUT CONSULTATIVE SELLING?

The most important and defining difference between transactional and consultative selling lies, predictably, in the area of value. Consultative salespeople create value during the sales process; transactional salespeople do not. From this difference comes a host of important consequences.

INVESTMENT OF EFFORT

In transactional selling, through which the salesperson communicates product value but doesn't add to it, you just can't afford the luxury of extra time spent with customers. It's the opposite with consultative selling. You can't afford *not* to spend the extra time. To create value, you must first invest in understanding the customer, and that takes time—much more time than most salespeople or their managers are ready to spend. As a result, salespeople habitually leap too quickly to solutions before they fully understand needs, and sales managers push inappropriately for short-term hits. Important accounts are often underresourced, and opportunities to create value are lost.

Working in a division of Kodak some years ago, we carried out an experiment that provided a convincing example of how dangerous inadequate time investment can be when a sales force is learning to adopt a consultative selling approach. We took 12 salespeople and asked them each to identify five accounts in which they were not making sales because, in their judgment, the customer had no needs to which they or their company could add value. These were "dead" accounts. In each of them, the customer had turned down the Kodak products that the sales force had been offering and had given Kodak no new business for six months or more. In these accounts, it seemed that the scope for adding value was small or nonexistent. Once a quarter, the Kodak salespeople visited the "dead" accounts just to check for new opportunity, and, on some of these calls, we traveled with them. From watching them in action, we concluded that the salespeople tended to sell very transactionally—in other words, they were product focused, and they saw their function as limited to communicating the Kodak product range and its potential value. Typically, the calls were short—about 15 minutes—and the salespeople would describe any new products or product enhancements that had been introduced since their last visit. Although they did a fairly good job of talking about Kodak solutions, it was rare for them to invest time in exploring the range and depth of customer problems where their solutions could add value. When asked about why they didn't spend more time in understanding the customer, their general reply was that there was no point because there was no opportunity to make a sale. In our experiment, we asked each salesperson to visit their five chosen dead accounts and, quite deliberately, not to attempt to sell or even to mention a single Kodak product. Instead, we asked them to spend the whole call just investing time asking questions to understand customers' issues, problems, and needs. Although they were understandably skeptical, they agreed. To their surprise, in over half of the accounts, they found new needs that neither they nor their customers had suspected. Even better, these non-selling calls ultimately led to over a million dollars of new business.

The moral of the story is twofold. First, salespeople accustomed to transactional selling will often fail to recognize opportunities to create value in consultative sales. Second, consultative selling starts with an investment of time to understand the customer. Without this investment, the value isn't created and the consultative sale fails. We should add that the Kodak case is an unusually simple example of consultative selling. It would be nice if the investment of a single customer call could normally guarantee sufficient understanding to allow salespeople to create customer value. Unfortunately, in most sales, value creation is far more complex and requires the investment of many calls, usually involving discussions with several customer employees or functions. Furthermore, it may require other forms of resource investment, such as costly technical or design support. In an age when sales force efficiency pressures are stronger than ever before, it's no wonder that sales management, and even salespeople themselves, are reluctant to invest enough time or effort to sell consultatively. Sadly, in our experience, most sales forces end up with the worst of both worlds—they don't invest enough resources to sell consultatively, but they invest more resources than they can afford for transactional selling. The result is an unacceptably expensive selling effort yielding suboptimal results.

LONGER RELATIONSHIP HORIZONS

Another important consequence of the shift to value creation is that the "relationship horizon" must extend beyond a single sale. What we mean by this ghastly jargon is that you can't usually justify the time investment and cost of consultative selling if your horizon is to make only one sale or sell just one product. As we've said, value creation starts with an investment of time. In complex sales, understanding the customer to a point where it's possible to create value may take months and cost tens of thousands of dollars. Unless the product or service is exceptionally expensive, it's unlikely that the investment in value creation can be recovered from a single sale. However, when it comes to further sales, the salesperson's investment in understanding the customer's business has already been made, so—for little or no incremental investment—the seller is already positioned to create value. The economics of consultative selling must be judged in terms of revenue from the relationship rather than from the individual transaction, and in terms of the product range or product stream rather than one specific product.

As Figure 5-1 shows, it may not be until the second or third sale that the up-front investment in understanding the customer brings a positive return. Many sales forces we've worked with have encountered problems here. Their metrics and management systems, derived from the days of transactional selling, have been based on single pieces of business rather than on the overall revenue stream potential. As a result, their selling efforts in new accounts seem disproportionately expensive. This leads to unproductive attempts to cut costs during the investment phase of the consultative sale. The result, once again, is that insufficient resources are invested to allow the level of value creation that consultative selling requires. It's easy for a sales force to lose nerve when transitioning to con-

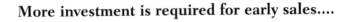

More investment is required for early sales....

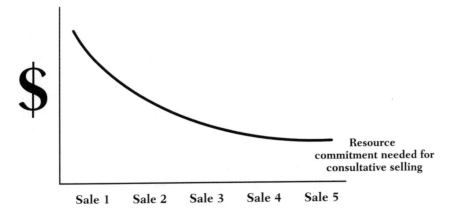

...while return on investment comes later

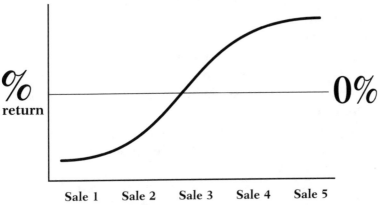

FIGURE 5-1   Getting a return on consultative selling effort.

sultative selling and, alarmed by the apparent high costs of the initial sale, to revert to selling transactionally.

DIFFERENT SKILLS

The skills involved in value creation are very different from those used merely to communicate value. At the most fundamental level, you can communicate the value of a product or service through *telling* about what you have to offer. Many very successful transactional salespeople learn to deliver value messages through polished, persuasive, or enthusiastic telling. A salesperson from Exxon Chemicals once told us that his success came from "turning myself from being just a talking brochure to being a singing and dancing brochure." In his environment, which was a classic transactional sale, there seemed no doubt that persuasive telling could be a recipe for success. But, although telling may sometimes be an effective selling style in transactional sales, there is increasing evidence that it is ineffective in consultative selling. In 1987, the book *SPIN® Selling* published the results of a massive 12-year research study of 35,000 sales calls; the research revealed conclusively that telling fails dismally in consultative sales. Instead, the key skills of consultative selling rest on *seeking*. Successful consultative salespeople sell through the questions they ask. The good news is that there are excellent well-researched and validated models of how to ask questions effectively during consultative selling. The bad news is that there's a huge gap between knowing what to do and actually doing it. Ask most sales managers how they want their people to behave in consultative sales, and they will readily tell you that they expect their people to ask skillful questions. In reality, based on findings from more than 50 consultative sale forces we've studied over the years, the majority of salespeople still tell more than they ask. The saving grace is that their competitors are generally equally incompetent.

If you doubt what we say, or if you feel that you don't have this problem, we invite you to try a depressing little experiment in your own sales force that demonstrates the strong telling orientation that is deeply ingrained in most salespeople. Ask a random 20 salespeople to define their job by answering the simple question "What is it that the company pays you to do?" Typically, you'll get answers like:

- "Show customers that our products are better."
- "Help customers see why they should buy from us."
- "Make sure that the customer knows what we have to offer and why it's worth the money."
- "Explain why we're a good investment."

The common factor in responses like these is that they are about communicating value, not about creating it. And, if salespeople see their role as value communicators rather than value creators, it's quite legitimate for them to use telling rather than seeking as their mode of selling. Once salespeople have ingrained the habit of selling through telling, it takes much more than a training program or sporadic coaching to alter their selling habits. It may seem a relatively simple task to shift a sales force from telling to seeking. But, as we'll see in Chapter 9, it's a shift that is rarely made successfully. Building the underlying skills needed for value-creating consultative selling is becoming a mission-critical task in many organizations, and few of them are doing it well.

METRICS

It's not just lack of the right skills that makes it hard for sales forces to transition from transactional to consultative selling. Another reason that it's difficult to develop a true consultative orientation is that most sales performance metrics are derived from transactional concepts of selling. One office products company we worked with had decided to take a consultative approach. Their products were changing from stand-alone boxes and were becoming increasingly customized configurations with a range of software solutions. As a result, there was real opportunity for salespeople to create customer value during the sales process. The company invested heavily in training, and everyone, from the senior VP of sales down to the humblest technical support person, knew all the right mantras about the importance of a consultative approach. Cards were even reprinted to use titles like "business consultant" rather than "sales representative." Despite all this effort, it was evident that the transition wasn't going smoothly. When we talked with salespeople, they raised a legitimate issue. "How can we sell long-term relationships," they asked, "when we're measured on call activity and 30-day sales volume?" They were right. The company still tracked the number of calls made per day—a miserably counterproductive measure if the idea was to encourage salespeople to invest much more time in understanding their customers. Even worse, the company's time horizon was the old 30-day period that they had always used when they had been selling transactionally. A typical complex consultative sale in their marketplace took about nine months. All that the 30-day reporting did was to focus effort on quick hits, which meant that the sales force was missing the larger and more profitable consultative opportunities. When we challenged senior sales management, they told us that while intellectually they agreed that these were the wrong metrics, practically they weren't prepared to change them. They feared that if they eased up on transactional metrics, call activity would decline, their people would become lazy, and sales would fall. They didn't have a clear idea of what consultative metrics would look like, and soft approaches like "trust your people" made them feel justifiably queasy.

It's easy to be critical of this inappropriate clinging to outdated transactional metrics. But the top management team had a valid point. You can't just abandon traditional metrics when you move to consultative selling. You need something better to put in their place. And most sales organizations are in the same position as this office products company: They don't have a clear idea of what the new metrics should look like. Consultative selling has been around for almost 20 years, and, in that time, we've gained a fairly good understanding of the *skills* required for effectiveness, even though few sales forces do a good job of putting those skills into practice But the metrics have unquestionably lagged behind.

THE RISE OF THE ROCK STAR

The idea of creating value through consultative selling isn't new. As we've seen, it has been gradually evolving for more than 20 years. Its practitioners haven't generally used the term *value creation* to describe their approach, but the intention has been clear. The mantras of consultative selling have been concepts like "focus on the customer," "understand customers' problems and needs," "provide solutions, not products," or "look after the customer's interests." All of these imply that the sales force is instrumental in creating value for customers. There is, however, one aspect of value that is a relatively new phenomenon and a troubling one. As consultative selling has become more sophisticated and as sales forces have generally failed in their attempts to develop strong consultative selling capabilities across the majority of their salespeople, organizations have become dependent on a few naturally gifted salespeople who can make consultative selling happen. Starting in professional services, where these talented individuals were generally called "rainmakers," the phenomenon of the consultative selling superstar has extended to other industries, notably financial services and high technology. The emerging term for these naturally talented people is "rock stars," and, as the name suggests, they are highly paid performers. In some areas of financial services, it's not uncommon for the top rock-star salespeople to command a million dollars a year for their ability to bring in business.

What's wrong with rock-star selling? Providing that the stars can bring in enough business, then, on the face of it, the rainmaker model sounds like a perfectly legitimate selling strategy. Unfortunately, increasing dependence on rock stars has made many organizations vulnerable. Even worse, in terms of value creation, reliance on sales superstars is an inefficient and ineffective way to create the highest value from a consultative selling effort. Before we look at the value creation issues, let's examine some of the associated business issues that make the rock-star selling model questionable.

THE ROCK-STAR TRAP

By definition, consultative selling superstars are a scarce resource. And, like any other scarcity, when demand greatly exceeds supply, the cost of rock stars inevitably rises. It's becoming common for talent-hunting sales organizations to offer signing bonuses and other inducements to tempt talent to come their way. Coupled with very high base compensation and commissions, this turns out to be a costly strategy. The CFO of one major financial services company once told us, "The only thing more painful to me than adding up the cost of these people is when I realize that they're getting paid three times my salary, and, despite that, they don't care a damn about the company that's paying them."

He has a point. Rock-star talent is notoriously fickle. When superstars are lured away by astronomical remuneration, stock options, or signing-on bonuses, they often take their best customers with them. It's not uncommon, for example, to hear of ad agencies that collapse overnight after a key rainmaker leaves. Other, larger, organizations may be less exposed, but the fundamental vulnerability remains. Dependence on rock-star talent is a serious business risk.

Despite the risk and the high cost, many companies still feel that, for practical business reasons, they have little choice but to depend on rock stars. "It's a different magnitude of problem for high-technology companies," says Sanjay Vaswami of the Center for Corporate Innovation. "Product life cycles are so short that the window for selling your way to market share may be weeks rather than months. Whatever it costs, rainmaker talent is worth it if it catches the window. You just can't afford to wait for the average salesperson to develop business. You need very high performers with a network of existing relationships, or you're dead." But, even in those cases where dependence on rock stars is sound strategy, the scarcity problem increasingly means that even if you can afford them, you can't find them. As Curt Wozniak, CEO of Electroglas told us, "At one time, if we wanted talent, we went to a recruiter to hunt it down for us. Now the recruiters are so busy they don't return calls. So I've had to find a recruiter to help me find recruiters."

HUNTERS AND FARMERS

The scarcity of rock-star talent—or even of proficient consultative salespeople—has led many organizations to think hard about the most efficient way to use the talent that they do have available. Sensibly, they have stripped away nonselling activities, such as administration, from their top consultative salespeople. As a result, their people have more time available for customers. The majority of organizations that have pruned routine non-selling activities report not only that their results have improved but also that their top performers seem more motivated.

This increase in motivation is certainly plausible. Some years ago we carried out a study in Xerox Corporation to find why high performers left the sales force. We discovered that one of the top three reasons they left was frustration with the time-consuming administrative and reporting systems the company imposed on them. Average performers, on the other hand, were much less upset by the burden of routine administration, so, for them, it was rarely a reason for leaving. Allowing top performers to spend more of their time on selling and less on paperwork would seem to be the proverbial no-brainer. Everyone gains, and results improve. What could be better?

As with any good concept, problems start to arise when a deserving idea gets taken too far. From the straightforward and sound notion that salespeople would be more effective if their nonselling activities were stripped away came the idea that some parts of the actual selling task were less valuable than others and should be stripped away too. This has led some people to revisit the old idea of "hunters" and "farmers" as a way to make best use of rock-star talent. The logic behind the hunter-farmer model goes something like this. The scarcest resource in most sales forces is the shaker-and-mover who knows how to bring in a significant piece of new business. These rare creatures—call them rock stars, rainmakers, or just top sales performers—don't only sell new accounts; they also spend a lot of time developing business from existing customers. But, so goes the argument, the skills are different. To open up a new account takes hunter skills. It requires aggressiveness, confidence, and the capacity to make an impressive initial impact. These are just the qualities that top performers are supposed to possess. However, once the first piece of business has been initiated by the hunter, a different kind of skill takes over. This is the expertise of the farmer. Farmers, says the theory, are the ones who grow the business. They plant seeds, they tend the account, they nurture the customer, and, as a result they harvest a stream of revenue season after season. By splitting the sales force into these two groups, hunters and farmers, it should be possible to make the highest and best use of top performers. We can strip away any farming activities presently carried out by expensive rock stars, so the thinking goes, and give these jobs instead to lower-salaried or less experienced people. Our top performers, the hunters, can then concentrate on generating new business. It's a seductively simple idea. The only problem is, it doesn't work.

BLEEDING TO DEATH AT BURROUGHS

What's wrong with the hunter-farmer concept? Why has it so often resulted in failure? Some of the practical issues are illustrated in the history of Burroughs Corporation before it merged with Sperry to become Unysis. Burroughs was one of the first companies to espouse the hunter-farmer model. Their case was fairly typical of other organizations that later adopted the same approach. To sell their product range—computers, specialist electronic equipment, peripherals, and software— increasingly required problem solving and a solution focus. In other words, they made classic consultative sales. They had tried to build a better level of consultative skills into their entire sales force, but with only marginal success. As a result they relied heavily on a few top salespeople—the rock stars— who brought in a disproportionate share of the overall business. In an attempt to use their top performers more productively and hoping to increase their market share by gaining new customers, Burroughs decided to create a hunter sales force that would originate business from new accounts. The rest of the sales force became farmers, and, once the initial sale had been made, accounts would be turned over to them for development. "When we heard about the hunter-farmer split at Burroughs, we were overjoyed," a Digital Equipment sales executive told us. "As soon as they took their top people off of existing accounts, we were ready to jump in. We beat the crap out of their farmers before they could get their act together."

The new strategy quickly started to get into trouble. Existing customers were lost by the farmers, and far fewer new ones were gained by the hunters than the company had anticipated. Burroughs was one of the early casualties among sales forces that adopted and subsequently abandoned the hunter-farmer model. What went wrong? Was it, as the DEC executive suggested, that they simply never got their act together—that it was a good strategy, which failed in the execution? Or were there more fundamental reasons? In hindsight, and from what we now know about creating value in the consultative sale, it seems clear that the hunter-farmer model was intrinsically flawed right from the start.

DUBIOUS ASSUMPTIONS ABOUT HUNTERS

One serious problem with the hunter-farmer model is that it rests on a transactional rather than a consultative concept of selling. The model started its life in the 1940s and 1950s in the insurance industry where producer sales forces originated business, while separate service sales forces went every week to collect premiums from the customers that the producers had created. It was clearly a superior use of sales time to let producers knock on more new doors, while less skilled people came behind to keep existing customers happy, to collect premiums, and to make the occasional add-on sale. But that's hardly an effective model for consultative selling. In the consultative sale, as we've seen, the first piece of business from a customer results from a disproportionate investment of time to understand that customer's needs in depth. But this essential time investment isn't consistent with the basic logic of the hunter model. The whole idea of separating hunters from farmers is to make more efficient use of hunter time. Companies expect their rock stars to justify their cost by producing new business quickly, and their metrics will often unwittingly penalize their people for time spent in learning the intricacies of a new customer's needs and issues. Many corporations that have created a hunter sales force have found, to their cost, that the new business they so confidently expected has been agonizingly slow in arriving. Even more alarming, the business stream from existing accounts that have been handed over to less experienced farmers has begun to dry up.

As companies look more closely at why the hunter-farmer model is failing them, they inevitably start looking for flaws in the logic that led them to adopt the model in the first place. They usually find that they made two questionable assumptions. First, they assumed that the skills and experience required for a successful hunter were different and deeper than the skills and experience needed for farmers. That might have been true in the transactional 1950s world of insurance producers and collectors, but there's much less evidence for such a belief in today's consultative selling. Existing accounts require just as much active selling as new; both hunters and farmers require equal skills in questioning and problem solving. The second doubtful assumption is that there's more business to be had from new than from existing customers. This assumption is sometimes justified, but less often than you might think. If your existing accounts have genuinely reached the end of their revenue-producing life, or if you've a large marketplace of new customers waiting to hear from you, then it may be a very sensible strategy to give your top performers the role of exclusively generating new business. On the other hand, if you are like most value-creating businesses, the bulk of your present and future revenue comes from the accounts you already have, and, unless you map your top resources to your most important existing customers, you are likely to lose opportunity.

The hunter-farmer model also assumes we are still living in the good old days of transactional selling, when customers would put their business out to bid annually, or even on a purchase-by-purchase basis. In the RFP era, before supplier consolidation, there were plenty of chances for new business from competitors' accounts every time the customer went out to bid. So the hunter sales force had a large pool of opportunities to choose from. Even if they failed in a particular account, it would only be a few months' wait before the customer would be looking around again, and there would be another chance to get back in the door. Those days have forever disappeared in an era of supplier consolidation where opportunities for significant new business are few and far between. Dick Canada, who was selling for Xerox at the start of the supplier consolidation movement and lived through some of its effects on sales, put it well when he said, "I suppose that the hunter-farmer idea might just have worked when the woods were full of herds of game waiting to be hunted. But try it when you're starving because the game's gone someplace else. Pretty soon your thoughts turn to how nice it would be to grow crops."

THE HIGH COST OF HAND-OVER

Even if the woods happen to be full of game—even if you're in the fortunate position of having as many new business opportunities as you could possibly want—there's one more issue that makes the hunter-farmer model less attractive than it superficially seems. In a consultative sale there are costs that often go unrecognized when an account is handed over from hunter to farmer. The hunter, in a consultative sale, makes a substantial investment in understanding the account and its needs. This effort, which could cost weeks or months, then has to be repeated all over again when the account is handed over to the farmer. Either the hunter must invest nonselling time in bringing the farmer up to speed, or else the farmer has to learn the account from scratch. When the farmer relies on the hunter to thoroughly brief and hand over the account, there's the inevitable danger that the briefing is incomplete or distorted. We've sat in on enough *post mortems* when promising accounts have been lost after an indifferent hand-over, to know how easy it is for information transfer to leave out crucial details or to introduce unintentional bias. Almost invariably, the pressure on hunters to focus on new opportunities acts as an active disincentive for them to take the time needed to ensure a seamless hand-over of the accounts they have generated. Some proponents of the hunter-farmer model shrug off the hand-over issue by saying that it's not the hunters' responsibility; it's up to the farmers to become educated by immersing themselves in their new account.

Unfortunately, such a reeducation is at the customer's expense, and they rightly resent the time and effort required to bring a farmer, or any new salesperson, up to speed. As Bill Budney, vice president of distribution systems for Public Service Electric & Gas put it, "It's a big investment of time bringing a new vendor aboard. You need to know that the time you spend with them is worth it. You can't just give a free education to everyone who comes knocking at your door." Yet that's so often what the hunter-farmer model asks of customers. Educate our hunter so we can sell to you; now start over again and educate our farmer so that we can sell you some more. From the customer's point of view, that's a value proposition that doesn't make much sense.

DRIVERS OF VALUE CREATION

It's easy to catalog the drawbacks of the hunter-farmer concept as an organizing model for consultative selling, but the practical question remains, how do you best use scarce top sales talent? If you shouldn't adopt the hunter-farmer split, then what's a better way? It's clear that the diminishing availability and increasing cost of top sales talent makes many sales forces vulnerable. Their whole sales effort is held hostage by the scarcity of rainmakers. They can't find enough of them, and the ones they have are constantly being tempted away by competitors. The expense is escalating, and, given the high cost of the rainmaker approach, there is always the question of when the price of making rain will exceed the value of the crop. Yet many companies feel they have no choice. They need rock stars, and they can't succeed without them. The top-talent issue is becoming an ever-increasing concern for organizations whose success depends on high-level consultative selling. How can you most effectively use rock stars, or—better still—how can you reduce your dependence on them?

Perhaps the best answer starts with an understanding of where value creation resides in the sales organization. For those sales forces that have adopted rainmaker models, almost all of the value creation capability resides in the rock-star sales performers themselves. There's often very little value created by the rest of the sales function. Cynics have suggested that the value contribution of most companies is limited to providing their salespeople with office space, a phone, and business cards. Some top salespeople would add, even more cynically, that their institution not only fails to create positive value, it actively creates negative value in terms of demands for reports, forecasts, and internal meetings that take time away from customers. This may be a pessimistic assessment of institutional value, but, unfortunately it's often close to the truth. For years many sales functions have been managed more by the compensation plan than by management. Sales managers have become remote from customers and have kept themselves informed through cumbersome and demanding reporting systems. All too often, the sales function has failed to see itself in value creation terms and has allowed itself to become a necessary cost incurred in monitoring the activities of salespeople. A major issue for consultative selling is how to build more value within the institution, through better sales tools, management, and improved sales process, so that ordinary mortals can perform well in the consultative sale. As rainmaking talent becomes ever scarcer, the need to shift value from the individual to the institution becomes ever more pressing.

DEFINING INSTITUTIONAL VALUE

What do we mean by *institutional value*? Put simply, the institution—in the form of the sales function or its equivalent—actively enables its salespeople to create more customer value than they would be able to create by themselves. So, as a result, salespeople are able to create customer value *because* of their institution rather than despite it. There are three principal ways to create value on an institutional level that result in a tangible customer impact:

- *Coaching and Training,* to develop the effectiveness of salespeople in the value creation skills of helping customers understand new needs, arrive at better solutions, and act as the customer's advocate.
- *Support, Tools, and Information,* to allow salespeople to identify and provide customer value more efficiently and effectively.
- *Sales Process,* to provide salespeople with a customer-centered road map of the steps and tasks required of them for effective consultative selling.

COACHING FOR CUSTOMER VALUE

Coaching is a powerful vehicle for creating institutional value. It's the principal tool available on an institutional level for improving sales effectiveness. No other activity carried out by sales management has so positive an impact on the success of consultative selling. Training alone, without substantial reinforcement through coaching, has a disappointingly small impact. A well-integrated combination of training and coaching can enable average salespeople to improve their performance dramatically. In the appendix to *SPIN® Selling* (McGraw-Hill, 1988), there are several studies showing that there are sustainable revenue generation increases of over 35 percent from consultative salespeople as a result of a systematic combination of training and coaching. Even when the coaching is less carefully implemented, a study of 1000 coached salespeople showed revenue increases of 17 percent compared with uncoached control groups. In the excellent sales forces we've worked with over the years, a strong coaching culture has been a hallmark of their success. We'll have much more to say in Chapter 9 about coaching and how to implement it. For now, we'll focus on two of the most serious barriers that must be overcome if coaching is to become an effective strategy for increasing institutional value.

Time for Coaching.   Simple as it sounds, the biggest single barrier to effective coaching is management time. On the face of it, this doesn't seem to be a particularly difficult problem. In reality it's a showstopper that, for many organizations, has been the prime cause of their inability to build an effective consultative selling effort. The most intractable time issues usually manifest themselves in two ways. First, many organizations have a span of control that has been derived from transactional selling models where it's imperative to contain sales cost. Transactional sales forces can often run efficiently with a span of control that involves 20 or more people reporting to a single manager. That's out of the question if your objective is to build a coaching culture. The best consultative sales forces we've worked with have a span of control of between 6 and 9 salespeople reporting to a sales manager. Once the number increases beyond these limits, it's almost impossible for a manager to provide the in-depth level of attention that's needed to create institutional value through coaching.

The second time problem is the perennial organizational issue of long-term time investments being squeezed out by short-term pressures. One Citicorp manager put it this way: "I know I should be spending more time coaching my people. But there are so many other immediate demands on my time that keep getting in the way. In my job, there's paperwork that I've got to complete, or we're in legal violation. If it's not done, I don't go home. And then there's usually at least one customer with a crisis that's time sensitive. I can't neglect things like that. But coaching doesn't have to be done by Friday, so it always gets put off until next week." Thousands of first-line sales managers will tell a similar story. Coaching doesn't have to be done by Friday, so it's forever left on the back burner of good intentions. Making time for coaching needs more than a cursory mandate from senior management. It requires a significant policy commitment, determined implementation, metrics to ensure it happens, and a reward system that encourages it.

A Shared-Effectiveness Model.   The difficulties involved in freeing up enough management time for coaching have sunk many an effort to create a coaching culture. But, even with adequate time for coaching, even with training in how to coach and even with the right rewards and metrics, the coaching effort can still yield disappointing results in terms of value creation. Many organizations have recognized the power of coaching and, having created the right conditions to allow coaching to happen, optimistically believe their problems finally are over. Soon they find that, although coaching *is* happening, it's not leading to the kind of improvement in sales results they had hoped for. Yet, on the face of it, they've done all the right things. They have freed managers to coach, and they have trained them in coaching skills and techniques. What could be going wrong? They have discovered the hard way that there's a missing ingredient. Coaching skills alone are not enough to help managers add value. Generic coaching techniques are useful but, by themselves, are insufficient to improve sales performance. Even more fundamental than coaching skills is the missing ingredient—an understanding of the performance to be coached.

To coach consultative salespeople, you must start with a clear picture of what good consultative selling looks like. And, alas, few sales managers have such a picture. As a result, they coach their people to use irrelevant or even counterproductive skills and strategies. For example, in Xerox Corporation, we found that the most common coaching advice from managers was that their people should ask more open, rather than closed, questions. Studies in Xerox that observed over 500 of their salespeople during actual sales calls found that there was no difference in the relative frequency of open and closed questions between top performers and average performers. So the most commonly offered coaching advice was, in all probability, irrelevant to sales performance. Unfortunately, skills are difficult to coach, and sales managers, unaware of the growing body of research on effective consultative selling skills, all too often coach their people in skills that neither add value to customers nor lead to improved results. It's much the same with selling strategy. Managers coach their people to call high and attempt to get in front of decision makers as early as possible in the selling cycle, bypassing influencers and secondary players. Yet evidence from research suggests that this advice may be dangerous. It's a risky strategy in a consultative sale to go to a senior-level decision maker before thoroughly understanding the issues and problems where you can create value. Most good consultative salespeople will first do their homework by working with those influencers in the buying organization who have the best knowledge of the problems and opportunities where the selling organization hopes to create value. For managers to coach effectively, they have to know what actually works in a consultative sale, and the majority of managers are badly in need of help in this area.

Despite these barriers, which can so often have a devastating effect on attempts to improve coaching performance, there's no doubt that a carefully implemented coaching program, supplemented by training, is a powerful way to increase institutional value. Good coaching allows mortals to succeed in areas that previously were the exclusive province of rock stars.

SUPPORT, TOOLS, AND INFORMATION

Another way for the institution to create value is through providing better support tools for their consultative salespeople. We saw in earlier chapters how improved information systems can add value by reducing selling costs in the transactional sale. In the consultative sale, customer-accessible information systems can allow the institution to create new value for customers. A good example is Haworth, a company that designs and makes office furniture. Their modular office furniture requires a fairly sophisticated consultative sale. Configurations are customized to solve customer space problems. Each customized solution involves the assembly of many components. In an average cubicle [or "cluster," as Haworth calls it] there are 14 visible components, but 72 items must be ordered to allow correct assembly. With 22 million orderable parts in their product range—excluding color and fabric variations—the logistics were a nightmare for salesperson and customer alike. To sell a large Haworth configuration took more than rock-star talent; it took a knowledge of the part numbers that bordered on mathematical genius. Very few salespeople had that knowledge. As a result, only a handful of their people were able to create customer value in terms of configuring the best customized option for customers. Haworth solved the problem by designing an elegant object-oriented software support tool that allows customers to see what they are getting. This tool gives a three-dimensional visualization and modeling capability so that customers can quickly see what a particular configuration looks like and can change it at will. The system, which runs on a laptop, accesses 25 million part numbers but does so in a way that's transparent to the customer. Kris Manos, director of customer service at Haworth explains, "We sell a complete solution, but what we deliver to the customer is a bunch of parts that we then assemble. The system allows us to do this more accurately, more responsively, and more cheaply for our customers. We're less dependent on highly experienced salespeople who are able to translate customer needs into part numbers." The configuration software is a tool that has enabled Haworth to transfer some of the value creation from salespeople back to the institution. It's worth noting that the Haworth software does more than shift value out of the experienced salesperson's head and back into the sales function; it also actively creates new value by giving customers a superior way to "see" new or better solutions to their problems. Showing customers new or better solutions, as we saw earlier, is one of the three pillars of value in the consultative sale.

There's an increasing use of information tools to create customer value. The tracking systems of a UPS or FedEx are another well-known example. It's likely that there will be an explosion in the use and availability of tools such as these that provide customers with solutions more easily, quickly, and conveniently than the sales force can achieve in conventional face-to-face selling. Even the most responsive salesperson can't track down the status of a package as fast as customers can themselves at the touch of a button.

In addition to tools that directly create customer value, the institution can increase its value creation capability by improving internal systems and providing tools that allow salespeople to perform their value creation role more effectively. There are two hopeful trends here:

- The shift from reporting tools to planning tools
- The shift from product communication tools to value identification tools

FROM REPORTING TOOLS TO PLANNING TOOLS

The reporting tools of most sales organizations add no value to customers. On the contrary, they are a source of negative value by taking up time that could otherwise be used by the salesperson to create customer value. Most organizations have reporting requirements that take salespeople a minimum of two or three hours per week to complete. With sales forecasts, call reports, expense and activity reports, not to mention all the other internal demands for information, salespeople often feel that the customer comes a distant second in terms of institutional priorities. Companies generally view their reporting demands as a necessary evil and excuse them saying that, on the whole, they are carried out after business hours and on the salesperson's own time. Nevertheless, the fact remains that the majority of reports are exclusively for the benefit of the selling institution, and neither salespeople nor their customers benefit from them.

Activity tracking may have a role in transactional selling, but in consultative selling, it can be downright counterproductive. In Rackham and Ruff, *Managing Major Sales* (Harper & Row, 1991), we describe a number of cases where the introduction of activity management systems in consultative sales forces actually led to a significant fall in sales results and in customer satisfaction. So it's refreshing to see a number of major organizations such as IBM, Microsoft, Procter & Gamble, and Johnson & Johnson shift the emphasis of parts of their reporting systems so that they have a more positive impact in terms of creating institutional value. The shift, put simply, is from an emphasis on reporting after the event to planning before it happens. A call report completed after a customer visit adds very little value. The call is over; it's history, and reporting on what happened won't change a thing. The same effort, however, put into call planning *before* the customer visit can result in a more purposeful and organized meeting that adds customer value. Call planning has the potential to change history rather than to catalog it. By providing better call-planning tools, especially if call plans are coupled with systematic coaching, the institution can create value that, in the execution of the plan, becomes visible to customers.

From Product Communication to Value Identification

Because most organizations see the role of the sales force as value communication rather than value creation, they provide their salespeople with a range of value-communicating tools such as product descriptions, brochures, or even multimedia presentations. In a limited kind of way, these communication tools do provide some customer value. They help customers to understand potential solutions, for example, and they may sometimes even cause customers to see a need that they hadn't realized before. The trouble with most of these tools is that they are one-way mechanisms for passing on information. They would work just as well if there were no sales force—if the brochures or presentations were sent directly to the customer. In transactional selling, value communication tools of this kind have a useful role to play. By informing the customer more cheaply than face-to-face human interactions, they can substitute for some face-to-face selling and allow cost to be stripped out of the transactional sale.

But relying on brochures doesn't work for the consultative sale, where product complexity and customized solutions make these one-way communication tools less and less effective. It would clearly be a more powerful contribution to value creation if the sales organization provided tools that helped their salespeople to diagnose customer problems or understand customer issues more deeply—tools, in other words, that played an active role in helping salespeople to identify and create value. Increasingly, there is a shift in consultative sales forces toward developing better analytical tools. Consulting organizations, for example, have developed a wide variety of diagnostic frameworks and tools to help them understand client problems, financial services companies have a range of financial analysis tools, utilities have energy audits, and so on. In consultative selling, these diagnostic and analytical tools allow the salesperson to do a more efficient and effective job of understanding the customer's needs. Without such tools to diagnostically identify customer value, the sales organization must depend on top talent that can create value through experience and skill without the help of the tools. The more that the institution invests in good diagnostics, the more the institution itself contributes to creating customer value and the less it depends on rock stars.

APPLYING PROCESS THINKING
TO SALES

We've seen how it's possible to build institutional value in consultative selling through systematic coaching and through sales tools that are designed to focus on value creation rather than value communication. A third promising area for creating institutional value lies in the application of process methodologies to consultative selling. Process redesign and reengineering have radically changed the internal workflow of most production and administrative functions in organizations. Like any idea that has had the misfortune of being widely promoted as an answer to all organizational ills, process redesign has become overly fashionable and is seen by many as a fad that is in decline. However, process thinking has great potential for reducing the reliance on rainmaker selling by redesigning sales jobs so that average salespeople can perform them more easily. As we'll see in Chapter 7, there are traps aplenty for those who seek to transport reengineering and process redesign concepts into the sales force. And, as we'll also see, there are rich rewards for those that succeed.

THE NEW ENTERPRISE SELLING

FROM LARGE SALES TO DEEP RELATIONSHIPS

"I'm responsible for two national accounts," a senior manager at Microsoft told us, "and they are as different as night and day. By coincidence, last year we did exactly the same volume of business with each one, but the way we did that business is so opposite that it's like another set of rules, or like speaking a different language." In the first key account, all customer contact went through the purchasing department. In order to talk to other players inside the customer's organization, the Microsoft team routinely submitted a formal request in writing to their purchasing agent for what they called a "permission to speak." Every sale—and there were a lot of them—required a separate contract and a new purchase order. Microsoft employees on the customer's premises were required to wear badges reading "Contractor: Escort required at all times." They were never shown any customer confidential information, yet each team member had to sign a fearsome confidentiality agreement every time a new project came up to bid. This wasn't a military client engaged in secret work. As it happened, the customer was a *Fortune* 500 company whose products were simple low-tech commodities.

The other key account was dramatically different. It too was a *Fortune* 500 company, and its products were in a variety of technology-related businesses. Let's call it Hightec, Inc. Microsoft people wore the same badges as Hightec employees. They had offices inside the company, they were listed in the company telephone directory. Although there was just one simple confidentiality agreement between Microsoft and Hightec, people in each company constantly shared deeply proprietary information with each other. Hightec had access to Microsoft's product development strategy and had been invited to help shape the direction that Microsoft's strategy was taking. Microsoft, in turn, had detailed knowledge of Hightec's business planning, and Microsoft people regularly attended Hightec strategy meetings, during which they were treated as equal and valued participants.

What accounted for the dramatic difference between these two customers? Was it just a matter of corporate culture? In part. There's no doubt that the first organization treated all outsiders with suspicion and built a wall around themselves that no supplier could ever penetrate. But that's only part of the story. It wasn't simply a case of a more open culture in Hightec—they were equally guarded about their internal affairs, to the point that they preferred not to have their real name used here. The difference between the two customers was less a matter of corporate culture and more a result of the selling relationship. As it happened, while Microsoft was sitting in Hightec corporate strategy meetings, at that very instant there were other software competitors visiting Hightec who were being treated as arms-length vendors and were even wearing "Escort required" badges. In the first customer's organization, Microsoft was a vendor, and relationships were transactional or, at best, consultative. In Hightec, Microsoft had achieved an enterprise relationship.

THE ENTERPRISE RELATIONSHIP

What's the fundamental difference between an enterprise relationship and the kind of long-term, trust-based relationship that a very effective salesperson can achieve in a consultative sale? The difference has little to do with the volume of sales to the customer. As we've seen, it's possible to achieve a huge sales volume with an account whether the relationship is consultative, enterprise, or even transactional. Enterprise relationships, however, *always* imply a substantial volume of profitable business to justify the resources they require. Consultative or transactional sales, because they use fewer resources, need not generate so great a return—which allows them to be smaller. The defining differences between high-level consulting sales and enterprise relationships lie not in the size of the sale but in the nature of the offering and the roles of the players.

THE ENTERPRISE OFFERING

Put simply, in the enterprise sale, the enterprise *is* the offering. The product is secondary. What the customer "buys"—although that word no longer adequately describes what happens in the relationship—is a supplier organization's total value-creating capability. The hallmark of the enterprise relationship, as defined here, is that it exists to create value at an institutional level; it leverages the whole business chain rather than a product or a single function. So Stone Container, for example, supplies corrugated and other packaging to Baxter, the giant pharmaceutical company. But, because it's an enterprise sale, the whole of Stone Container's business chain is harnessed to hunt for ways to create new value for Baxter. Stone's research and development teams work with Baxter on simultaneous product and packaging design; engineers from each company operate in the others' plants to improve performance and bring new thinking to each other's problems; Stone's trucks are transporting Baxter's products. The two organizations have undertaken more than 200 joint projects, in every area of their respective businesses, to reduce costs or create new value. The "product" that Stone sells Baxter is a total enterprise capability.

In this respect, enterprise selling is sometimes different from a partnering relationship. It's possible for a single function within the supplier organization to partner with a single customer function. Many outsourcing arrangements are set up and managed by a single function. So, for example, our engineering services department might take over the maintenance of all electrical equipment in your factory, or we might outsource all our graphics work to your design function. Although arrangements such as these have some of the superficial characteristics of an enterprise relationship, they are generally much narrower and more tightly defined. However, terminology in this emerging field is still very loose. There's little enough agreement between writers and experts on how to define "partnership" or "strategic alliance," let alone what makes these things different from enterprise selling. The term *partnering,* in particular, has become so widely misused that, if it were a person, it would be suing for misrepresentation and making its lawyers rich. Many, if not most, of the things said in this chapter about enterprise selling could apply equally well to partnering as defined in the book *Getting Partnering Right* (Neil Rackham, Lawrence Friedman, and Richard Ruff, Mc-Graw Hill, 1996). At the risk of introducing a complication, almost half of the partnering relationships studied in that book had been set up with the sole and specific objective of reducing costs. These partnerships often had limited duration as well as narrow objectives. So, for example, the partnership might aim to cut three warehouses out of the distribution chain. Often they were created to enable one or both parties to compete better in transactional marketplaces, and, once the specific objective was achieved, then the partnership had met its purpose and was dissolved.

Although cost reduction opportunities are eagerly recognized and exploited in enterprise sales, the fundamental purpose of the enterprise relationship is to create new value by any means possible. This is likely to lead the enterprise partners on a comprehensive hunt for new and creative sources of value rather than merely to contain or reduce cost. When a division of NEC that manufactured PBX telephone switches made an enterprise sale to a major hospital, one part of their effort was to help the hospital reduce the cost of its internal telephone and paging operations. However, the greatest rewards came from the creative thinking that the parties put into finding new value where none had existed before. So, for example, they knew that with the increasing pressures to keep hospital stays short, it was often the case that patients were moved out of rooms or even discharged from the hospital without friends and relatives finding out about the move. As a result, the next patient got the last patient's calls. NEC was able to program the switch so that the number moved with the patient, which meant that when patients were transferred, relatives could find them easily and the next patient in the room was left in peace. In dozens of other small ways, for example, by using the telephone system to punch in and capture medication records, the enterprise sale led to new benefits and created new value.

When the enterprise becomes the offering, several things fundamentally change. A salesperson, or even a sales team, can no longer control the relationship. It's too complex, and there are too many people involved. Early on in the Baxter-Stone relationship, for example, several hundred people were included in the discussions. Jean Brock, who was Baxter's program manager for supplier relations at the time, told us:

> Very early on we structured it so that all our plants and all of their [Stone's] plants had an opportunity to gain and share in the relationship. We went out to 18 Baxter locations and 16 Stone locations that were involved, and we got the materials manager and the purchasing manager and the plant manager from our side, as well as the plant manager and the sales manager from Stone's local plant, involved in the relationship.

Not only are there more people involved in terms of absolute numbers, there are also more *types* of people. Enterprise selling is intrinsically cross functional. In the Baxter-Stone case, in addition to sales, purchasing, and sales support people, there are production staff, plant engineers, materials managers, and others all actively working together on a daily basis.

EQUALITY IN THE RELATIONSHIP

There's another fundamental difference about how the enterprise participants work together that goes beyond the number of players involved and the functions they represent. In the enterprise sale there is an important shift of role. If you sit in on the discussions in transactional sales, or even in most consultative sales, it's easy to see who represents the supplier and who represents the customer. In transactional sales, being a vendor is clearly an inferior role in terms of status and power—and some customers go to great length to remind their suppliers that vendors are a lower-life form. As one purchasing agent from a large oil company remarked, "With vendors our motto is 'Keep them waiting, keep them sweating, and keep them from getting too good an opinion of themselves.'" The transactional sale is rarely a discussion between equals. The enterprise sale, on the other hand, is about business equality. As Randa Rosenblum of FedEx described it:

> If we just move boxes for a customer on a price-per-package basis ["transactional sale" in our terminology], then we're not very high up the food chain, and we're probably going to be treated like an inferior because, basically, that's just what we are. Even if we go in and solve problems ["consultative sale"], or we move *important* boxes, then we're still not on their level. But when we partner to help our customers provide better value to their customers ["enterprise sale"], then everything changes. We're in it together, it's our shared mission, and we're on their level.

The hallmark of an enterprise relationship is that it's almost impossible to tell the relative status of the team representing each side. It's not the age-old transactional ritual between overbearing buyers and deferential sellers. "Two business equals working together to create value for the customer's customer," to paraphrase Ms. Rosenblum, isn't a bad way to express it. Unfortunately, though, inappropriate old habits die hard. In the early stages of an enterprise relationship some customers will still treat suppliers as vendors, with all the baggage that the label brings with it. Even worse, salespeople will often push customers for short-term transactional gains and, in doing so, sabotage the new relationship before it can become productively established. As we'll see later in the chapter, it's crucial to establish the role of a business relationship between equals early on in the enterprise sale.

CREATING VALUE AT THE BOUNDARY

We've defined one element of an enterprise sale in terms of the players and their roles—we've said that it's a multifunctional relationship involving many players on each side who are working together as business equals to create new customer value. But where does that value come from? Is it just that bringing in more people and more resources allows more value to be created—that it's really only a consultative sale but on a bigger scale? Or is there something intrinsically different about the nature of enterprise value? We believe that there *is* a fundamental difference in how value is created that makes the enterprise sale unique and very different. Put in one sentence, the enterprise sale creates its value by redesigning the boundary, or interface, between the supplier and the customer.

Most readers will be familiar with one of the central ideas of the reengineering methodology, that when there's a sequence of tasks to be performed with hand-off from one function to another, enormous productivity improvement is possible at the boundary between the functions. Inside each function things may run smoothly, but at the boundary—or interface—with the next function in the chain, things generally go awry. So, for example, marketing may come up with a truly awesome launch plan for a new product, but somewhere at the boundary during the hand-off to sales for execution, the launch plan begins to unravel because it isn't designed in a form that lets the sales function execute it most effectively. The next chapter will discuss the idea of boundary redesign in depth in the context of the design of the sales process. For now, let's assume that if the reengineering gurus are even half right in the claims they have made for their method, redesigning the boundaries between functions can result in dramatic improvements in performance. Their logic is simple enough: Most of the available productivity gains within functions have already been captured. There's now more productivity to be gained by looking at how the functions fit together than by looking within the individual functions themselves.

Now let's apply that same logic not to the boundaries between functions inside the company but to the boundaries between the company and its suppliers or customers. The internal boundaries between functions inside the company may, as the reengineering proponents suggest, be a rich vein of opportunity for productivity gain. However, in comparison to internal boundaries, the external boundaries between customers and their suppliers are an absolute productivity gold mine. The room for improvement is almost inexhaustible. The way most suppliers have historically worked with their major customers is all too often a model of inefficiency and waste. Typically, you'll find issues such as:

- The supplier's production schedules don't match the customer's demand pattern, and, as a result, the supplier is either overproducing, which leads to excess inventory, or underproducing, which leads to loss of product availability and therefore loss of sales.

- Each party has its own logistics system, including separate paperwork, transportation, and warehousing. As a result, there's a lot of duplication and waste.

- The customer is doing things internally that the supplier could be doing much more competently and more cheaply. However, these things that the customer is struggling with aren't in a mainstream area where the supplier is selling a product or solution.

Traditionally issues like these have gone unaddressed because problems of this sort don't belong to anybody. What does it matter to a customer if the supplier's production schedules are inefficient? As long as the supplier meets the contractual obligations of price quality and delivery, it's not the customer's problem. And why should a supplier care if a customer has excess inventory or inefficient logistics? If a customer is prepared to take the agreed supply and pay their bills on time, it's their problem, not the supplier's.

In an enterprise relationship, issues like these become everyone's problem. The goal of the enterprise sale is to redesign the boundary between supplier and customer to make it significantly more productive for the benefit of both parties. Let's see how boundary redesign worked with actual cases involving some enterprise relationships that were facing the three typical scenarios we've just quoted.

Supplier's Production Schedules Don't Match Customer's Demand Pattern. The customer Public Service Electric & Gas (PSE&G) got together with their cable supplier Okonite to jointly plan Okonite's production scheduling to link it more efficiently with the emerging cable needs of PSE&G. Before the enterprise relationship, Okonite's scheduling issues would almost certainly have brought an "it's not our problem" response from PSE&G. After an enterprise relationship had been established, PSE&G was prepared to make significant changes to help Okonite optimize their scheduling. They cut the number of cable types they used from 27 down to 9 and changed their internal systems. As Ken Doyle of PSE&G told us, "We had to forecast differently and much more accurately." With better integration of the supplier's production and the customer's demand, substantial savings were generated that both could share.

Each Party Has Its Own Logistics System, and the Two Systems Don't Mesh. One of the classic cases in enterprise relationships has been the Wal-Mart–Procter & Gamble (P&G) partnership. By streamlining the logistics process by which P&G goods reach Wal-Mart stores, cutting out unnecessary steps, and reducing duplication of paperwork and administration, the partners have made multi-million-dollar savings. Before the redesign of this boundary issue, each grumbled about elements of the other's logistics system but, as Mike Milligan, senior vice president for worldwide sales of Procter & Gamble put it, "At the time, the inefficiencies in their system didn't seem as though it was any of our business."

The Customer Is Doing Things Internally That the Supplier Could Be Doing More Competently.   Hillenbrand runs a fleet of 400 trucks, but that's not one of their core competencies. They make such things as surgical beds, hospital equipment, and infusion pumps. They ship their products all over the world using their own fleet and outside shippers. One of these outside shippers is UPS, and the relationship, at one time, was typically transactional. Price and delivery were the only things that mattered. Since starting to work with Hillenbrand on an enterprise level, UPS has used its considerable expertise in fleet management to enable Hillenbrand to save $2 million per year in fleet and other logistics costs. In the old transactional days, the existence of Hillenbrand's fleet would be just a piece of bad news for UPS. As Larry Rutherford of UPS told us, "As a vendor, you'd see their fleet as taking away business from you so—in a way—the less well it operated, the better because you'd always get some crumbs falling your way because their fleet couldn't deliver. But when you get into a continuous-improvement partnership, then any area where you can add value gets to be your sandbox to play in—and we could certainly add value in logistics and fleet management because that's our business."

In each of these three cases, and hundreds more like them, enterprise selling has meant a redesign of the boundary between organizations to create new value.

ASSESSING ENTERPRISE SALES POTENTIAL

Many organizations have been attracted to the idea of building enterprise relationships with their customers. The advantages are seductive. Enterprise sales usually involve long-term, high-volume business that—in some cases at least—can offer excellent margins. Frequently these relationships are single source and lock competitors out of the account. Drawn in by these apparent riches, companies have hastened to set up any arrangements they can make to capture the long-term business of key customers. Under a variety of labels, such as "partnering," "strategic alliances," "superaccounts," or "special relationships," they have created their own version of the enterprise sale. In doing so, many of them have stepped unwittingly into a minefield. The failure rate of these relationships is high. A common statistic, one that most experts in the field seem to accept, is that 70 percent of these arrangements collapse within 12 months. What goes wrong? More often than not, it's a failure by one or both parties to understand the preconditions needed for an enterprise relationship. As a result, it's easy for organizations to get drawn in to an expensive and frustrating journey to failure.

PRECONDITIONS FOR A SUCCESSFUL ENTERPRISE RELATIONSHIP

Most of these failures could have been avoided if organizations had asked themselves five fundamental questions before deciding to pursue an enterprise sale. Each of these questions is a potential showstopper. Each has to be answered with an unequivocal yes. They are:

- Will *both* parties be prepared to make changes to create value?
- Is there sufficient potential for new value creation that would not be possible from a transactional or a consultative relationship?
- Is there cross-functional capability and commitment on both sides?
- Will there be access to each other's strategy?
- Is there compatibility of organizational values?

A thorough exploration of each of these questions is a useful insurance policy for anyone considering an enterprise relationship. As many companies have found to their detriment, failure is expensive in both monetary and psychological terms. A few hours of caution can prevent months of recrimination and an irretrievable rift with a crucial customer. Richard Crew, president of BEST Logic, expresses it this way:

> In partnering relationships, there are greater risks if things go south. No harm, no foul, if you're purely in a price relationship. But it's a major hit if you're partnering. In transactional relationships you have far less invested, and it's easier to accept those losses. Plus the fact that more times than not you can get back in next month or—at the worst—next year. But enterprise relationships really hurt if you lose them because you've usually lost them forever.

Let's look at these five questions and at how each one can raise red flags about the chances of setting up a successful enterprise relationship.

Will *Both* Parties Change?   The first question, on the face of it, seems an odd one. As long as there is value to be created, what does it matter whether the change is by both parties or just by one of them? There are two answers to this, one practical and one theoretical. The practical answer is that when we've interviewed participants in failed enterprise relationships, over and over again they have told us, "One side was prepared to change but the other one wasn't," which turned out to be a primary reason for failure. The theoretical reason, for us, is even more compelling. An enterprise relationship—as we've defined it—is about the mutual redesign of the boundaries between supplier and customer to create new value. If only one party is prepared to change, then the scope for redesigning the boundary is severely limited. As Frank Waterhouse, manager of project development at Bechtel, told us:

> You're looking at the work processes and methodologies that your two organizations can use to become more integrated,

more common. You'll never get there by insisting on our way or your way. You won't have the Bechtel way of doing business, you won't have the customer's way of doing business, you'll have the team way of doing business. That requires investment by *both* parties. One's own work methods are no longer employed. Rather, we have a blending and an optimization of those processes.

That's easy to say, but history suggests that it's far from easy to do. Organizations tend to cling to their familiar ways of doing things. Unless both parties are seriously committed in advance to giving up turf in exchange for greater impact, then it's going to be a tough task to redesign boundaries.

Is There Value Creation Potential?   Ask yourself, "What, specifically, will we do differently in an enterprise relationship to create new value?" Unless you have a very clear answer—or at least a strong hypothesis—then you're probably in trouble. The best maxim we know comes from André Boisvert of Seer Technologies, who says:

> One plus one better be greater than two; otherwise you're just swapping four quarters for a dollar.

It's all too common for companies to enter into an enterprise relationship, to reconfigure their boundaries, to merge processes and systems, only to find that one plus one—plus, of course, many hundred thousands of implementation dollars—adds up to a paltry 1.7 or 1.8. Ruthless and probing questioning about potential impact, from both sides of the table, is vital. Unfortunately, many people—and suppliers are more guilty than customers here—are reluctant to prod too hard for fear of breaking the fragile emerging agreement. But another good maxim is, "Any arrangement that's too fragile to survive tough questioning before the agreement will never stand up to implementation afterward." It's everybody's obligation to raise hard questions about the impact that the enterprise relationship will create. In the end there's no escaping the fundamental question, "What are we going to do in this new relationship that we can't do right now through transactional or consultative selling?" Anything other than a clear and convincing answer should be a red flag to warn you that you're heading for serious trouble down the road.

Is There Cross-Functional Capability and Commitment on Both Sides?   Enterprise selling is intrinsically cross functional. No single department or function is likely to be able to harness the total resources of the enterprise. Before entering into an enterprise relationship, it's important to review your capability to deliver value across the whole organizational spectrum. A national account manager in the telecommunications industry related a typical case study of how vital this is, yet how easily an enthusiastic organization can delude itself in terms of its capability:

> They [the potential enterprise customer] had asked us to set up and help manage a totally new communications network. It involved just about everything we knew about. We were going to design and build a number of telemarketing centers and work with them to produce an online information system to integrate into their marketing effort and give them new voice, data, and video capability. There was intranet design and integration; there was billing and data capture. It seemed there was no end to the opportunity—and they were *BIG*. We started with the telemarketing centers. We had put up two of our own, and we knew a lot of stuff, so we were confident we could deliver. Anyhow, without going into all the detail, our design people got into a fight with the architects we'd brought in. The facilities people got out of phase, and then we couldn't get the software guys working right with the hardware provider. We'd have these meetings with the customer, and we'd be fighting each other while the customer just watched. Each piece we worked on was potentially OK—we just couldn't fit them together. We're out of the account now, and the only people still talking are the lawyers. I've thought hundreds of times since, we should never have got into the mess. What sucked us in was that we knew each department could deliver individually, so we

thought that the whole would just be the sum of the parts. Well, it isn't. The whole is far bigger, and you need to get your act together across a lot of groups if you're going to work at this level.

It's hard enough for an organization to work effectively across its own functional boundaries. It's even harder when the cross-functional efforts of one organization have to mesh seamlessly with the processes of their enterprise partner. In reality, the match is rarely or ever perfect. The prerequisite for success is effective cross-functional teamwork within each organization and an extraordinary willingness to be flexible and accommodating when working together across the two organizations. Before initiating an enterprise sale, the participants would be well advised to look carefully at their own and each other's history of working cross functionally. As Jim Morgan, chairman of Applied Materials explains, "Understanding how your customers work across their whole business chain is the most important success factor. While it's important to understand things like technology and products, it's a deep knowledge of how the customer organizes their processes, workflows, and systems that makes this kind of collaboration succeed."

Will There Be Access to Each Other's Strategy?   Nobody in their right mind—whether supplier or customer—sets up an enterprise relationship unless the supplier's products, services, or capabilities are genuinely and centrally strategically important for the customer's success. So, for example, a thermoplastics company might supply a car manufacturer with millions of dollars per year of plastic components used in automobile assembly. It's a large sale when measured in dollars, but—in the overall scheme of things—which vendor is chosen to supply the components is unlikely to be strategically important to the customer. So it makes little difference whether it's United Thermoplastics or Amalgamated Moldings that produces those mysterious little plastic parts that most people find kicking around loose on the floors of their cars about 1000 miles after they have left the showroom. Chances are that the automobile manufacturer, whom we'll call "Gasguzzler, Inc.," buys those parts transactionally and squeezes every last hundredth of a cent out of the transaction. Even if both parties were willing, it's unclear what either would gain from the enormous investment and change that an enterprise relationship would require.

But now let's imagine that United Thermoplastics comes up with an exciting new product concept. They believe that, with suitable R&D investment, they could perfect a plastic substitute for steel that would allow the automobile manufacturer to build lighter, cheaper car bodies. Whom do they sell this to at Gasguzzler? Not to purchasing, to be sure. Purchasing has no authority to develop innovative car body options; they are too far down the customer acquisition chain.

The role of purchasing at Gasguzzler, assuming that the company has a fairly typical purchasing function, will primarily focus on the last two steps of the acquisition chain shown in Figure 6-1. Purchasing identifies suppliers who can provide solutions to needs that have been defined earlier in the acquisition chain and then selects the best of these suppliers. If United Thermoplastics wants to sell their innovative car body idea, they will have to move much further back along the chain. If their concept had been less radical, for example, if they just wanted to introduce a new composite material to replace an existing plastic or metal part, then they would have to move back only one more step to the point in the Gasguzzler acquisition chain where problems and needs are defined. By consultative selling, they could influence the car company's design engineers to specify their new material in place of the existing formulation. But their idea is far too strategic for design engineers to make decisions. Replacing the whole metal body would require a very significant shift in corporate policy and direction. To make this shift happen, United Thermoplastics would have to change the car maker's strategic agenda. This would require selling on an enterprise level.

Unless you have access to your customer's strategic agenda, you are unlikely to be in a position to sell effective enterprise solutions. An enterprise relationship requires a

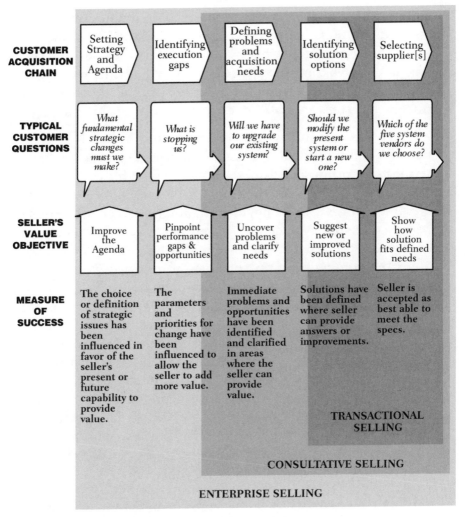

CUSTOMER ACQUISITION CHAIN	Setting Strategy and Agenda	Identifying execution gaps	Defining problems and acquisition needs	Identifying solution options	Selecting supplier[s]
TYPICAL CUSTOMER QUESTIONS	What fundamental strategic changes must we make?	What is stopping us?	Will we have to upgrade our existing system?	Should we modify the present system or start a new one?	Which of the five system vendors do we choose?
SELLER'S VALUE OBJECTIVE	Improve the Agenda	Pinpoint performance gaps & opportunities	Uncover problems and clarify needs	Suggest new or improved solutions	Show how solution fits defined needs
MEASURE OF SUCCESS	The choice or definition of strategic issues has been influenced in favor of the seller's present or future capability to provide value.	The parameters and priorities for change have been influenced to allow the seller to add more value.	Immediate problems and opportunities have been identified and clarified in areas where the seller can provide value.	Solutions have been defined where seller can provide answers or improvements.	Seller is accepted as best able to meet the specs.

TRANSACTIONAL SELLING

CONSULTATIVE SELLING

ENTERPRISE SELLING

FIGURE 6-1   Adding value to the customer acquisition chain.

huge investment of people, resources, and corporate energy. Nothing short of radical change in the customer's way of doing business can justify its cost. Yet, in order to bring about radical change, you must influence customer strategy very early in the acquisition chain. Too often, hopeful organizations try to create enterprise sales too far down the chain. Like our fictitious plastics example, they are talking with the equivalent of design engineers whose job is to define discrete problems and solutions, when they should be working to influence the customer at a much higher and much earlier policy level. Unless you have a means of access to the customer's strategic agenda—and unless you are prepared to share yours—it's unlikely that you can make an enterprise relationship happen.

Is There Compatibility of Organizational Values?   The final precondition for a successful enterprise sale is arguably the most important and is certainly the most difficult to measure. Unless the two organizations have very similar underlying values, there's little hope of creating a successful enterprise relationship. Values are shared beliefs and assumptions about the world that align and guide the actions of people within the company. Some elements of an organization's values are relatively easy to spot. It's usually not difficult to tell whether a company genuinely cares about quality or whether it has a strong customer orientation. Other elements can be harder. Do they have a collaborative culture? How open are they to change and to new ideas? Are they risk averse? In interviews with many experienced practitioners who have set up enterprise sales, almost without exception, they stress how important it is to get a "feel" for both the declared values of the customer and the subliminal values that you can sense but you can't measure. As Frank Wingate, president of Industrial Computer Corporation, told us:

> I think you have to look at the corporation that you're going to be doing business with, and look at the values of the corporation. Both the established values and the values that your antennae pick up on early in the sales cycle. If the ethics are not the same and the business practices are not the same, it's just going to really inhibit the relationship.

It's particularly valuable to develop the "antennae" that Frank Wingate talks about. Most organizations have a gap between the pious values expressed in corporate mission statements and the sordid realities of everyday business practice. For some companies this gap is a yawning chasm. One of the authors attended an internal purchasing group meeting in a major company located near Chicago. The topic of the meeting was relationships with key suppliers. On the wall was a poster with phrases like "mutual respect," "valued partners," and "win-win relationships." However, the principal speaker at the meeting—the company's chief procurement strategist— was saying things like "Lure them in with promises of partnership, then skin them alive." This gap between declared values and actual business practice is a dangerous one that has destroyed many high-potential enterprise relationships.

The five preconditions we've suggested here provide a useful initial test of whether an enterprise relationship is worth pursuing. In our experience **all five of these preconditions *must* be present** for the enterprise sale to succeed. Unlike transactional or consultative sales, one really bad enterprise sale can put the whole corporation at risk. And, almost by definition, neither the true costs nor the full benefits from an enterprise relationship can be predicted with any precision in advance. For example, Motorola and United Parcel Service built a successful enterprise relationship to handle the complex logistics involved in the "seven-day factory" concept by which Motorola products were to be ordered, assembled, tested, and shipped from Asian factories to customers' North American loading docks within seven days. The partners were both fairly clear in advance about the potential for cost saving and reduction in cycle time. However, neither party fully realized at the outset that leveraging their enterprise capabilities would—among other things—create new trademarked products and services for each of them. Was there a way for Motorola and UPS to predict in advance whether an enterprise relationship would succeed? In terms of the five preconditions, it was a pretty safe bet that it would:

- *Will both parties be prepared to make changes to create value?* Both Motorola and UPS had a history of making fundamental changes to accommodate the needs of customers and suppliers. In fact, this flexibility on the part of UPS was probably the most important factor in their favor when Motorola began looking around for an enterprise partner.

- *Is there sufficient potential for new value creation that would not be possible from a transactional or a consultative relationship?*   Again, this was a relatively straightforward question to answer in this case. Motorola had a clear vision of the seven-day factory. The vision could be achieved only by a close operational integration of the two organizations. There was not the remotest chance that a transactional or even a consultative relationship would permit the seamless working together that the concept required.

- *Is there cross-functional capability and commitment on both sides?*   Both organizations were highly experienced in process management and in the setting up and operating of cross-functional teams. Without this experience, it's unlikely that they could have worked seamlessly together to pull off the tight coordination that was required. Had one or the other been less experienced, this might have been a red flag.

- *Will there be access to each other's strategy?*   Motorola was driven by a strategic vision different from anything else they had done before. They involved UPS at the strategy and agenda point of the customer acquisition chain shown in Figure 6-1. As a result, UPS had input to the design of the strategy and its implementation. Had this not been the case—for example, if Motorola had worked alone to plan all the details of the seven-day factory and then sought a vendor to handle specific logistics—it's unlikely that the venture would have worked. By sharing at the strategy stage, the parties ended with a significantly better solution.

- *Is there compatibility of organizational values?*   Motorola and UPS have a surprising number of deep values that are common. Both organizations put a high premium on operational excellence. Both grow their own people from within, and—as a result—they both value depth of company and customer experience even more than technical ability. Both live by continuous-improvement quality methodologies. The list could go on, but the point is clear. Here are two organizations that are highly compatible in terms of their values.

In terms of our five preconditions, the enterprise relationship between Motorola and UPS looked promising even before the parties began serious discussions. Unfortunately, it's rarely the case that all five questions can be answered with such a clear and resounding yes. It's more usual for at least one of the conditions to be absent, unclear, or a little uncertain. Unless both parties unequivocally recognize and plan to address the problem area—for example, by giving better access to strategy—then we would be very pessimistic about the chances for success. So, if you are considering the viability of an enterprise relationship, we urge you to ask each of these questions ruthlessly and thoroughly.

INITIATING AN ENTERPRISE RELATIONSHIP AT THE TOP

For all five of these preconditions to be met, it's unlikely that an enterprise relationship can be initiated by individual salespeople or even by the sales function. The need for a top-level, corporate-wide initiative is plain. How else can an organization make the serious cross-functional commitment that an enterprise sale requires? We've said "unlikely," but it's not impossible. Out of over 200 successful partnerships we studied, there were a few that started lower down in the organization and gradually expanded into enterprise sales. Mead Packaging and Pillsbury, for example, evolved from a consultative sale that went wrong. Mead's machines were not performing to Pillsbury's needs, and each party had a legitimate set of reasons for blaming the other. In a last-ditch attempt to avoid litigation, the parties met and began to discuss an alternative relationship to the vendor status that Mead held. This new relationship grew into an enterprise sale, involving each company's R&D and design functions, in addition to their engineers and production people. But cases of this kind are relatively rare. The evolving-from-below model of the enterprise sale is haphazard and risky. There are successes to be sure, but the casualty rate is high. As a good basic rule for initiating enterprise relationships, start at a very senior level in each organization. With an increasing top management focus on growth, there are few better ways for a CEO to have impact than to initiate selective enterprise-wide value-creating relationships with customers, suppliers, and collaborators.

STARTING AT THE TOP: HOW IBM AND MONSANTO SEARCHED FOR ENTERPRISE VALUE

Few CEOs have confronted as many serious internal problems and headaches as those that Lou Gerstner faced when he stepped into the chairman's job at IBM. If anyone could have been forgiven for taking an internal focus, his circumstances made him a uniquely deserving candidate. IBM was in deep trouble, and it must have been tempting to turn energy inward to resolve internal difficulties rather than to become actively involved with the company's sales effort. Yet the way in which Gerstner and his senior executive team have handled enterprise selling is a model of how top management should act as a stimulus and catalyst in the creation of enterprise relationships.

The enterprise relationship with Monsanto, the St. Louis-based agricultural and pharmaceutical giant, is a good case in point. Gerstner hosted a number of one-day strategy seminars for small groups of chief executives from significant companies in a variety of industries. Robert Shapiro, the chairman of Monsanto, was an attendee at one of these events. During the discussions there was talk of research collaboration—an area where IBM's long history of breakthrough research was a clear corporate competence. Monsanto was engaged in genetic research, and Shapiro asked whether any of IBM's research or cutting-edge technology might have an application for

Monsanto in this area. Immediately after the meeting, IBM combed their research units looking for any relevant research. They found some interesting material on gene mapping in both animal and plant cells that they thought might be useful to Monsanto. A few weeks later an IBM executive team, armed with this information, arrived at Monsanto headquarters, and discussions began. Some of the genetic research was indeed useful and gave IBM the proverbial foot in the door. But, as discussions progressed, it became apparent that IBM had other more important enterprise-level contributions to make. Within a year, Monsanto and IBM signed a contract, reputedly worth several hundred million dollars, that had IBM running the total Monsanto mainframe and PC network, including all installation, maintenance, programming, and applications development for the 20,000 personal computers in the system.

In addition to illustrating how enterprise sales start at the top, the IBM-Monsanto relationship shows several of the other essentials discussed in this chapter. For example:

- It leverages the whole business chain, from fundamental research through day-to-day support capability—so it is cross functional.
- It involves IBM products, but these are secondary to the value created by the overall enterprise relationship—so the enterprise is the offering.
- It is a relationship initiated by the chairmen of each company and continued by their respective teams—so it's a relationship between equals based on an understanding of each other's values.
- It redesigned the boundary between the two organizations to create new value—so both IBM and Monsanto had to make substantial changes.
- It began at a strategic level and was integral to each company's strategic agenda—so there was no problem about access to customer strategy.

DUE DILIGENCE: PREPARING THE ENTERPRISE GROUND

Although the involvement of senior executives is essential to creating enterprise relationships, there are many more ways to initiate enterprise sales than running CEO meetings along the lines of IBM's strategic seminars. One of these ways is to set up a joint cross-functional team consisting of people from each company. The charter of the joint team is:

- To determine whether an enterprise relationship will create new value that could not be achieved from a consultative or transactional relationship—what we call the "is there a bigger pie?" question

- To make a quick-and-dirty quantification of the value that the relationship might reasonably be expected to generate—the "how much bigger is it?" question

- To specify the changes that each party would have to make in order to create the potential value and to put a rough cost to those changes—what we call the "do we need a new oven for the pie?' question

- To identify the barriers and issues that need to be addressed to make the enterprise relationship a practical reality—the "what if we don't like the way you bake?" question

Armed with the output of this joint team, each party is in a position to make a more realistic assessment of whether an enterprise relationship is worthwhile. We should emphasize that we have seen this joint team model work very effectively when its role was clear from the outset. It is not set up to manage the relationship or even to make a definitive set of recommendations backed by precise numbers and data. Its role is preliminary due diligence. If the team comes up with encouraging findings, then it's appropriate for each company to take on a greater level of commitment and to begin more definitive work together to move the relationship forward. Too much initial detail is generally a mistake. We worked with one company that had set up a team of seven full-time people who struggled for 15 months to lay out an agonizingly detailed plan for an enterprise relationship with a key customer. It was impossible for the team to include senior people because of the time commitment required. And, because top executives on either side had not yet seen real value in going ahead, there was a 15-month vacuum culminating in the two companies' moving apart and never forming the enterprise relationship.

MAKING ENTERPRISE RELATIONSHIPS WORK

This chapter has focused on the prerequisites for an enterprise sale and how to initiate the enterprise dialog. Relatively little has been said about how to manage enterprise relationships once they have been established. One reason for this is that the skills of managing an enterprise relationship are the skills of managing a business, rather than the skills of selling. So, for example, enterprise relationship management requires planning skills, resource optimization skills, cross-functional team management, and financial skills. It demands a high level of general people skills and extraordinary creativity. The leader of the team that creates enterprise value has an almost identical skill set to the manager of a strategic business unit. There are some differences of emphasis. Two are particularly important but are often lacking on both sides of the typical enterprise relationship:

- *Value-based metrics.* As we'll see in Chapter 9, good metrics are the guidance system that keeps the enterprise sale on track as it hunts for opportunities to create and increase value. Successful management of the enterprise relationship rests on the ability to develop metrics that both parties can use to assess how effectively value is being created and whether each party is capturing their fair share. This is a new and difficult field for many enterprise managers. The most common question we get from people actively involved in the management of enterprise relationships is, "How can we do a better job of measuring value creation?"

- *Sitting on the partner's side of the table.*   The skills involved in managing a business unit include an entrepreneurial, almost aggressive, approach to the market. In the enterprise sale these skills are valuable in terms of seeking and creating opportunity. However, they often conflict with another crucial skill set—the ability to view the world as your enterprise customer sees it. In an effective enterprise relationship, both parties look out for each other. Both, so to speak, sit on the same side of the table and view the world in terms of the overall good of the relationship rather than the exclusive good of the party they happen to represent. It's unfortunate that many people who are skilled at other elements of enterprise selling, such as resource allocation or cross-functional management, often have real difficulty in seeing the world from their partner's side of the table. There's a particular personality type that raises red flags here. We've seen several cases where an executive has been spectacularly successful in managing an internal business unit or function. As a result, the executive has been given responsibility for managing a major enterprise relationship—and has failed spectacularly to the detriment of all concerned. Looking closely at these cases, there seems to be a common factor. The unsuccessful enterprise manager is highly competitive and tends to work through negotiation rather than collaboration. As a result, these managers view the world from the perspective of themselves and the companies they represent. They don't sit on the same side of the table as their partners—and the enterprise relationship deteriorates as a result.

But, in general, the skills of the enterprise sale are those of good business management. If you are a good creative consensus manager inside the business, chances are you'll be effective in managing an enterprise relationship.

ALIGNMENT OF VALUE CREATION SKILLS

By definition, enterprise sales involve many people in the value creation process. It may take the personal involvement of only a few top executives to initiate the sale, but the long-term success of the enterprise relationship depends on the day-to-day work of dozens or even hundreds of people. We believe that there's a risk here for many companies but an opportunity for those who think ahead. We've watched enterprise teams in action where day-to-day opportunities to create value have been squandered because the team is not aligned in its value creation skills. Some members of the team may be well focused on understanding issues from the customer's standpoint and are clear about their roles as creative problem solvers. Others, without that clarity, or lacking training, still see themselves in their old functional roles as representatives of their companies. As a result, they impede understanding, block problem resolution, and polarize people back to old supplier-customer ways of thinking and behaving. Most organizations see the need to train their more senior people whose job is to initiate or steer the relationship. Very few train the day-to-day team members in customer-centered problem solving or take active steps to ensure that their people are aligned in terms of understanding their roles in the enterprise sale. We think that this neglect damages the potential of many enterprise relationships, and, in extreme cases, we've seen relationships fall apart primarily as a result of misalignment among team members.

MAINTAINING THE ENTERPRISE RELATIONSHIP

The cost of setting up an enterprise relationship is high for both parties, and it therefore follows that the cost of terminating an unhappy relationship, or replacing it with a substitute, is likely to be equally high. "No doubt about it, divorce is messy and expensive," says David Montenaro of NEC. "It should give everyone an incentive to invest in the marriage and to make it work." What is it that, so to speak, keeps the romance alive in a good enterprise relationship? Like any other relationship, the biggest risk is to take the other party for granted. The high switching cost has sometimes led suppliers into the tempting strategy of raising prices, or reducing value creation, in order to profit from a relationship that the customer will be reluctant to terminate. This is a dangerous course of action, as the next case illustrates. Chapter 4 discussed Free Markets OnLine who provide a bidding forum that allows suppliers and customers to meet and trade online. An organization that had an enterprise relationship with a totally integrated just-in-time supplier decided to try Free Markets OnLine as a way to give them a feel for prices in the marketplace. Because they had a sole-source relationship with their existing supplier, they had lost touch with pricing, and they thought that it might be smart to periodically check on the current state of the market. They invited the supplier to participate in the bidding along with eight other potential alternative suppliers. On hearing about their intentions, the supplier immediately offered a 10 percent price cut if the customer would call off the experiment. The customer, understandably, felt disturbed by this tactic and became even more determined to press ahead. In the final bidding, the existing supplier won, but only after reducing price by 38 percent from the historical level they had been charging. The relationship, however, had been severely damaged.

There are several morals from this story. The first one is that an enterprise sale is not a license to steal. The second moral is about metrics. Perhaps a 38 percent premium is justified if the supplier has been creating extraordinary value for the customer by, for example, making large R&D investment. But unless the supplier has metrics to justify the cost in terms of added value—and unless those metrics have been shared and agreed in advance—the supplier is rightly exposed to the charge of price gouging. The final moral is that in the information age you can't hide. Free Markets OnLine made it easy for this customer—or any other—to quickly find the fair market price. Any enterprise sale supplier who decides to use the high cost of switching as an excuse for exploitation is vulnerable.

THE FUTURE OF THE ENTERPRISE SALE

There's every sign that the enterprise sale will play an increasingly important role in the future as business attention turns to redesigning the boundaries between organizations as a rich source for creating new value. Although we've emphasized that enterprise selling is a very selective strategy because of its high costs in terms of investment, opportunity cost, and risk, there's little doubt that it offers one of the few avenues left for dramatic performance improvement. Those companies with the most experience of enterprise selling generally report a very positive impact. One area of concern does seem to be emerging. Enterprise partners have a disproportionate influence on strategic direction, for good and for bad. On the plus side, an enterprise relationship sometimes leads a company into entirely new and profitable ventures, as happened to American Sunroof Corporation when their partnership with Honda led them into painting non-sun-roof components and from there to become a world leader in automobile component parts painting. On the down side, an enterprise customer can virtually control their partner's research and development effort and can lead them away from other profitable market opportunities. But, on balance, the news is good. Enterprise selling promises to bring a powerful and stable value creation orientation to a world in which transactional pressures so often pull towards cost stripping and commoditization. It is also another force for breaking down the old and increasingly unproductive functional boundaries that separate sales from the rest of the organization. For that alone, enterprise selling deserves the organizational equivalent of a Nobel Prize.

SALES PROCESS

LIGHT IN THE LONG DARK TUNNEL

O nce upon a time, the worst thing that could happen to a good idea was that it lay unnoticed so that its potential value languished in obscurity. Today, overenthusiastic acceptance is proving to be a much worse fate than neglect. Any concept that has the misfortune to be caught up in the unforgiving world of business fashion has a meteoric rise to fame followed, almost invariably, by an equally rapid fall into discredit. A few years ago there was just such an idea. It was called *business process reengineering.* Its advocates described it using the kind of powerful imagery that attracted a huge corporate following. They used terms like *revolutionary, unprecedented change, dramatic improvements in performance,* and *breaking all the rules.* They created expectations that this would be the most fundamental and exciting business advance since the industrial revolution. Inevitably, business process reengineering attracted the usual seekers of magic bullets and simple answers. With equal inevitability, when the revolution turned out to be hard work for modest but worthwhile gain, the fad collapsed and process reengineering became the subject of scorn and vilification from the very people who had been its most uncritical supporters. That's a great pity because it's hard to find anyone who is neutral when it comes to process approaches to business problems. Somewhere between the fervent enthusiasts and vociferous detractors there is a middle ground that says, "Here's a useful set of

ideas. It's not a free lunch, but it's a good meal for the money."
That's the approach we intend to take in this chapter.

PROCESS 101

The fundamental principles of process thinking are elegantly,
almost dangerously, simple. A process, says Michael Hammer,
one of reengineering's founding gurus, is any linked group of
tasks, carried out by several groups or functions, that together
create customer value. An obvious example is the product
development process, by which a company's offerings are created, which would traditionally involve such organizational
functions as research and development, design, engineering,
and manufacturing. Another important process is the order
fulfillment process by which a customer order is turned into a
delivered and installed product, service, or solution. In a typical company, this order fulfillment process may involve a
dozen or more separate groups ranging from order entry
through materials scheduling and industrial engineering to
installation and customer service. The chain of tasks that
make up the design process or the order fulfillment process
are so important to most companies that they form the backbone of company activity and are termed *core processes*. Sales,
say the reengineers, is part of yet another core process that
brings in orders from customers. The emerging label for this
process is the *order acquisition process*—a ghastly term that
might suffice for transactional sales but is woefully inadequate
for describing the complex business relationships of most consultative or enterprise sales.

Core processes, such as the horribly named order acquisition process, cross the organization's functional boundaries
and are not confined within a single traditional organizational
function. So the reengineering theorists frown on the term
sales process because it is normally used to describe the
sequence of linked tasks that occur solely within the sales
function. They prefer to think of sales as a subprocess, which
they define as a linked series of tasks that form one part of an

overall value delivery process. Sales is therefore part of the overall customer value creation and value delivery generated by the order acquisition process. This way of thinking, despite its awful terminology, has some real merit. First, it expresses the function of sales as part of an overall process that creates customer value. Obvious though this may seem, for many organizations it's a surprisingly counterintuitive idea. Most companies still see their sales forces as providing value for the corporation, not for the customer. At a recent meeting of chief executives, we asked 40 CEOs to describe, in a single phrase, the mission of their sales force. The most common response was a variant on "to bring us business efficiently and effectively"—in other words, to provide value for us as a corporation. Few of these CEOs mentioned customer value.

The second merit of an overall process approach is that it highlights the cross-functional links that become increasingly crucial for developing the successful enterprise selling that we saw in the last chapter. Enterprise selling, by definition, is cross functional. It creates value by leveraging the resources of the whole business chain and, to be effective, requires the kind of seamless continuity between functions that business process reengineering was designed to produce. Even in the consultative sale, as we'll see later, there are many functional boundaries where the classic process redesign approach can pay enormous dividends in terms of creating greater customer value. No wonder an increasing number of organizations are reorganizing their sales effort around process-based models. A recent survey by Andersen Consulting found that 18 percent of companies have already built their sales effort around a customer-centered process model. And another 49 percent plan to build customer-centered sales processes within the next five years.

BOUNDARY PROBLEMS

One of the most powerful ideas that underpins mainstream process thinking is the concept of boundaries or hand-offs between different groups or functions. Organizational functions, such as design, sales, or customer service, have—so the process theorists say—learned how to operate relatively productively within the boundaries of their own functions. They have more or less evolved a workable way to organize themselves. So, as a result of this evolution, there is an efficient design team, a responsive customer service unit, or a smoothly operating sales branch. However, at the boundary with other functions, things run much less well. Marketing, for example, is at war with sales, engineering can't execute the design team's concepts, or billing is continually making life miserable for customer service. The problem is that each function has built itself into a silo that may be very internally productive but is monumentally incapable of working smoothly with the other silos that make up the organization. The answer, any process neophyte will tell you, is to break down the silo walls, to dissolve the boundaries, to redesign the hand-offs and to move with amazing haste to a process-driven organization based on cross-functional teams.

This makes good business sense, at least on a theoretical level. But, as so many organizations have found to their cost, it has proved a very hard concept to execute. However, the difficulties of executing a cross-functional team approach shouldn't detract from the fundamental logic of the idea. The problems, and therefore the productivity opportunities, lie between functions, not within them. There is gold to be mined at the boundaries between functions and between groups. Let's take an example of a typical order acquisition process, illustrated in Figure 7-1. Where the process starts is some-

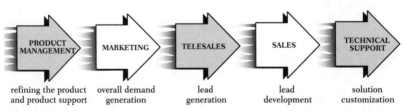

FIGURE 7-1   Typical order acquisition process.

what arbitrary—it could begin within product development or, as in this example, within a group or function called *product management* that is responsible for taking a new product, refining it, supporting it, and bringing it to market. For the sake of simplicity, let's assume that—unlike most real-life product management—the new product, once tuned to the market, will be handed off totally to a second function, *marketing.* At this hand-off, product management must pass on all their experience and wisdom in terms of what it will take for this product to succeed. Unfortunately, marketing will almost inevitably have a very different perspective on the question. "The cost structure is wrong," they'll say. "You overengineered the product. It doesn't benchmark well against competition. We can't come up with a decent value proposition. It needs better differentiation." Assuming marketing's view is accepted, then the product goes back to product management's proverbial drawing board with the inevitable delays and increases in cost. Alternatively, marketing is saddled with a product they feel they can't position, that they don't believe in, and that may indeed be fatally flawed. Either way, at the boundary between the two groups there is unlimited opportunity for waste, ineptitude, and recrimination.

Marketing, in turn, hands over to the *telesales* group, whose function is to generate leads for the new product. But, inevitably, there's another hundred potential disconnects waiting at the boundary. Attractive market segments that marketing had planned to capture may not fit the databases in telesales, or possibly marketing's value proposition is too abstract for telesales to use. Again, the result is waste, delay, frustration, and cost. When telesales finally succeeds in generating leads, it hands them over to *sales.* Alas, it's yet another boundary with trouble at the border. Sales complains that the leads are low quality and not worth the high cost of follow-up. Predictably, this quality problem isn't diagnosed for several months, so that when sales complains, then telesales responds with the obvious comeback, "Sounds like the problem is that you can't sell. The leads we set up were OK until you blew them." Finally, in our simple example, sales has succeeded in developing some of the leads to the point where customers are ready to discuss customized solutions, special configurations, or technical details of installation and use. At this point in comes *technical support*. These folks are mightily irritated with the technical ineptitude of sales and, as a matter of professional pride, feel obligated to tell customers how badly sales has advised them and what a shamefully poor job sales has done of diagnosing their true needs. "Truth-blurters" was the term the Motorola sales force gave to technical support; in turn, the technicians and engineers called salespeople "snake oil merchants." It spoke volumes about the problems that existed at the boundary between the groups.

As you can see in this somewhat simplified account of a typical order acquisition task sequence, the boundaries and hand-offs are the source of the problem. Even though we created this little example to show a worst-case picture, it's amazing how many people have told us, "You've obviously worked in our company. That's exactly the way it happens here." So it's hardly surprising that the idea of improving the hand-offs should be attractive. As a result, there's a whole slew of consulting jargon terms for working on the hand-over points in the chain of tasks that constitute a process. Depending on your favorite gurus, you would talk about reengineering the interfaces, redesigning the borders, dissolving boundaries, breaking down the silos, creating hand-off transparency, seamless process design, step minimization, or dozens of other terms that convey the same simple message—get rid of the boundaries and you'll get rid of the problems.

PROCESS IN ENTERPRISE, TRANSACTIONAL, AND CONSULTATIVE SALES

The concept of removing boundaries is the central tenet of traditional process redesign as a way to improve sales performance. The strength of the tear-down-the-boundaries approach is most apparent in the enterprise sale. Here the issue is how to leverage the total assets of the enterprise to create customer value, so that smooth transition between the supplier organization's many contributing groups and functions is essential. In many enterprise sales, good cross-functional teamwork, based on a process that has made seamless hand-off possible, has been the cornerstone of success. In a different way, the redesign of sales process is substantially transforming many transactional sales. Here the issue is one of cost. By cutting out unnecessary steps in the process, by reducing the overall completion time for the sequence of order acquisition tasks, or by reducing errors and waste, good process design enables cost to be taken out of the system. As a result, significant value can be created for both supplier and customer. Process redesign can therefore play a centrally important role in both the enterprise and the transactional sale.

In case we're beginning to sound overly enthusiastic about the benefits of process redesign in sales, we should sound one note of caution. In the consultative sale, process approaches have often failed to deliver the anticipated value. Part of the problem, as Michael Hammer says, is that consultative sales forces seem "curiously resistant" to process approaches. Another issue is that the central idea of getting rid of boundaries may be precisely the wrong approach to take to process design in consultative selling. But, before we tackle the thorny issues of sales process in consultative selling, let's first look at some examples of the positive impact that process thinking has had in terms of creating customer value in transactional and in enterprise selling.

PROCESS IN THE IBM ENTERPRISE SALE

One of the best overall examples of a process approach to enterprise selling comes from IBM. Its development was a consequence of the lean years between 1990 and 1993 when revenues, net income, and earnings per share were all in a steady decline that many inside the company feared was irreversible. Part of the problem, everyone acknowledged, was a strategic failure to predict profound changes in the technology marketplace and the significant shift in customer needs. Another part of the problem was the sheer size of the organization and its consequent inability to respond to rapid changes. But, despite these dismal and difficult issues, people in IBM still generally thought of themselves as preeminent in terms of customer care and customer satisfaction. "We have our difficulties," acknowledged one IBM executive at an industry meeting in late 1992, "but we also have our strengths—and the greatest of our strengths is the excellence of our customer service and the satisfaction of our customer base." Others in IBM were beginning to find that the news was bad even in this area. Benchmarking studies of customer satisfaction between 1990 and late 1993 were showing a progressive decline in customer satisfaction. During this period IBM was losing ground, month by month, measured against the best of the competition. These benchmarking studies showed that customers were increasingly dissatisfied with the growing number of invoicing errors. They had quality issues with products and with service levels, and they were also unhappy about the complexity of doing business with IBM. One cause of these problems was the reduction in IBM's worldwide workforce. Since 1986, year by year, IBM had been shrinking until, by 1993, it employed less than half the number of people who were on its 1986 payroll. While this might be a plausible excuse for some increase in errors or fall-off in service levels, there was no escaping the message that while competitors were getting easier to do business with, IBM was not. By the end of 1993 it was clear that radical change was needed if IBM was hoping to keep its enterprise customers.

For example, it would be fair to say that from a customer's perspective, in 1993, IBM was an international company but not a global one. So, while one of IBM's enterprise customers, McDonald's was operating in more than 90 countries—as was IBM—McDonald's needed standard solutions that could be delivered to any location globally. But, despite its presence in all of McDonald's major markets, IBM was poorly equipped to deliver the consistent solutions that the world headquarters of McDonald's was seeking. McDonald's needs in Indonesia were handled very differently by IBM's Indonesian operation than, say, the way in which IBM UK dealt with McDonald's requirements in London. Each local operation of IBM had evolved its own processes, so that global customers didn't have a single worldwide way to work at an enterprise level with IBM. Not only did each IBM locale have its own set of processes and procedures but the quality of these processes varied widely. In some areas, notably the Nordic countries, France, and Canada, there were some real success stories in terms of breaking down the traditional silos, creating cross-functional teams, and removing some of the boundaries that were slowing down IBM's responsiveness to its customers. In other areas the news was less encouraging. Old functional thinking persisted and, as a consequence, it was hard to deliver the full potential of IBM's value to its enterprise clients.

Starting in 1994, IBM began to rethink its process approach to its whole market, including its enterprise customers. The company designed a *customer relationship management process*, beginning with the best local practices and adapting them for worldwide use. The process redesign put the issue of creating customer value firmly in the center of the new strategy. As John W. Thompson, general manager of IBM North America, explains, "Our intention was to create value for our customers worldwide, and that meant centering everything on customer wants and needs. We could no longer afford the old functional ways of thinking—in value creation terms the functional approach provided less for our customers than the process approach." A sign of IBM's determination to break down the boundaries was the policy, articulated across the organization, that read, "When conflicts occur, process management will have priority over functional management."

Ned Lautenbach, IBM's senior vice president in charge of worldwide sales and service, explains the role of process in the new IBM: "Success in a global marketplace demands disciplined processes. You can't run a successful business without them. To be the best solution provider, we must have processes that allow us to leverage all of our strengths and resources on a worldwide scale. Customer relationship management (CRM) is the way we run our business. It gives us the ability to support our customers anywhere in the world. It's what brings the different parts of our business together to design, develop, and install unique solutions for customers, large or small." In practice, the process-driven customer relationship management approach has transformed the way IBM deals with its enterprise clients. In the case of McDonald's IBM has created a cross-functional global team to operate with McDonald's global headquarters in the United States. The structure of the team has been designed to mirror McDonald's own worldwide management structure. It includes a senior IBM executive sponsor and specialist food service representatives for McDonald's major markets in Asia Pacific, Europe, and Latin America. Coupled with global pricing and improved responsiveness to McDonald's needs, the process approach has been successful in creating customer value on an enterprise level. As Chris Foster, IBM's client executive for the McDonald's team, says, "Our ability to communicate efficiently and effectively a common message around the world is a tremendous competitive advantage."

The extent of that competitive advantage can be seen in IBM's marketplace turnaround that started at the time when the first phases of the customer relationship management process were being implemented in 1994 and has continued since. Revenue, earnings per share, and net income have all risen. Even more important, from the 1993 low in benchmark studies of customer satisfaction, IBM has shown a year-on-year improvement. By the end of 1996, for the first time in seven years, IBM was level with the best of the competition and is now well placed to continue the upward trend in customer satisfaction.

ENTERPRISE PROCESS: THE LOGICAL NEXT STEP

In the book *Getting Partnering Right*, Rackham, Friedman, and Ruff (McGraw-Hill, 1996), we defined *partnering* as a redesign of the boundaries between organizations. We said, "The biggest productivity opportunities of the last five years resulted from rethinking the *relationship between functions.* The opportunities of the future are likely to result from rethinking the relationships *between organizations.*" Since the book was published, events have continued to move in just that direction. Successful partnerships have increasingly integrated the supplier and customer organizations and have adopted common processes and metrics—particularly where the partnership has been created around a continuous-improvement model. As we saw in the last chapter, enterprise selling is frequently working in just such a partnering mode. It's not within the scope of this book to go deeply into the impact of process on partnering or enterprise relationships. However, it's worth noting that the logical next step, in terms of creating a more effective enterprise selling process, is to merge the customer's processes with the supplier's and to make the boundaries between the supplier and customer increasingly transparent. The JIT II model developed at Bose Corporation would be a good example of this next process step at an enterprise level. In Bose, the distinction between supplier and customer has become blurred to a point where, driven by a common process, it's sometimes hard to tell who represents whom.

BREAKING DOWN THE SALES AND MARKETING SILOS

One of the hardest silos to break down in any cross-functional sales effort is the pernicious and often impenetrable wall that has grown up in many corporations between the sales and the marketing functions. As we saw in the last chapter, the lack of integration between marketing and sales is a perpetual source of difficulty, particularly in the enterprise sale. Sales behaves as if marketing were an impediment between the sales force and its customers. Marketing treats sales as a low-level execution arm. The new marketing myopia, all too common among marketers who should know better, is that "marketing creates value, sales communicates value." It was difficult enough to support that idea 10 years ago. It's an impossible way to look at the world today if you believe even a small part of the message of this book. One useful role of sales process is to dismantle unhelpful stereotypes like these and to create better ways for marketing and sales to work together in mutual creation of customer value.

An example of an organization that has used a process approach to attack the unhelpful boundaries between marketing and sales is Ortho-McNeil Pharmaceutical, part of the Johnson & Johnson organization. Jack Lemelle, director of business reengineering at Ortho-McNeill, describes the problem in terms many readers will recognize all too well:

> One symptom that tells you something's wrong between marketing and sales is what happens to product launches. In our president's words, our last five product launches had been "dismal at best." Marketing knew where the blame lay—clearly it was sales. "Those damn sales people aren't following the plan," they complained. Sales had another explanation, "Those marketing imbeciles in Raritan don't have a clue about the real world," they said. "This stuff doesn't work..."

Sadly, it is a typical story. The old functional divisions between sales and marketing had done for Ortho-McNeill what it has done for so many similar companies. An almost adversarial relationship had been created. There was little synergy between the efforts of each group. Finger pointing was inevitable. And the end result was reduced ability to create customer value. In other words, Ortho-McNeill had a typical marketing and sales structure. At the root of the problem was the lack of a shared business planning process. This wasn't just an issue between sales and marketing. There were, within the old functional organization, 15 separate business planning processes. "The nicest word for it," says Jack Lemelle, "was 'smorgasbord.' Basically, it became one big hand-off." To address the problems, the process redesign team created a single-market planning process as the backbone for their efforts. Sales and marketing both gave input to the new planning process. More importantly, they jointly owned the result. Their two functions were combined into a single sales and marketing group. Their separate cost systems were merged into a single cost structure. The new organization was vertically aligned into customer-based groups, such as Women's Health Care. One acid test of this new process-based integration of sales and marketing is the effectiveness of product launches since the redesigned structure was put into place. Jack Lemelle says:

> We've launched three important new products since the change. ULTRAM has been the most successful launch of an analgesic in history, selling $119 million within nine months. TOPOMAX was launched six weeks early. It was approved in December and was on the shelf in January— which is an industry first. Finally, there's LEVAQUIN. To give you an idea of how that's gone, I'd compare it with our earlier launches of Quinolone. Quinolone gained a 1 point share in three months. In contrast, LEVAQUIN has made an 8.1 share in the same three-month period. With each share point being worth about $8 million, that's not bad.

Evidence like this suggests that breaking down the sales and marketing boundary can indeed speed time to market and improve sales results. More importantly, in Ortho-McNeill, it has allowed sales and marketing to work together to create customer value. In an increasing number of organizations, similar approaches have led to the redesign of enterprise selling boundaries between sales and other functions, such as customer service, generally with positive results.

PROCESS IN THE HEWLETT-PACKARD TRANSACTIONAL SALE

It's clear that a cross-functional process approach adds customer value in enterprise selling. In the transactional sale, the role of process is generally rather different. Process, in the transactional sale, primarily contributes to customer value in two ways:

- It reduces the cost of the transaction by cutting out steps or substituting cheaper methods and channels.
- It increases the convenience and ease of acquisition for the customer.

A good example of a transactional selling process that achieves both of these objectives is Hewlett-Packard's series of process-linked tools used to quote, configure, and manage customer orders. The largest division of Hewlett-Packard is its Computer Systems Organization. Within this organization there are enterprise, consultative, and transactional sales. During the last three years, H-P has seen a significant increase in overall orders while, at the same time, slightly reducing the size of its sales force. During that time the cost per order dollar has dropped by over 40 percent. This reduction in selling cost has largely been achieved in the transactional sales area. Hewlett-Packard was one of the first companies to segment its sales force by the value it was able to create, and one of the first to recognize that in the transactional sale, alternative and cheaper channel options would be essential for survival. Their 1997 distribution of order fulfillment was 50 percent direct and 50 percent channel. In the year 2000 they anticipate that 80 percent of fulfillment will be indirect.

With this in mind, H-P has designed a series of Internet-enabled tools that allows both direct and channel sales to quote, configure, and manage transactional customer needs. Unlike many Internet-based systems, this was not aimed at the small customer or the home office market. It was initially designed for four of Hewlett-Packard's biggest customers who, although they were buying in large volume, were nevertheless buying transactionally. Today the electronic commerce tool, called *order@hp.com*, has as its value proposition that it "allows selected large customers to simplify the process of choosing and buying their pre-agreed configurations." In other words it increases the convenience and ease of acquisition for the customer—one of the ways in which process provides value in the transactional sale. It also does an excellent job of achieving the other purpose of transactional process in that it greatly reduces the cost of the sales transaction. The simplification that the tool promises is particularly important given the complexity of the Hewlett-Packard product range. H-P, at the time when *order@hp.com* was being designed, had 5500 products, twice that number of product options and several million possible combinations and configurations. The selected customers each had an online catalog specifically designed for that particular customer's requirements. This allowed customer employees to browse the options, configure their requirements using a "virtual shopping basket," and trigger their orders electronically. As the system has been tested and refined, increased functionality has been added, and it is being made available to all customers. For the truly transactional customer it's possible to order cheaply and conveniently without the need for sales force or other human interaction. When coupled with consultative or enterprise selling, it becomes an information channel and delivery option that can be combined with face-to-face selling either by a direct sales force or through channel.

There are many other examples where transactional sales processes have been designed to reduce cost while simultaneously increasing customer convenience. In most of these examples, electronic or other media have been used to substitute for a face-to-face salesperson. Given the definition of a transactional sale—that the salesperson can communicate value but cannot create it—it's logical that most transactional processes should try to design out the salesperson role and replace it with alternative customer-driven forms of communication. So, for example, "interactive stores," such as the New Brunswick Telephone Company's Interactive Phone Store, are becoming increasingly common in transactional selling. NBTel's Interactive Phone Store allows customers to remotely access billing details, make account inquiries, or buy a range of products and services. Access is either by touch-tone tele-phone or by screen. The result has been an increased conve-nience for customers in terms of 24-hour availability. For NBTel there has been a dramatic reduction in the cost of each transaction. Before the new process, the cost per transaction was just over $11. It's now less than half that and, by the year 2000, is projected to be below $2.50 per transaction.

Good transactional sales process is geared to adding value in terms of the key decision criteria that matter most to buy-ers—stripping out cost and making the transaction as painless as possible. Cost reduction can be achieved, as in the Hewlett-Packard example, through substituting electronic sell-ing for salespeople. However, there are other ways to take cost out of the sales process. Progressive Insurance, for example, has cut its claims settlement cycle dramatically by eliminating unnecessary steps in the process and streamlining the claims procedure to a point where it has become a significant com-petitive advantage. Other process approaches in the transac-tional sale have reduced cost by shifting some sales tasks to lower-salaried people or have focused on identifying and pur-suing more attractive customer segments. But, in designing transactional sales processes, the two fundamental questions always remain. First, how will the new process take cost out of the system? Second, how will the process make acquisition as convenient and painless as possible? If you can achieve one or both of these objectives, then your process can create cus-tomer value in the transactional sale.

PROCESS IN THE CONSULTATIVE SALE

We've seen how the design of sales process can allow smoother integration of functions in the enterprise sale and can reduce costs or increase customer convenience in the transactional sale. The cases cited here are fairly typical of the benefits that can come from breaking down the traditional functional boundaries between sales and other parts of the organization. On the face of it, a process methodology would seem to have so many advantages that it's hard to imagine *any* sale—whether enterprise, transactional, or consultative—that would not benefit from a process approach. But here's the paradox. While process methodologies have proved valuable in both enterprise and transactional selling, the overall record of process in the consultative sale is much more uneven. Many companies that have set out to redesign their consultative sales processes have ended up with very little to show for their efforts except resentment and confusion. What has gone wrong? Why is it that process design in the consultative sale has such a spotty success record?

Let's first look at where process redesign has worked best in consultative selling. In certain consultative sales, particularly those requiring customization, installation, or ongoing support, a process approach has generally brought about worthwhile improvements. Whenever there are a series of sequential hand-offs in the chain of events that lead from first contact to a satisfied customer, value can be created by improving the chain and making hand-offs as seamless as possible. In this respect, removing and improving the boundaries is no different in consultative sales than it is at an enterprise level. In each case, inefficiency and ineffectiveness lurk at the task boundaries. The familiar mantra is true: Remove the boundaries and you remove most of the problem.

So why has process redesign had such an indifferent record when it comes to consultative selling? One possible reason is that sales forces are, as reengineering guru Michael Hammer puts it, "curiously resistant to a process approach." Hammer's explanation of this resistance is that selling attracts lone-ranger individualists who see sales as an art form and hate being tied down. But the same could be said for many professionals in other functions. Engineers and design professionals, for example, have historically had many of the same "loner" attributes as salespeople but have generally responded well to process approaches. Others have suggested that the problem lies with sales management. Many sales managers do very little managing of their people's performance. All too often, it's the compensation plan rather than management that drives performance. Sales managers, so the argument goes, have difficulty implementing processes and process coaching because they have never managed *anything*. While there may be some truth to these points, we believe that there's a far more significant reason for why process often fails to deliver results in the consultative sale.

WHERE'S THE PROCESS PROBLEM?

The fact is that process methodology often fails in the consultative sale because it's the wrong method being used to attack the wrong problem. As we've seen, the primary success of classic process design comes from the removal of boundaries. That's fine if the performance problem of the sales force lies at the boundary with, say, billing, marketing, or customer service. However, in our experience, that's rarely where the greatest problems lie in the consultative sale or where you'll find the greatest opportunities to create value. In the consultative sale, salespeople add value through their interactions with customers. Unless the process design somehow changes or improves the way salespeople interact with their customers, it has little or no impact in terms of creating value. In the typical consultative sale the hand-off problems between sales and other functions pale into insignificance compared with the problems, issues, and opportunities that lie along that mysterious and generally little understood sequence of tasks that make up the typical sales cycle.

INTO THE LONG DARK TUNNEL

The selling cycle problems are not those of boundaries or hand-offs. Just the reverse. In a consultative sale, a salesperson, or sales team, characteristically handles the whole sale from start to finish—or from contact to contract, as some express it. There is no handoff, so there are no boundaries to dissolve. The sales cycle may take months, or even years, and

Why the consultative sales process is different

Classic process models must *remove* boundaries

| DESIGN | MANUFACTURING | ENGINEERING |

~ Each function works on one step of the process then hands it off to the next function.
~ The handoff (or boundary between functions) is a source of ineffectiveness and must be dissolved.
~ Creating seamless boundaries is the prime source of the process improvement.

Consultative sales process models must *create* boundaries

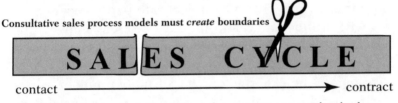

SALES   CYCLE

contact ————————————————————————➤ contract

~ Each salesperson or team works the whole cycle form contact to contact with no handover.
~ There are no boundaries to dissolve.
~ Without boundaries there is no clear way to measure progress across the cycle.
~ Creating boundaries in the form of milestones becomes the prime source of process improvement.

FIGURE 7-2   Why the consultative sales process is different.

during that time few organizations have any clear idea of what their salespeople are doing or what progress they may or may not be making toward the ultimate goal of a large sale. As Figure 7-2 shows, consultative sales process design may often require exactly the opposite approach from the boundary removal that underpins traditional process thinking.

The selling cycle, in many consultative sales, is like a long dark tunnel—the company puts in sales resources at one end and hopes a contract comes out at the other. But, as to what goes on inside the tunnel during the months in between, they generally have little information beyond questionable assurances and optimistic forecasts. It's hard to talk convincingly of improving the creation of customer value if what goes on during the selling process is so little understood by sales management. There's a disturbing analogy here with the manufacturing process. Assume, for a moment, that the whole manufacturing process might be a similar tunnel. In at one end goes raw materials (equivalent to sales opportunities), and out at the other comes a finished product (equivalent to sales contracts). What sort of yield would you legitimately expect from the tunnel? The exact number would obviously depend on your specific process, but a yield of less than 50 percent would have most manufacturers tearing the tunnel apart to find what was wrong. In sales, it's common for the tunnel to have a yield of 10 percent or less. A million dollars of opportunity becomes, at best, $100,000 of orders. Other processes don't have this 90 percent (plus) reject rate partly because the process owners understand and improve discrete steps within the overall process. Unfortunately, because classic process design is so concerned with boundaries and hand-offs, it is poorly equipped to tackle the long dark tunnel problem, where there are no hand-offs and there is not a boundary in sight.

THE IDEA OF "INDIVIDUAL PROCESS"

To bring light into the selling cycle tunnel requires a fundamental rethinking of process methodology. Process designers, such as Hammer, distinguish between two levels of process:

- *Process.* A linked group of tasks that together create customer value, such as the order fulfillment process. Such processes are normally cross functional.
- *Subprocess.* A linked group of tasks within a single function that is a part of an overall process, such as the sales process.

We believe that there's a need for a third level of process:

- *Individual Process.* A linked group of tasks carried out by an individual or a team without hand-off to other individuals, groups, or functions.

Most process reengineers don't find this idea particularly enchanting. Process theorists believe that process is intrinsically about hand-off, not about better performance of the sequence of tasks. Yet, for most sales organizations, the key performance issue is not about hand-off or cross-functional boundaries. Boundaries can be improved, for sure. But with the long dark tunnel of the selling cycle giving such a poor overall yield, the bigger problem lies in how to improve a sequence of selling tasks that has no boundaries or hand-offs. We believe that applying the logic of a process approach on an individual level can help shorten the sequence of selling cycle tasks and improve the yield in the tunnel. By improving individual process, most consultative sales organizations can have more impact on value creation—and on sales results—than by reengineering their boundaries with other functions.

DESIGNING INDIVIDUAL PROCESS

How do you design an individual sales process? As we've seen, the central rule of conventional process redesign—dissolve the boundaries—doesn't seem to apply. Like any other process, the consultative sale consists of a series of linked tasks. But that's where the similarity with conventional process thinking ends. We can't eliminate or improve the boundaries between these tasks where no hand-offs exist. In a typical consultative selling cycle, that takes a year or more to complete, there may be upward of 100 "tasks"—that is, sales activities performed by the individual sales person or sales team. Only a very small proportion of these tasks is handed over to another function. Few of these tasks, if any, have clear boundaries with other groups. So, if we can't remove boundaries, what *can* we do to help the average salesperson perform these linked tasks more effectively? We believe that a great deal can be achieved by following three basic design principles for creating individual process:

- Create boundaries in the form of process milestones.
- Link selling steps to the buying process.
- Design process selling steps that add customer value.

Each of these design principles can help with the central issue of individual process design—how to break up the long dark tunnel of the sales cycle in a way that increases its yield, shortens its length, and creates more value for customers.

CREATING PROCESS MILESTONES

The role of individual sales process is to put light in the tunnel. It must take this long seamless journey into night and provide in its stead a clear and measurable series of steps for assessing progress. Too many salespeople wander haphazardly in the sales cycle tunnel. As a result, they are both inefficient and ineffective. The inefficiency comes from wasted time and effort that, ultimately, the customer pays for in terms of increased selling cost or misuse of customer time. A simple measure of this inefficiency is the average length of the selling cycle. In one division of Xerox, for example, there was an average selling cycle for a large printing system product of 13 months. Yet some salespeople had an average cycle length of only 6 months. Clearly they were more efficient. We found that they were selling differently. By looking for patterns in such things as their sequence and level of customer contacts, the points at which they introduced product solutions, or the way they involved other Xerox resources, we were able to build a series of steps, or milestones, that were characteristic of efficient sales cycles. Using these steps as a model, managers were able to assess their salespeople's progress along the selling cycle and coach their salespeople to adopt the more efficient sequence of selling tasks associated with shorter selling cycles. In other words, by studying efficient performers, we were able to create a more efficient individual process model.

We should confess that although this sounds easy on paper, in practice it's hard to do. In the Xerox case we were lucky. There were some clear patterns associated with shorter selling cycles. However, we have not always been as fortunate. Sometimes, especially when the sales force is selling to a very fragmented customer base across different industries, there's no clear pattern associated with shorter cycles. Nevertheless, the principle is sound enough—look for patterns associated with efficient selling, and use these patterns to put light in the tunnel in the form of steps or milestones that allow managers to coach and assess progress through the tunnel.

The same fundamental method, and some of the same difficulties, apply to creating milestones based on effectiveness rather than efficiency. To improve the efficiency of individual processes, you analyze the patterns of shorter or lower-cost sales cycles. To improve an effectiveness-based process, look for consistent high-yield selling cycles. So, for example, in an average sales force there are some people whose "tunnel" consistently yields better results than others'. Given a million dollars of opportunity, they will reliably create half a million dollars of invoiced revenue. Others in the same sales force have difficulty getting half that. By studying the high-yield performers, it's possible to build effectiveness models that lay out the steps, or milestones, that are used by high performers. These can then be used to provide a process road map for less successful performers to follow. Once again, this isn't easy work. It's outside the scope of this chapter to delve into the detailed methodology of building effectiveness models. Our book *SPIN® Selling* describes the results of research into sales effectiveness models for the consultative sale. Developing these models is a complex undertaking. However, once developed, the results are worthwhile. Studies of over 1000 average performing consultative salespeople from a variety of industries showed an average 17 percent increase in sales volume following training in consultative selling models derived from analysis of successful performers.

Even without extensive research, it's possible to group the tasks in the tunnel into a series of steps that form the basis of milestones. We define a *milestone* as an objectively measurable step in the sales process that allows both the salesperson and the sales organization to assess progress in the selling cycle. A simple example is shown in Figure 7-3.

In this case an instrument manufacturer, supplying control instrumentation and software to the petrochemical industry, had a selling cycle that was taking experienced salespeople between six and nine months to complete. The manufacturer's

FIGURE 7-3   Milestones in one manufacturer's selling cycle.

less experienced salespeople generally required twice that time. In an attempt to shorten the tunnel for less experienced people, management created four subsales—what we would call "milestones." These were the following:

- *Joint Study Team.*   At this point in the process, the customer's instrument engineers agreed to spend a day with the manufacturer's technical people to go through a carefully designed meeting agenda that reviewed current instrument performance and covered the major technical issues involved in instrumentation changes. This was considered a "sale," and the manufacturer's salespeople were entitled to 10 percent of initial sales commission once the meeting had been completed. Notice that this meeting has one of the characteristics of a good milestone in that it is an objectively measurable event. In order to get the 10 percent commission, salespeople had to meet certain clearly articulated criteria in terms of such things the authority levels of customer staff attending, and they had to collect and prepare specific information on existing instrumentation problems that the customer was experiencing. From the point of view of an inexperienced salesperson, this milestone brought a focus and purpose to a series of tasks, such as data collection. Selling a major instrumentation change seemed an impossibly difficult goal—selling a one-day meeting was much simpler to achieve.

- *Technical Test.* The second "sale" was to set up a test of one of the manufacturer's products within the customer plant. Again there were clear criteria for determining what type of instrument, how long the test would last, the nature and severity of the customer problem that the instrument was designed to solve, and so on. On satisfactory completion of this milestone, the salesperson became eligible for a further 25 percent of the initial sales commission.

- *Customer Contract.* When the customer signed the order, the third milestone was achieved and the salesperson was entitled to a further 35 percent of commission.

- *Successful Installation.* The final milestone was an installation that met certain defined performance standards, including customer satisfaction measures. The final 30 percent of commission was payable on completion of this final step.

As a result of these simple steps, the selling cycle was reduced by an average of two months. Overall volume of business increased by 60 percent although, to be fair, it's not clear how much of this increase was the result of product changes and other market factors. The reduction in selling cycle time, however, does seem to be a result of the installation of a milestone-based individual process model.

A milestone-based approach involves the artificial creation of boundaries, not the dismantling of them that is so central to a classic process approach. The sales cycle must be broken up into steps, each of which culminates in a milestone that is an objectively measurable event that, in essence, provides a subgoal for the sale. In this way, forecasting is in smaller increments that are less uncertain, and management can pinpoint areas of failure or competitive risk and devise tools to help the sales force succeed. In other words, a process that breaks the sales cycle into steps and milestones enables the sales organization to add value and be less dependent for success on individual salespeople. A word of warning here: Effective selling demands flexibility. So steps and milestones in an individual sales process that become rigid quickly evolve into counterproductive rules that reduce sales effectiveness.

Another important point to consider in designing individual process milestones is always to use results-based, rather than activity-based, measures. This is particularly important if, as in our instrument manufacturer example, your compensation plan is linked to milestones. In the instrument company, for instance, the first "sale," or milestone, is a joint study team where manufacturer and customer staff meet to go through a prepared agenda together. That meeting is a *result* of the salesperson's activities and, as such, represents the achievement of a customer action that moves the sale forward. To get to that result, the salesperson would have to make calls on several people in the account, would almost certainly have to write letters, send out technical information, and make many phone calls. All of these things are *activities* that are undertaken by salespeople in order to achieve the result of a joint study team meeting.

Many companies confuse activities and results. As a consequence, they make the mistake of designing a process that sets out milestones in the form of activities that must be carried out during the sales cycle. Salespeople have a genius for doing what's compensated rather than what's effective. If your process has an activity such as "submit proposal" or "make cold call," then that's just what your people will do. No matter that the calls were to the wrong customer or went nowhere. No matter that the proposal wasn't submitted at the right point in the buying decision or contained inappropriate information. The process asked for activity, and activity was what it got. Salespeople have done what was asked for. "Garbage in, garbage out" they will delight in telling you. "It's not our problem, it's this dumb process."

Finally, it's important for any good process to build in a continuous-improvement capability. It's particularly vital for the individual level of process that puts light into the tunnel of the consultative sales cycle. A good individual process is a living and evolving methodology that develops a sense of common understanding throughout the organization.

LINK TO THE BUYING PROCESS

The idea of a series of selling steps is far from new. Xerox, for example, had a sales pipeline model in the early 1970s called "JAWS." Most sales organizations, at some time or another, have experimented with similar pipelines or sales funnels. Unfortunately, most of these models have laid out a series of selling steps—such as suspecting, prospecting, approach, proposal, close—that are not closely related to the buying process of their customers. Good sales process models begin with a thorough understanding of the customer's acquisition process. What would the most fundamental model of a buying process look like? In Chapter 3 we introduced a simple buying process model with four distinct buying phases or steps. As shown in Figure 7-4, these steps are as follows:

- *Recognition of Needs,* where the buyer comes to understand the problems that make a purchase necessary and decides to go ahead with the decision to look for a solution
- *Evaluation of Options,* where the buyer sets decision criteria and evaluates the alternatives against those criteria

FIGURE 7-4   A simple buying process model.

- *Resolution of Concerns,* where the buyer resolves perceived risks and barriers to purchase
- *Implementation,* where, following the decision to buy from the chosen source, the buyer focuses on how the preferred solution will be implemented or installed

Any useful sales process model must take, as the starting point for its design, a valid model of the buying process, whether it is broad and universal like the one suggested here or more focused and industry specific. Failure to start with a buying model has led hundreds of sales organizations into designing a series of selling steps that are unrelated to how their customers buy and have little or no positive impact on sales performance.

DESIGNING PROCESS TO ADD CUSTOMER VALUE

So far, we've looked at the creation of milestones in the sales process from the point of view of the selling organization. We've seen how milestones allow better forecasting, how they can shorten the selling cycle or help less experienced salespeople perform. But good process design is primarily about creating value for the customer. How do you design an individual sales process that helps a consultative salesperson to add customer value?

To illustrate how individual process can be designed to create customer value, let's contrast a traditional pipeline approach to selling steps with an alternative approach that is specifically designed to add customer value. First, let's look at a fairly typical example of a conventional pipeline process (Figure 7-5).

In this example, each of the steps is about selling. Not one of them creates any value for the customer. How, for instance, does a customer benefit from the prospecting step that has as its objective "generate 25 leads per week"? Cold calling has a quantity objective, not a customer value objective. What value does it create for customers if the salesperson succeeds in generating two meetings with decision makers per week? Everything in this pipeline process is couched in terms of sales

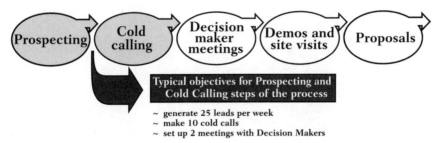

FIGURE 7-5 Traditional milestones in the selling process.

activity. There's not a word or thought about value for the customer. The sad thing is that this isn't an extreme case—it's horribly typical of the way that sales organizations create steps or milestones in their individual sales process. Certainly any series of steps—even these—puts some light in the tunnel, and, if it results in more efficient selling, it adds some value to the transactional sale. But in the consultative sale, the lights won't lead in the right direction unless the sales process is designed to allow salespeople to create customer value.

THE VIP PROCESS

What would a value-based process look like? Here's an example from a small consulting company (Figure 7-6). The first two steps of the traditional model, prospecting and cold calling, are replaced by what the company calls a "value identification process" (or VIP). The purpose of the *value identification process* is, as the name suggests, to allow salespeople to identify potential areas of value creation. Unlike the traditional prospecting and cold calling pipeline steps, the VIP process is designed with the basic premise that the function of the sales force is to add customer value and that the first steps in the process must be to identify where the greatest potential lies for value creation. Let's look more closely at the steps of this process and the metrics that allow salespeople to know that they have achieved each milestone along the process:

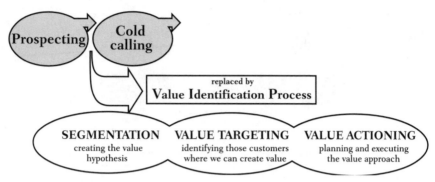

FIGURE 7-6   A value identification process.

- *Segmentation.*   The purpose of this step is to help salespeople target particular industries, segments, or types of customers where the company's products and services could add the most value. The ultimate measure of successful segmentation is that the salesperson has a clear hypothesis about how to add value to the segment, in terms of trends that affect the segment's business performance, needs arising from those trends, and how value could be created for customers with these needs.

- *Value Targeting.*   To achieve the next milestone, salespeople must select potential or existing customers from within the segment who are likely to benefit from the value hypothesis chosen for the segment. In this step, salespeople research customers to validate the value potential and make initial estimates of the value to be created and captured.

- *Value Actioning.*   Once the high-value-potential customers have been identified, the next milestone is to turn the generic value hypothesis into a specific hypothesis tailored for each individual customer: In this final step in the value identification process, salespeople identify named players within the potential account and meet with customers to jointly validate and quantify the value hypothesis

What can we learn from these new value-driven approaches that replace the traditional tasks of prospecting and cold calling? Two things: First, it is clearly possible to redesign traditional sales process in terms of customer value. In today's sophisticated consultative sale there's no longer a place for the old process that is designed exclusively from the point of view of the sales organization. The second lesson is more subtle. Notice how the steps in the value identification process model sound much more like marketing than selling. Terms like *segmentation* and *value hypothesis* are common enough among marketing people, but they are very new to selling. In the old days it was perfectly acceptable to believe that marketing created value, sales communicated value. If process thinking should teach us anything, it is that distinctions like these are inappropriate and not helpful. Everyone creates customer value. The role of process is to ensure that value creation is as efficient and effective as possible.

SEVEN CHARACTERISTICS OF A GOOD SALES PROCESS

How well does your sales process stack up against the principles outlined in this chapter? One simple test is to ask yourself these seven questions:

1. *Does your sales process reflect your customers' acquisition process?* Selling steps, as we've seen, are of no value—or even detrimental—unless they are firmly rooted in how your customers buy. So ask yourself how well your sales process maps the customer acquisition process, and redesign any areas where there's a gap.

2. *Is your process self-correcting?* Can your sales process learn from real-world feedback? Too many sales processes are theoretical dreams generated in the bowels of some corporate staff office. There's nothing wrong with a theoretical process model as a starting point, provided that it's continuously improved by real-world feedback from customer experience. Good sales process—like any other—learns from its environment. Yet few sales processes do this.

3. *Does your process create value?*   Good sales process earns its keep by adding value to three separate constituencies. First and foremost, it must add value to customers. Ask yourself whether your process makes life easier or better for the customer, and, if not, be prepared to go back to the drawing board and redesign it. The second constituency is the institution. As we've seen, good process provides institutional value by reducing dependency on rock stars. The final constituency is salespeople themselves. Rest assured that unless they feel the sales process actively helps them, they will fight and ultimately subvert it. So, if your present process is encountering resistance, ask yourself whether it could be improved to create more value for your salespeople.

4. *Does your process increase efficiency?*   Good process doesn't just put light in the tunnel, it actually makes the tunnel shorter. So a good test is to ask yourself whether your selling cycle has become shorter as a result of your sales process. If not, it's a red flag that should alert you that you may need to redesign the process by reducing steps or building in new thinking based on analysis of what your successful performers are actually doing to reduce sales cycle length.

5. *Does your process allow mortals to succeed?*   The test of good process is not the performance of top salespeople; it's whether or not middle-of-the-road performers are doing better. So ask yourself how your process is affecting the performance of your average salespeople. Is it, for example, bringing them more quickly up the learning curve to proficiency? Are they getting better results from a given amount of selling effort?

6. *Is your process scaleable?*   One of the great strengths of good process is that it provides a track to run on that is replicable and scaleable. In other words, it allows for quicker and more certain performance that, in turn, permits growth. Sales forces without good process must learn by trial and error—mostly error—and that makes it harder for them to grow. Conversely, bad process can

inhibit growth. Rigid sales procedures out of touch with how the customer buys often masquerade under the name of "sales process." So ask yourself whether your present process is a growth enabler or a growth inhibitor.

7.   *Are your milestones objectively measurable events?*   Good process, as we've seen, is based on objective events, not on activities. Review your process and cut out garbage in–garbage out activities such as "make presentations" or "submit proposals" and, in their stead, put objective milestones like "complete a three-week product trial" or "take the customer on a site visit to see the equipment in action."

We find these seven questions can form the basis of a simple process audit that lets you look at your existing sales process to see whether it deserves a clean bill of health. A process that passes on all seven questions is unusually good and will almost certainly be creating significant customer value.

PROCESS AS INSTITUTIONAL VALUE

Sales process clearly has an important role to play as a means of value creation for customers. Good process also creates value for the sales organization. In Chapter 5 we discussed the problem of rock-star selling where all the value creation capability lay in the heads of talented superstars who, increasingly, can hold the institution to ransom. Good process is a powerful way to attack the rock-star problem. A fundamental strength of a well-designed sales process is that it allows ordinary mortals to do work that was once the sole province of the rock stars. A well-articulated process not only provides milestones and guidance for salespeople; it also gives a framework for their coaching and development. Perhaps the most tangible benefit of a process approach for many organizations, especially for those whose sale is consultative, is that process shifts the value from the individual to the institution. That's a shift that would benefit many organizations.

RETHINKING CHANNELS TO CREATE AND CAPTURE VALUE

Channel management is a hot topic. Virtually every company today, regardless of industry or region, is facing a slew of new channel players or channel options. Some of these players are potential partners, some potential competitors. Some new channel options are rooted in new technologies like the Internet, intranets, and extranets, while others are emerging in more traditional areas such as new retail formats. And in just about every instance, there are conflicting sentiments about whether to embrace or reject these new options. Some see untold opportunity in these new channels for those with the foresight and courage to take advantage of them. Others are equally convinced that these same innovations portend "death and destruction," or at least large financial loss, for those who venture into the uncharted waters of emerging channels. It's hard to know whether to believe the proponents of unlimited opportunity or the prophets of gloom and doom. Many companies are adopting a wait-and-see approach, but that might be the most dangerous strategy of all. The risks of inaction are becoming ever more apparent. Those who are choosing not to make any channel changes are fast realizing that their competitive position may be severely compromised by the channel actions of others.

One thing is for sure: Channels are taking on increasing importance. In any number of categories, it is the channel—not the product—that has become pivotal in the buying decision. In areas where there are few product differences, or where differences are perceived to be of minor importance, the key differentiating value often comes from the means of acquisition—the channel. For example, people who believe they get roughly the same product quality and price from a catalog company as they would from a store, might buy from the catalog because they valued the convenience of shopping from home. They could have bought the same or a similar product at a store, but they preferred to avoid the hassle of mall traffic. Their decision to acquire was influenced more by their preferred channel than by any product factors. Similarly, in a business-to-business sale, a buyer might turn to the supplier or distributor who offered the best or easiest delivery options if the product itself was roughly equivalent to others.

Even in situations where distinctive product differences exist, channels may still hold enough value to play the deciding role in customer choice. In the world of consumer products, for example, customers may have a very strong preference for a specific brand of laundry detergent based on their experience with the product, the strength of the brand's reputation, or advertising effectiveness. But if those customers unexpectedly run out of detergent on laundry day, they may make a quick trip to the nearby convenience store so that they can finish their laundry. If that store isn't stocking their favorite brand, they will probably buy the brand that's there rather than go to another store. The value of quick and easy acquisition, of being the most conveniently available option, is likely to have a lot more influence on which brand is purchased in this instance than will the product characteristics, advertising, or even price. A similar situation may arise as customers make stock-up trips to club stores or come across grocery items while shopping in drugstores. If their favorite brands aren't there, they are likely to choose among the alternatives that are. Along the lines of Woody Allen's axiom that "80 percent of success is just showing up," ready availability is taking on increasing importance. This doesn't mean that package goods companies can stop worrying about their product formulations, advertising, or pricing and simply work on availability. But it does mean that they can't afford to treat channels of distribution questions as issues of little consequence.

And neither can we. With the increasing importance and rapid rate of change in channels today, it would be impossible to write a book about rethinking the sales force without directly addressing channel issues. But the changing world of channels is a vast subject that would be hard to cover in a single book, let alone a chapter. So we'll confine ourselves here to channel opportunities from the perspective of creating and capturing customer value and the key challenges presented by the evolving channel landscape.

Before we go any further, we should agree on some definitions to help us explore this area with less chance for confusion. The concept of "channel" covers an enormous amount of territory, and the term is applied in widely different ways in different industries. In its broadest and most inclusive sense, a channel can be defined as any organization, or network of organizations, involved in sales transactions and physical flows of products or services between suppliers and end users. In effect, any and all means companies use to reach end customers are channels. But while it is important to consider all of the competing ways of reaching customers, there are some fundamental differences between traditional "direct" sales forces, third-party intermediaries (like retailers, distributors, and brokers), and "electronic" sales approaches (like telesales, the Internet or extranets). If we approach channels in a sense that is too general, we'll blur many of those fundamental distinctions and also miss some of the interesting things that are happening with different types of channel players. Before we begin the discussion of channels, it makes sense to group the different types of channels into categories so we have a common frame of reference.

First of all, it's helpful to classify channels along two dimensions:

- *Ownership and/or control.* Who owns the channel raises some important strategic issues for value creation and capture strategies. There are basically four different types of ownership models. At one end of the spectrum are *owned channels,* that is, direct sales forces or owned stores that are totally controlled by the manufacturer. At the other extreme are open, *arms-length channels,* such as retailers, where competitors' products are also offered and each manufacturer has relatively little formal control or influence on the channel. Between these two extremes are two *hybrids.* One type of hybrid is *tied channels* that are owned by agents or franchisees but only carry the manufacturers' products and whose fates are largely linked to the manufacturers' success. A second type of hybrid is a *shared channel* where one company uses another's sales and/or distribution system to reach customers. Moving along the continuum from totally owned to arms length generally lowers that cost and commitment of suppliers, but it also lowers the degree of control or influence the supplier can have on the channel. In addition to the fact that there is another owner to contend with, there are also very significant legal restrictions on what suppliers can and cannot do with regard to channels they do not own.

- *Customer targets.* Channels target their customers differently, and the second dimension groups this targeting into two distinct types. The first includes *direct channels* that focus on a set of identifiable customers. These are outreaching channels that include direct sales forces or distributors. In direct channels, the channel generally proactively initiates the sale. The second group, *retail–mass-market channels,* are less likely to have specific accounts and are more reliant on attracting customers to their sites. In simple terms, direct outreach channels go out to their customers; in retail–mass-market channels their customers come to them.

The different types of channel players are shown along each of these dimensions in the chart in Figure 8-1 to illustrate the broad range of options that exist today. This range continues to explode with a continuing stream of new concepts and channel variations.

	OWNED	TIED	SHARED	ARMS-LENGTH
Direct Outreach Channels	• Direct field sales forces • Intranets • Telesales • Electronic catalogs	• Agents • Exclusive distributors	• Brokers • Manufacturers' reps • Joint ventures/comarketing	• Wholesalers • Distributors • Independent agents • Value-added resellers
Retail Mass-Market Channels	• Company-owned retail stores • Internet sites	• Franchises • Dealerships	• Authorized dealers	• Direct mail and catalogs • Independent retailers • Internet intermediaries

FIGURE 8-1   Channel types.

CHANNEL ROLE IN VALUE CREATION

A central premise of this book is that sales forces must create value—not just communicate the value that is inherent in the products or services that they sell. It follows that all elements of sales and distribution channels should be held to that same standard. Channels need to create customer value or they will begin to erode value for the suppliers who use them, and they may even threaten a supplier's competitiveness. First of all, customers aren't willing to pay for unnecessary inefficiency— they are concerned with the value they receive, regardless of what it costs to provide that value. Repeatedly, suppliers learn that they can't pass along their cost problems to customers, and excessive costs ultimately come out of their own bottom line. On the other hand, channel players, whether employees or independent entities don't come free. Everyone in the "food chain" wants to take a piece of the pie for themselves, and if they have not grown the pie through value creation, then their piece, sooner or later, is going to come out of the supplier's profit.

But while the need for channels to create value is self-evident, few suppliers are acting in ways that suggest they fully understand this. Most suppliers will need to change their thinking about channels in some very fundamental ways. First of all, suppliers have historically thought about the value channels created for *them*—but seldom about the value created for customers. Talk to companies who use agents and they are likely to tell you that this is an attractive channel option because agents "variabilize" sales costs. Agents are paid only when they make a sale, so suppliers who use them have no fixed-sales-cost base to worry about. But suppliers are much less likely to be able to tell you what the experience is like for customers and what value agents provide to end users. Similarly, suppliers with direct (owned) sales forces or company-owned stores will tell you about the advantages of "control" over sales operations that this form of channel provides—but they are unlikely to recognize that their control may be coming at the expense of customer convenience or cost. This does not mean that value to suppliers isn't important—just that it's no longer enough. Success in the future is going to require thinking much more about value both to end users and to the channel players themselves.

In addition to focusing on value for the customer, suppliers need to rethink their role in ensuring channel performance, especially when it comes to intermediary channels—those that are not supplier owned. One of the major mistakes most suppliers make is to treat intermediary channels as self-managing and to assume that the channel doesn't need the management time and attention that it would get if it were a direct, owned sales force. "They know their business," the argument goes. "We'll only mess things up if we try to interfere. Besides, they are entrepreneurial, which is one of their major advantages—they don't want our help, and we shouldn't try to push our way in." As a result of this logic, many suppliers focus little or no attention on how the agent or franchisee is running the business. When there are supplier's people devoted to the channel, they are usually spread very thinly, and they tend to view their role as "relationship management" with the agency or franchise principals, or as "selling to the franchisees" who then do whatever they think is right to sell to the end customer. Unfortunately, this hands-off posture toward channels causes a great deal of damage and results in substantial value destruction for everyone. Every supplier using channels needs to play an active role in improving the value that each channel is creating for customers.

DEVELOP CHANNEL VALUE CREATION POTENTIAL

There are three types of actions that can be taken to increase the value creation potential of channels (Figure 8-2).

1. Improve or enhance the current channel's operating capability and performance.

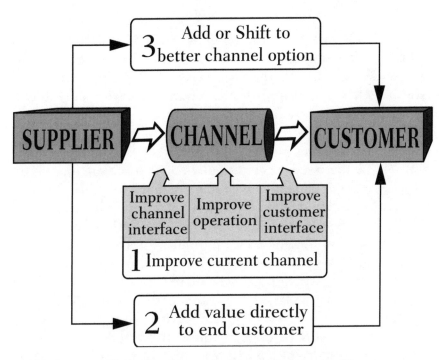

FIGURE 8-2 Channel management value creation opportunities.

2. Shift to a different type of channel with lower cost or higher performance potential.

3. Add value directly to end customers.

In the remainder of this chapter we will explore some of these opportunities and look at specific examples of how some companies have taken advantage of them.

OPPORTUNITY 1: IMPROVE CURRENT CHANNEL

We're going to start by looking at the potential for improving existing channels because although "new" channels always seem to get the most attention, there is usually more value creation opportunity in improving what you already have. In addition, having a clear sense of what you can do with your existing channels will put you in a better position to evaluate new channel opportunities. The following five ways to improve channel performance should help you get the most value creation potential out of existing channels.

Adapt Channel to Changing Market Conditions.   In today's rapidly changing markets, it's imperative for sellers to continuously rethink their channel strategy and to assess whether they are continuing to create value for customers. Markets move even faster, and channels that at one time added unique value to customers quickly lose that capacity if they are not adapted to fit evolving market requirements. One example of the need to continually adapt to changing market requirements is gasoline retailing, which has gone through numerous market evolutions. A few years ago, adjacent to just about every gas pump, you'd find a service station that made a good deal of its income from automotive repairs and service. Over time, automotive dealerships took on an increasing portion of the repair and service business, as did specialized chains, such as AAMCO for transmission work, Midas for mufflers, and Jiffy Lube for basic service. To replace this lost income, successful gasoline retailers converted stations from automotive repair stations into combined convenience store stations, adding grocery and beverage items to the site. Over time better operators refined the concept to adapt the mix of products and prices to provide better customer value. Today, gas retailing is going through further evolution, using a variety of models to suit location needs—adding dry cleaning drop-off–pick-up at some locations, fast food and beverages at others, and for yet another set of sites, a broader selection of convenience goods. Successful companies have adapted their channel strategy to meet changing market conditions and customer needs. Other players, who have let the channel remain grooved in an old format, have found that the groove has all too quickly become a rut, and they have woken up to find themselves with outdated, money-losing franchises that ultimately eroded sales and profits.

Keep Channel Participants Financially Viable and Healthy. For as long as suppliers have used channel intermediaries, there has been a struggle over how much of the value belongs to the channel and how much to the supplier. The bias to date on both sides has been to get as much as you can for yourself and to disregard the impact on the other party, despite what is generally a fairly symbiotic relationship. Unfortunately, when the supplier is too successful at keeping its share, it erodes the financial viability of the channel and ultimately destroys value for everyone. To illustrate this, let's look at a well-known baked-goods manufacturer in the United States. This company had long used a system of franchised route drivers, who sold and serviced local supermarkets, delivering fresh goods, managing the shelf, and removing stale goods from the market. Each individual franchisee made an investment to buy the franchise and was responsible for any labor or equipment costs. In return, they received an exclusive territory and were paid a commission on their net sales. The company focused almost exclusively on its own interests in negotiating franchise agreements and market coverage. Over time, pricing decisions were made based on the manufacturer's profit needs rather than the franchisee impact. Little was done to react to market or competitive shifts within territories. As a result, profitability for a large percentage of franchisees declined to unsustainable levels. Franchisees couldn't afford to make necessary repairs or keep up their equipment, and service levels to supermarkets started to decline, while old, dirty delivery trucks began to hurt the brand image with customers. To help shore up failing income, many franchisees began taking second jobs, further taking attention away from route management and accelerating the decline in shelf conditions. Franchisees couldn't afford to invest in technology to help manage shelf assortment, and while competitors were making smarter decisions about what items were moving in different stores and adjusting the mix to optimize sales and reduce "stales," the franchisees fell further and further behind. It was getting harder for customers to find fresh products. Serious value destruction was occurring, and eventually the situation reached crisis proportions for the manufacturer as well, with declining brand shares, an eroding customer base, and a soaring expense of stale and returned product. With the situation dire, the supplier finally realized that their interests depended on financially healthy franchises that could provide a value-adding function for end-user customers. They took a much more positive stance in supporting the channel itself, bought back some franchises, and restructured territories to create financially viable units. In addition, they developed route management systems and shared technology investments to assist franchisees to become competitive, and they took a more active role in developing franchisees' business management skills. These actions reversed the decline.

Improve Supplier-Channel Interfaces.   There are a number of opportunities that are appearing at the interface between suppliers and their channels. Electronic data interchange (EDI) for example, that lets a manufacturer's and retailer's computers deal directly with each other for order entry and billing, speeds up the process, eliminates manpower, and lowers system costs. Rethinking many of the traditional ways of doing business between the manufacturer and intermediary is also yielding some improvements. For example, inventory costs are generally very high because of buffer stocks held at the intermediary and the manufacturer. By jointly managing these inventories—in effect, managing it as if they were one company—many channel players have made substantial progress in bringing down the size and cost of excess inventory in the system.

In another case of adding value at the interface with the channel, an insurance company moved its underwriters out of head office and located them in the broker firms that constituted its principal channel. This gave the channel instant access to advice and expertise that had previously been difficult to obtain and the faster response created new value for the end customer.

Improve Channel Operations.   There are also opportunities to improve channel operations—either its efficiency or effectiveness—by focusing on individual elements within the channel. For example, many buyer-seller relationships are a combination of consultative and transactional elements. Often, the initial sale may be quite consultative, but the day-to-day reordering and customer care is quite transactional. You still need a consultative salesperson to uncover new customer needs or to help problem solve and customize solutions, but this person's time can be overwhelmed by the demands of day-to-day transactions. One solution is to offload some of these day-to-day transactional activities to a lower-cost model, like telesales, or electronic ordering. Unlike the hunter-farmer model, the consultative salespeople remain involved with, and responsible for, the account. They've simply been teamed up with a lower-cost transactional force to better meet customer needs and improve their economics. The quicker and less expensive phone call for reorders is also less time-consuming for purchasing people and can free up their valuable time as well. Intranet ordering, while saving the supplier money, is at the same time eliminating paperwork and processing costs for the customer in addition to creating new value by providing automatic expense reporting and order control.

In other cases, there are opportunities to improve channel effectiveness rather than costs. Canon USA was faced with the problem of introducing digital copiers to a dealer network that had previously sold only analog products. The company quickly realized that dealers in the channel would have great difficulty adapting to the new technology. Through a series of sophisticated dealer training programs and support tools, they were able to create value for their channel that enabled dealers to sell the new products effectively and, in turn, create value for the end customer. Others have used their own employees to help increase the effectiveness of channel intermediaries' selling efforts. For example, many technology companies have teamed their salespeople with resellers to create a more valuable diagnostic and advisory capability for their large important accounts.

Improve the Channel-Customer Interface.   The customer interface is another area where technology has been well used to provide better value to customers and to lower the supplier's cost. Financial institutions, for example, are harnessing technology to significantly change and improve their interface with consumers. PC banking lets consumers access their accounts directly to obtain information (balances, past activity, check clearing, and so on) and to make transactions electronically by transferring funds between accounts, paying bills, or setting up recurring payments. This is clearly a lower-cost transaction system for the bank, but the real benefit is the value that is created for the customer. Customers get the convenience of 24-hour, 365-day-a-year access to their accounts so that they can do their banking whenever they like. Customers realize savings in postage fees, and they save money by setting a delayed payment date, which enables them to earn interest on their balances until the last possible day, while eliminating the risk of missing the payment due date and incurring late fees. The investment side of financial services is also taking advantage of these newer technologies, providing electronic account access to brokerage accounts and enabling online trading, buying, or selling of securities. Some are also taking advantage of automated telephone response technologies. Fidelity Investments, for example, provides customers with the ability to phone in, enter their social security number and a password, and obtain account balances and other information, from a fully automated system. It is clearly a lower-cost channel, but for many customers it is a greater value because they can avoid the nuisance of asking someone to look up the information for them. Thus they are able to get it more quickly, with no hassle, and in complete privacy.

OPPORTUNITY 2: ADD VALUE DIRECTLY TO END USERS

In some instances, the best way for suppliers to add value through channels is by augmenting channel efforts and adding value directly to end users, rather than trying to work everything through the channel. Packaged-goods companies have long operated in this manner. Third-party retailers, such as grocery stores, drugstores, or mass merchants, are the only practical channels for distributing products to consumers. Each manufacturer would find it impossible to distribute directly to end consumers at anywhere near the economics or customer convenience that these retail outlets can provide. But these channels aren't very effective at explaining the differences between products or at helping customers understand product use or benefits. For these tasks, packaged-goods companies have gone directly to the end user via advertising commercials or longer "infomercials." Or they have gone directly to consumers with coupons or rebate offers to entice consumers to try their products, or in some cases they have hired demonstrators to augment normal channel activities with distributing product samples or answering customers' questions.

Recently, business-to-business suppliers have begun to adapt some of this thinking to their channels. For example, in the technology sector, *value-added resellers* (VAR) have been a key channel for many in the industry, and they have executed a large share of the business. For most sellers, however, they have not been an especially effective selling channel. They have been happy to install whichever product or system the customer has wanted, but they haven't played the consultative role, which is often essential for helping customers get all the value a manufacturer might be able to provide. This gives rise to the cynical definition of a VAR as a black hole existing in the space between supplier and customer designed to suck in value from the supplier and ensure that none of it ever escapes to the end customer. Accordingly, many suppliers are going directly to end customers with their own direct force to do the selling, but leveraging the VAR's ability to install, maintain, and service a customer at a local level. In other cases, companies have used 1-800 numbers to be able to answer end-user questions, provide information about products, or to perform troubleshooting or service by phone. In addition, some are adding Web sites that can deal directly with customers on these issues. In still other cases, suppliers are creating product and service enhancements, such as manufacturer-provided training for end users or the design of easier-to-install products to add value directly to end users and augment the basic channel functions.

Opportunity 3: Add or Shift to Better-Performing Channels

Beyond looking for ways to improve current channel performance, suppliers must also be willing to add new channels or even replace channels with better-performing alternatives. For example, a company selling specialty audio components through an expensive distributor sales force found its products were increasingly being treated as commodities. It could no longer afford the overall expense of face-to-face selling so it moved part of its business to a new low-cost telesales operation, lowering its overall sales cost by 30 percent without significant loss of business. Another company took the opposite approach. Its products were becoming more complex, and it found that its old distribution network of dealers or manufacturers' reps was no longer up to the task of selling the more sophisticated product. By changing to a specialty distributor who brought technical support and expertise that its existing network lacked, the manufacturer was able to increase sales by 28 percent.

The types of channel options that make sense for a supplier to consider depend largely on the type of sale involved.

In a transactional sale, channels that can lower selling costs substantially or improve convenience for end customers can create significant value for customers and suppliers alike. Shifting from a direct sales force to a telesales channel, for example, can make a considerable difference in the overall economics of the selling effort. A direct sales call costs several hundreds of dollars, a telesales call less than $10. And, since transactional sales deal with well-understood products and needs, telesales can often be an effective tool. GEICO, for example, has enjoyed considerable sales success using a telesales channel instead of a direct sales force to sell standard auto insurance, creating customer value in the form of lower prices and convenience.

Channels can also be used to increase value creation potential in the consultative sale. For example, although the direct selling model is generally favored for consultative sales, it is not always affordable. In some cases, customer potential is simply too small to justify the high costs associated with a direct, in-person, sales force. Most companies in this situation automatically shift small customers to lower-cost transactional models, with little success. The nature of the sale doesn't really change for the smaller customer; they need the same kinds of help in understanding their needs better and in getting new insights into products, and they need help in customizing solutions to their specific situation. Some might plausibly argue that smaller customers, because they tend to be less sophisticated, need consultative sales even more than large customers do. It is just that the economics don't support traditional consultative sales resources.

One of the smarter answers to this dilemma is to find lower-cost consultative sellers to take care of smaller customers. Montsanto's agricultural division is a good example of this innovative approach. Some of their products help dairy farmers get better yield from their herds, and salespeople play a critical role in helping herd owners understand the product and how to customize its use to optimize each farmer's economics. For large herds, Monsanto can afford to devote dedicated direct salespeople, but for small herds, just sending a direct salesperson to these farms will cost more than the profit that might be gained. The solution they arrived at was to use *farmer agents*—local people who might be retired farmers, or others experienced in the industry, who can be effective in counseling the smaller farmers in the area. They generally work part-time and are an effective way to provide the benefits of a consultative sale to small customers economically.

These channel options involve shifts to better-performing traditional channels. There are also new channel options that appear to have very strong value creation potential—electronic channels and shared channels. Let's look briefly at some of the opportunities emerging in each of these new areas.

Electronic Channels.   It is already clear that the new electronic channels will offer fresh possibilities for many suppliers by dramatically lowering the cost of reaching customers, which is especially compelling for transactional sellers. Further, electronic channels can provide an economically viable way to reduce the dependence on intermediaries, allowing suppliers to go directly to end customers. Electronic catalogs, intranets, and the Internet do not require the bricks-and-mortar investments that have been a barrier to some, nor do they require the scale and cost of the traditional retail outlet approach that combines the offerings of many manufacturers. Newer technologies are also offering innovative ways to improve customer benefits. Electronic catalogs, for example, can be tailored to individual customers' needs quite cheaply. Employees can search through the catalog and select items needed, then directly place orders to the supplier, eliminating the cost and hassle of requisitions or purchase orders. Controls can be built into the system as well to assure that the item is within the purchasing authority level of that individual. The electronic catalog can even limit the access of individuals to a specific range of items that are approved for their selection.

For consultative selling, the applicability of electronic channels is less clear-cut. The effectiveness of consultative sales is determined early in the selling process by helping customers gain new insight into their problems and needs. Moving more new business to lower-cost channels is, therefore, problematic since an up-front investment in thoroughly understanding and diagnosing needs forms the basis for most consultative sales. Low-cost channels, such as the Internet, have generally provided insufficient consultative capability. There are some attempts under way that start to break through the problem of offering consultative capability through a lower-cost channel. These provide interactive diagnostic tools that can help customers do their own needs assessment and gain insights on their own. Home Account Network has attempted to create such a system. They have developed an automated financial planning and advising product that can be used by customers to acquire a richer understanding of their financial position, objectives, and risk tolerance. If successful, this type of self-diagnostic tool could open up great potential for consultative selling on the Internet, leveraging its interactive capability.

Shared Channels.   In addition to emerging electronic channels, the use of alliances and the practice of sharing channels is increasingly common. Shared channels offer a great deal of increased potential for value creation and capture by suppliers. The concept is fairly simple—linking up with another supplier to share a channel, thereby gaining sales coverage at lower cost than an exclusive channel. And because the sharing is between only two suppliers, there is much less risk of losing control or of being held captive by a strong intermediary who can play suppliers off one another to squeeze down prices. In addition, it is often structured as a fee-for-service arrangement, reducing the conflicting interests of intermediary and supplier. Finally, these shared channels can be set up as temporary arrangements to meet specific needs.

In the pharmaceutical industry this type of approach is fairly common because the stakes are so high. A new drug with superior performance may hold enormous profit potential—but there is a limited time period to capture it. Once a drug goes off patent and generic drugs enter the fray, the bulk of the profit opportunity is gone. So there is enormous pressure on these sales forces to get new drugs accepted and to fully penetrate the market as soon as possible. Every day that goes by can mean literally millions of dollars of lost profit. But pharmaceutical sales forces are very costly—among the most expensive of any industry—so there is a big penalty to having excess, unused capacity waiting for the next drug introduction. Further, even if it were feasible to hire up to meet the challenge of new drug introductions, there's a learning-curve issue. It's unlikely that these newly hired people could learn quickly enough how to win the battle against other established competitors' representatives for that ever-shrinking slice of time that doctors will set aside to meet with sales reps.

Sharing someone else's sales force is one approach that these companies have used to help resolve the dilemma. Instead of trying to staff up to meet this spike in requirements to quickly cover and distribute samples right after approval, they let another sales force "codetail" their product. In effect, a sales rep splits the call, devoting the first half of the doctor visit to promoting their own product and then turning in the second half to copromoting the other company's drug. Pharmaceutical manufacturers have often used this approach to expand their own capacity. The owned sales force gets paid for each codetail call they make, giving them extra revenue and/or income. The sharing company gets faster market penetration while saving the cost of building up an additional force of their own. Finally, the doctor gets some relief from ever-increasing pressure to see more and more reps and gets to see more patients instead.

In pharmaceuticals, the sharing concept has usually been used to supplement the efforts of the manufacturer's own sales force. However, in other industries, smaller players have used spare capacity of larger forces instead of creating their own channel. For example, for many years, the Kraft sales force handled Pillsbury's refrigerated products in supermarkets. Kraft had a large interest in the refrigerated category with their high share of cheese sales, and they deployed a large retail sales force to cover retail stores. Pillsbury, on the other hand, had most of their business in "dry" categories, such as flour, and a rather small part in the refrigerated section. The incremental costs for Kraft to also handle Pillsbury's refrigerated products were quite small—they were going to the stores anyway—while Pillsbury avoided a great deal of expense. Both benefited greatly. The arrangement worked quite well for a number of years, until both companies were acquired by larger, more diverse food enterprises: Kraft by Philip Morris, who also owned General Foods, and Pillsbury by Grand Met. These two giants did have competing product lines. Even though it still made economic sense to share the refrigerated products sales force, there was discomfort in having a competitor's sales force handle Pillsbury's sales, and the arrangement was terminated.

Today we are seeing a great increase in these types of joint activities, and some very interesting new versions of channel sharing are developing. For example:

- Members of airline frequent-flyer programs open their frequent-flyer mail and find an offer to earn "miles" or program points by making MCI their telephone long-distance provider. For MCI it provides a rather efficient sales channel to reach a very attractive set of potential customers— frequent travelers. The airline earns fee income for sharing its access to its customers, and it is paid for the frequent-flyer miles given to subscribers. The customer gets an opportunity to earn miles that have high perceived value without more travel or added expense.

- Most charities, universities, and other nonprofit organizations have by now linked up with a credit card company to provide "affinity cards" to their supporters. The nonprofit earns fee income and a share of purchase revenue on the cards their patrons use, while the credit card company acquires an attractive set of customers at lower cost than other approaches they might use on their own. And the nonprofit supporter gets a card with a competitive rate and the satisfaction of knowing that their normal credit card spending will benefit their favorite nonprofit organization. One of the misconceptions of these programs is that they are merely a ruse to charge higher rates because of the charity tie-in. In fact, the rates for most of these joint ventures are quite attractive—the card companies make more money because of lower acquisition costs and lower default rates—not by gouging the customer. Most nonprofits are quite protective of their supporter base, and they generally ensure competitive rate offerings as a condition for lending their name and mailing lists, while consumers appear to be less likely to default on credit that is tied to a charity that they support.

- Key Corp, an innovative bank, has agreements with insurance providers USF&G, Kaiser, and United Health Care to sell competitively priced insurance products to Key Corp's 400,000 small-business customers. The insurance and health care companies get broader customer access; Key Corp gets more value from its direct sales channel, and customers get attractive new-product offerings with easy acquisition and access.

The list continues to grow as the number of new channel-sharing arrangements mushrooms. We believe this trend will accelerate. Channel sharing has the advantage of creating value by splitting sales costs and thus lowering them. And, because the arrangement is between a limited number of parties, it remains fairly controllable. The success of these newer models will inevitably trigger thoughts for other creative ways to share channel resources.

Choosing to Enter New Channels.   These new and emerging channel options are exciting, but it would be foolish to simply rush into every emerging format and location. A spray-and-pray approach will simply raise overall selling costs to unsustainable levels, and it is almost certainly doomed to failure. Judicious selection of appropriate new channel options is a strategic necessity for remaining competitive. There are a number of key questions to ask to help guide decisions about whether it's strategically smart to enter or expand a new or emerging channel.

Does the channel reach a new or different type of customer? New channels that tap new markets or new users can be extremely attractive because they can be strong growth drivers. Telesales or catalog sales, for example, can expand reach to new geographies, or new customers, with relatively minor investments. In other cases, different channel formats may simply provide current users with an alternative way to buy. While this isn't by itself a "knockout factor" for the new channel, it should be approached more cautiously because cannibalization of existing channels may make the new approach considerably more costly than it might appear at first.

Will the new channel expand consumption—or just divide it among more players? In some cases, additional outlets or offerings increase the total category sales among those who are already users. More and different types of fast-food outlets, for example, have done a great deal to expand the total amount of fast food consumed. In other cases, however, additional outlets or formats do little to expand the overall size of the category and simply wind up splitting up the same amount of business among more players.

Does the channel offer real new value to customers? In many cases suppliers have no choice. Failure to participate in emerging channels may simply eliminate the chance of competing for sales in that channel. Many consumer goods manufacturers, for example, refused to serve club stores when they first emerged, fearing backlash and retaliation from their traditional grocery channels. But both the value to consumers and the economics of the new channel proved overwhelming, and those who shunned the club store channel simply watched their overall market position erode.

Can you delay entry until the channel potential becomes clearer? Market leading brands will almost always have a chance to enter a channel at a later time, when the channel is more "proven"—but the same doesn't apply to weaker brands. A less-than-sterling brand has a smaller window of opportunity to enter the fray in emerging channels, and it will have a much less favorable position—or no position at all—if they wait until the leaders have entered before making their move. This doesn't mean that market leaders should wait indefinitely, or that there are no consequences to being a very late mover, however. Kirin beer learned this lesson when it refused to enter the discounter channel in Japan, believing it would be a temporary fad, and it would not impact the bulk of beer purchases through mom-and-pop liquor stores. They continued this stance while the discount channel grew, strengthened, and became mainstream and only then entered the channel. But by then it was too late. They had already lost their number 1 market position to Asahi, which had quickly capitalized on this emerging channel. A similar situation occurred with building material suppliers who took too long to recognize the impact that Home Depot would have on the marketplace. In a number of categories, the leading manufacturers lost their number 1 market positions to the number 2 or number 3 player who recognized Home Depot's value creation potential early on and were able to ride it to leading market share positions.

CHANNEL CONFLICT

Inevitably, discussion about entering new channels raises the topic of channel conflict. For decades, suppliers have backed away from high-value opportunities simply because they might cause a negative reaction from their existing channel partners. But attempts to avoid channel conflict are proving less and less successful. With the continuing expansion of channel options, suppliers are finding that not participating in certain channels often excludes them from substantial market segments, which can erode both their competitive position and their capacity to create customer value. Most are concluding that succeeding in evolving markets will require participation in multiple channels. Instead of conflict avoidance, the winning players are accepting channel conflict as a normal part of business life and are looking for ways to manage conflicting channel demands. We are unable to cover this topic in great depth in this book, but we suggest those interested might look at the very interesting work that Christine Bucklin and Pamela Thomas-Graham of McKinsey & Co. have done in this area. In the balance of this chapter, we'll look at some of the actions companies have taken to create value through the channel while successfully avoiding, minimizing, or resolving conflict. Basically there are three emerging strategies for dealing with conflict situations:

1. Offer different brands, products, or services to each channel.
2. Reconfigure rates and/or terms or commissions to buffer the economic impact on channel players.
3. Leverage a strong competitive position and accept risk.

Let's explore each of these strategies with some market examples.

STRATEGY 1: DIFFERENT OFFERINGS FOR EACH CHANNEL

As consumers, we all view channel competition as a great thing—the more outlets there are selling the same item, the more likely it is that each outlet will be a bit sharper on pricing and be more willing to give discounts or run sales to move merchandise. And with careful comparison shopping, we can get the product at a very cheap price. The same situation looks a bit different from the retailer's perspective. It's the retailer's bottom line that is funding the consumer's good deal. So it's pretty easy to understand why channel conflict occurs when suppliers want to begin using more and different types of outlets.

One of the more successful strategies for mitigating this conflict has been to develop different offerings for each channel. This can be done by having different brands for each channel, different products, or different services, which permits each channel to develop a more distinctive competitive offering and reduces the comparison shopping between outlets that can drive out all of the profit for the channel. For example, in the early 1990s Black and Decker, the well-known U.S. power tool and small-appliance manufacturer, faced serious competitive threats and channel conflict. Black and Decker was selling its products through a broad variety of outlets, dealers, home centers, and discount stores, and its products ranged from very low cost household items, like cordless drills, to expensive power tools suitable for contractors and builders. Black and Decker was losing its position in the professional end of the market, and dealers were increasingly reluctant to carry Black and Decker products. As one dealer put it, "It's tough to sell a $130 drill to a contractor when the same brand sells to do-it-yourself customers at home centers for $30." To resolve the conflict, Black and Decker relaunched their "professional" products under the DeWalt brand in 1991, focusing the brand on dealers only, while keeping the low-priced, more hobby-oriented items under the Black and Decker name for discount stores. In 1993, they introduced a midrange Quantum line, distributed at home centers like Home Depot, and focused on serious do-it-yourself consumers. This differentiated brand and product strategy regained channel support and enabled Black and Decker to recapture the number 1 position in the dealer segment. By adopting this strategy, Black and Decker was able to provide value for both the low-priced household buyer and the professional user.

Levi Strauss has followed a similar brand and product differentiated strategy. Levi's 501 jeans with fashion finishes and Levi silver Tab jeans are distributed in specialty retailers and department stores, Levi's 501 jeans with basic finishes are sold in middle-market retailers and chains such as J.C. Penney, while Brittania jeans are targeted at discount chains such as Wal-Mart or Target. Similarly, Slates casual slacks are sold through high-end department stores, Dockers in middle-market retailers and, Levi's brand men's casual wear in discount chains.

These strategies can also be extended to other industries as well. For example, in financial services a bank could use its own brand name on customizable mortgage products, sold through its own consultative selling channel, but use a separate name on a very standard, easily understood and well-priced offering sold through the Internet. Both products—and more—could be processed through the same mortgage application processing center, mitigating conflict without adding to the overall cost base. For the consumer, these product and brand strategies create value by increasing choice, both in terms of product range and in terms of availability at a variety of outlets.

STRATEGY 2: BUFFER ECONOMIC IMPACT ON CHANNEL PARTICIPANTS

A second strategy for dealing with channel conflict is to restructure the financial arrangements with a channel to buffer the economic impact for current participants. Bang and Olufsen provides a good illustration of this strategy. Traditionally, Bang and Olufsen, a manufacturer of high-end electronic audio equipment, sold through independent specialist dealers. As the market increasingly shifted to broader chain retailers, Bang and Olufsen recognized that, unless they were represented in these other channels, they would be excluded from a large portion of the market. However, they also recognized that expansion into this other channel could erode independent dealers' willingness to continue to support the brand. To offset the impact on smaller dealers Bang and Olufsen restructured the financial support for the specialty channel. They developed master contracts with dealers that rewarded dealers for services aligned with their marketing policy and for displaying the full range of products. They sponsored product specialists in the stores, funded designated Bang and Olufsen listening rooms, and designated areas within a store. They also shifted rewards away from volume rebates, which disadvantaged smaller dealers, and launched an aggressive direct-marketing program, leveraging database-marketing techniques to bring people into the traditional dealer outlets. These actions permitted them to expand their channels while offsetting the negative reaction from their dealers, and to strengthen their market position.

GE's appliance division is another good example of effective use of this strategy. In the early 1990s, GE's dealer and home builder networks were threatened by increasing growth and success of national retailers in the major-appliance market. GE concluded that it needed both channels to be able to effectively cover the market, and they undertook a restructuring of the financial support to the dealer channel. They revised purchasing discounts to make the dealer-builder channel more competitive with retailers, and they installed computerized inventory systems in the dealers' facilities to help them increase turns and reduce carrying costs. They also leveraged the financing capabilities of GE's sister divisions by providing loans for equipment purchase, new-store construction, or store remodeling, and extending GE's corporate phone rates to its channels through the GE Exchange Telecommunication Program. Finally, they arranged for GE financial planners to assist channel participants in developing business plans and strategies. These actions not only defused conflict but gained GE greater support from its channels, which accelerated its growth rate well above that of the market.

Strategy 3: Leverage Strong Position and Accept Risk

In many instances, suppliers can't effectively mitigate channel conflict, and they must decide whether to forego new channel opportunity or simply bite the bullet and accept the negative reaction from existing channel participants. It's always a difficult decision because of the emotional issues and the difficulty of accurately estimating the cost—and likelihood—of retaliation. But often, despite the sword rattling, there are few, if any, negative consequences, especially when suppliers are in fairly strong positions relative to the channel.

Further, there are many instances where channels have become uneconomic, and suppliers can't afford to keep subsidizing an inefficient system.

The airline industry provides a good illustration. Prior to 1995, travel agents generated 85 percent of all airline ticket volume, and they were paid a flat commission rate of 10 percent for all ticketing activity. This structure had been in place for some time, but with the changing competitive environment driven by deregulation and the shift in ticket pricing, the channel had become a very significant expense problem for all airlines. In 1978, ticket commissions represented only 4.2 percent of airline operating expenses, but by 1993, they represented 11.3 percent, the third-largest and fastest-rising cost for the airline industry. In February, 1995, Delta overcame the fear of channel conflict and announced that it would cap the 10 percent commission structure for certain fares, replacing it with flat fee of $25 one-way/$50 round-trip. This structure, which lessened commission cost by roughly 25 percent, was quickly followed by the other major U.S. airlines. In September, 1997, United further reduced agent commissions from 10 to 8 percent, and Delta and American airlines followed immediately. These commission changes, not surprisingly, elicited a large outcry from the agents and led to an antitrust suit alleging collusion among the airlines. In the end, the airlines paid close to $100 million to the agents to settle the suits, but the settlement did not change the new commission rates, which have been estimated to reduce commission cost by some $500 million a year. There really wasn't much the agent channel could do to retaliate against the airlines. The agents ultimately responded to the new cost structure by making some basic changes to their own cost structure and pricing to offset some of the lost commission income.

Skillful management of channel conflict is becoming an ever more important aspect of customer value creation. Done well, channel management strategies like the ones we've covered here provide customers with an increased choice of options that meet their value needs. Needless to say, done badly, channel strategy and conflict management can be a potent destroyer of value for all parties, whether supplier, channel, or, most importantly, the customer.

THE FUTURE OF CHANNELS

Channels are evolving rapidly, and, predictably, everyone is trying to guess the direction that their evolution will take. In this chapter we've concentrated on just one aspect of channel strategy—the use of channels in creating customer value. As suppliers search for ways to make decisions in the face of conflicting channel demands, the concept of creating customer value can provide them with a useful perspective. All too often, channel management degenerates into a brawl between suppliers' self-interest and the competing self-interests of the various channel players. The end customer is forgotten, to the ultimate detriment of the whole selling effort. By introducing the notion of creating value for the end customer into channel management, it's easier for all parties broaden their perspective and to focus channel resources where they really count—on the creation of customer value.

CHANGING
THE SALES FORCE

One of the authors, traveling on an overnight flight from the West Coast to New York, was sitting next to the vice president, sales, of a *Fortune* 1000 company. The VP woke from one of those fitful dozes that are the nearest approximation to sleep that air travel allows and said, "I had a such a weird dream. I dreamt my whole sales force vanished overnight and I had to start again from scratch." He thought for a moment, then muttered, "What a great dream!"

Many managers would know exactly how he felt. The idea of throwing out the rascals and starting over is an irresistible fantasy for those who have suffered from the problems of an underperforming sales force. Unfortunately, few if any sales forces can realistically start again with a clean slate. It's unlikely that you'd be able to hire enough new talent fast enough, and, even if you could, you would still have to teach them your business after you hired them. Besides, in a going business, you can't just stop everything while you put in place a complete change of salespeople—very few companies can afford the disruption to revenues, or to customers. So realistic organizations, while they may dream of a fresh start, will settle on the sensible notion that their best option will be to work largely with what they have and try to effect change over time.

Sales forces, as we've said several times throughout this book, are curiously resistant to change. Building new value creation capability in a sales function seems to be much more difficult than doing so in, say, manufacturing or customer service. One of the authors recently interviewed a highly success-ful executive whose career had been the archetypal model of a high-flier. He had transformed a sleepy and unimaginative design function into a powerhouse of product ideas. He took over a bloated distribution function and turned it into a lean efficient logistics system that was the envy of the industry. "I've succeeded in changing everything," he told us, "with one exception—sales. Trying to change the sales force was like try-ing to build a skyscraper out of Jell-O." He deserves our sym-pathy. Many talented executives remember their time in sales as the one blot on an otherwise shining résumé.

What makes sales force change so hard? For one thing, most executives grossly underestimate the difficulty that is involved in changing the sales force. The actions they will take are generally too small and too piecemeal to bring meaningful improvement. We've seen it often enough. Sales organizations simply don't recognize the stubbornness of old habits or entrenched ways of thinking. They don't understand the power of all of the reinforcing mechanisms that can snatch inertia from the jaws of change. "We'll hire some new people," they say. "Get a new head of sales to shape things up"—only to find that these new brooms are quickly overwhelmed by the great mass of existing people and the traditional way of doing things. Others will take the training approach to change. They'll commission a brand-new training program for all sales-people on the "new way of selling." Alas, after several days of very fine training, they discover that there's little or no lasting impact once salespeople are returned to the old environment. A study Huthwaite conducted for Xerox a number of years ago, published in the *Training and Development Journal,* found that within one month of leaving the training program, salespeople had lost 87 percent of the new skills they had learned during the training period. That's 87 cents in the training dollar evaporated—and it happened in a company widely acknowledged as having some of the best sales training in the world. With that kind of a loss rate, it's no wonder that training or retraining alone will have little or no lasting impact on sales performance.

Perhaps the most frequent action people take to change sales performance is to change the compensation system. "Just get the incentives right and the sales will take care of themselves" goes the myth. And a great myth it is. Companies have whole departments devising compensation systems that they fondly believe will change the way their sales force behaves. The effort and ingenuity that goes into inventing these new compensation models is exceeded only by the creativity that salespeople put into defeating them. Managing by the compensation plan, as most companies ultimately discover to their cost, is no substitute for managing by management. The fact is that no compensation system can make people sell smarter. At best it can encourage greater effort and cause people to sell "harder."

Implicitly, if you accept the notion that changing the incentive plan is all that's required, then you have to believe that salespeople already have everything they need for sales success, except effort. You have to believe, for example, that they know exactly what to do, that they know how to do it, and that they have the tools they require to be effective. The only thing stopping them is that they simply don't want to do it, and so the new incentive plan will make them sell harder to achieve the goals they could have reached all along. When it's put that way, it's a pretty hard notion to accept. Don't get us wrong—we're not saying that measures and rewards aren't important, but we *are* saying that they are only one part of the answer. By themselves they can have, at best, a limited chance of success. Incentive plan changes are most likely to succeed in transactional sales, but those are the very sales that can least afford higher-cost incentives. Certainly, a new incentive plan can generate a flurry of activity in consultative sales, but in more than 90 percent of the cases, sales performance doesn't improve, and often it gets worse as a result of the new plan.

So the most commonly used tools—or levers—for improving sales force performance have a spotty success record at best. They rearrange the deck chairs when they should be turning the ship. In this final chapter, we'll take a fundamental look at how to change the course of a sales force. But first, let's look at four specific cautions that will help keep change efforts out of trouble.

CAUTION 1: IT TAKES LONGER THAN YOU THINK

Once you have a clear sales strategy, implementing it would—on the surface at least—seem to be a fairly quick process. "I've a definite vision of how my sales force can create new value for customers," the CEO of a technology company told us. "For years we've been a 'hot-box' company that communicates to buyers the value of our bells and whistles. But bells and whistles aren't cutting it any more. Our sales force needs to abandon its product focus and work instead on configuring customized solutions for customers. That's what our customers are asking for, and that's what I want to provide. I've been working at it for a year now. I've overcommunicated the idea to the sales force until they're heartily sick of hearing me. I've spent millions training them. But it's not happening—they still only have a superficial understanding of customer business needs, and they still push products. What am I doing wrong?"

In slightly different words, the same complaint might have come from almost any executive who has faced the uphill task of changing a sales force from a value communication role to value creation. The first caution of improving sales force performance is that it will take longer than you could decently imagine. As a general rule, efficiency can be built more quickly than effectiveness. It's a faster job to improve efficiency by stripping costs out of a transactional sale than it is to build the levels of skill and effectiveness needed for a consultative sale. If we had to give a rule of thumb, we've rarely seen a significant improvement in the effectiveness of a consultative sales force that has come from less than two years of concerted effort. So don't look for instant results.

CAUTION 2: THERE'S NO SILVER BULLET

The second caution is that improved performance doesn't happen as a result of any single action or change. It is about aligning lots of actions, ranging from the strategic all the way down to the sordidly petty. You build performance by aligning every aspect of your selling effort to support the capability you want to achieve. You align your training, your reward systems, your coaching, your recruitment, your sales tools, and every aspect of your sales process. No single change lever is powerful enough to transform sales performance on its own. The best training in the world won't change your sales force if it is contradicted by supervision or by the reward system. Over and over again we meet sales forces that are training their people to sell strategically while their compensation package continues to reward the quick tactical hit. The inevitable result is mediocre improvement in performance. The bad news for sales organizations is that there's no silver bullet for changing sales capability. Fortunately, the good news is that lead bullets will do quite nicely if they are well aimed. And that's what alignment is about—how to aim bullets that individually might not be armor piercing but collectively have enough force to do the job. At the risk of pushing an analogy beyond its useful limit, sales forces that pin their faith on one single change lever—whether it be sales force automation, sales process, or training—are shooting themselves in the foot.

CAUTION 3: YOU CAN'T HIRE YOUR WAY TO CAPABILITY

Another common trap is to pin hopes for change on upgrading the sales force through recruiting new and more competent people. "Our present salespeople can't cut it," so the argument goes. "We've tried training them, and they don't seem any more effective. We've got to hire new people." While we're all in favor of hiring the best salespeople available—and of replacing poor performers—you can't quickly change a sales force through hiring. For one thing, the pool of available high performers is limited. Any attempt to upgrade the sales force through recruitment usually means an intense and often fruitless search process—not to mention a substantial price premium if you are lucky enough to find the superstars you are seeking. For another thing, in complex business-to-business sales, it usually takes at least a year before new people—even those with talent and industry experience—are up to speed. But, perhaps the most serious problem of all, new salespeople quickly adopt the strategies, tactics, techniques, and work habits of the existing sales force. Rather than becoming a force for change, they themselves are likely to be changed by the critical mass of those around them. As the vice president of sales of an office products company put it, "All I've seen so far from these latest salespeople we've brought in is a 20 percent increase in sales costs—these new brooms quickly get clogged with the same old dust—and I'm having second thoughts about whether recruitment is the answer to our problems."

CAUTION 4: YOU CAN'T IMPROVE SALESPEOPLE WITHOUT IMPROVING SALES MANAGEMENT

One of the most common mistakes in efforts to improve sales performance is to focus exclusively on salespeople. In our experience, sales supervisors are even more critical for creating durable performance change. In fact, if we were forced to choose whether to invest our change efforts in working just with salespeople or just with their supervisors, then the supervisors would win every time. Really proficient sales supervision can do wonders to improve the skills, strategies, and competencies of average salespeople. Conversely, mediocre supervision can put a big dent in the effectiveness of quite good salespeople. Why is the role of sales supervisor so pivotal to performance change? For one thing, the supervisor is the primary performance coach, which is a crucially important role, particularly in the consultative sale. Studies of high-performing consultative sales forces consistently show that systematic high-quality coaching is the most important single, tool for developing performance. Another reason that sales supervision is so important is that effective supervisors ensure alignment of the many factors that influence salespeople's performance. It is they who can best link strategy and planning tools with selling and execution skills. They are the ones who tie sales function objectives to individual performance plans and help their people understand the overall strategic direction and how to align with it. So efforts to improve the performance of salespeople are likely to be ineffective unless first-line sales managers are an integral part of the process.

FOUR CHANGE LEVERS

The common thread in these four cautions is that creating major or sustainable improvements in sales performance requires a sustained and systemic change effort. To shift from existing value-communicating models of selling to value-creating models is an enormous task. Its success rests on the active involvement and leadership of top management, not just on management within the sales function. In particular, changing the sales force will require actions along four change levers, aligned to support the shift to value creation:

1. Clear vision of where and how to create value in the market
2. New structures to focus on value creation strategies
3. Capability building to enable value creation
4. Metrics and compensation aligned to value creation strategies

None of these levers can work alone. Each is an essential tool for a successful sales force change effort. In the remainder of the chapter we will explore each of these four change levers and the different ways they should be applied to transactional, consultative, and enterprise sales.

CHANGE LEVER 1: A VALUE CREATION VISION

"If you don't know where you're going," the White Rabbit told Alice, "then any road will take you there." And that's the root cause of so many failed initiatives in the sales and channel arena. Too many change initiatives are taken along whatever road happens to be available, without a clear understanding of where the organization has to get to and what barriers they must overcome to succeed. Interestingly, the most important factor that separates organizations that create real improvement in sales performance and those that don't is *focus*—having a clear sense of which customers really count and what has to be done to succeed with them. It isn't enthusiasm, or effort, or aggressiveness, or size of investment, or new people, new training, or new pay plans. Each of these can play a role in changing a sales organization, but if they're done without this focus or vision, then they have little or no chance of working.

An effective sales vision is a powerful change tool in three ways. First, it exposes the gaps in the current sales force value creation capability, and it illuminates the size and nature of the changes that are required to close those gaps. Second, a clear vision serves as a guidance system. It provides a "north star" that helps the organization make the day-to-day decisions that collectively shape what the sales force will become. With a vision, the organization has a sound context in which to make these decisions. Without one, each decision becomes as random as the White Rabbit's choice of roads. Third, a vision communicates the future to both salespeople and customers.

So the first step in changing a sales force has to be the development of a clear sales vision. But what's involved here? What do we mean by a "clear sales vision"? We don't mean sales wishes—all too often what passes for a sales vision is a statement like "increase sales by at least 20 percent," or "improve sales productivity by 15 percent." Statements like these don't provide much helpful direction for how to get there. Real direction represents a choice between competing paths—what *not* to go after, as well as what to pursue. Hard choices are what real focus, or vision, is all about.

How do you develop a vision? A good place to start is with some fundamental judgments about the nature of your customers and the type of sale that you are making. Are your targeted customers primarily intrinsic value buyers, for whom value is only in the product itself? If so, you are in a transactional sale and your strategy must reflect the severe cost pressures of transactional marketplaces. Or are they extrinsic value buyers, for whom a large part of the value lies in the seller's ability to advise and educate buyers about their needs and to customize products to fit those specific needs? If that's the case, then your sale is consultative. You will need a different type of organization, smarter salespeople, and a different level of sales supervision. For enterprise sales, are you equipped or willing to enter into the kind of deep relationship with strategic buyers for whom value goes well beyond today's products and largely lies in longer-term institutional capability? If so, and if you have strong cross-functional capability, then you may be able to enter the challenging but rewarding arena of extraordinary value creation that constitutes enterprise selling. Clarity about your customer targets will begin to illuminate the nature of the sales challenge and the magnitude of change that the sales force will require.

Generally, the greater the shift in customer target or sales mode, the greater the magnitude of sales force change required and the greater the effort it will take to break the inertia and put in place the right approach. For example, a transactional sale implies a "lean-and-mean" approach, with tight cost control and focus on facilitating the acquisition process. If you've got a high-cost direct sales force that is used to more consultative selling, then you're facing a very major change to adapt to the harsh realities of the transactional sale. Your vision for prospering in a transactional environment would involve such things as simplifying product design, standardizing manufacturing, aligning your logistics to ensure easy low cost delivery, stripping costs out of your direct sales effort, and migrating to cheaper channels. With so many factors to align, it's not a simple change.

Shifting from transactional selling to consultative selling may be even more difficult. A technology company we worked with, for example, had been able to succeed in the past with a product-based transactional sales approach. Their products had been technology leaders, with clearly superior price-performance characteristics. Dealing with savvy buyers in a rapidly growing market, the sales force had been able to sell on the product alone. Over time, however, conditions changed. Growth slowed and the market became more competitive. The price-performance gap between products narrowed, with feature differences becoming more subtle and less important. The transactional sales approach for this company had run its course. Success would depend on the company's ability to quickly transform a product-oriented sales force into one that could shift its focus to customer needs assessment and shape the product offerings to better meet those needs. Such a shift is hardly a trivial task. But the company has made the critical first step toward changing its sales force. They have recognized that the nature of their sale has changed dramatically and that they will have to fundamentally alter their selling approach and capability. Heeding the White Rabbit's advice, they understood where they needed to go so that they were able to choose the best road to get them there.

Often, clarifying customer targets highlights an additional challenge: the need to serve different types of customers. For many companies, especially larger, more established market players, it simply isn't practical to focus exclusively on transactional sales or exclusively on consultative sales without dramatically shrinking business. Many companies are forced to serve multiple types of buyers to reach or maintain dominant market positions. Unfortunately, the most common response of companies in this position is to try to cover their different types of customers with the same sales approach, only to find this one-size-fits-all answer simply doesn't work. Transactional sales approaches are doomed in consultative situations, and vice versa, and the compromise solution that tries to straddle the two is doomed in both. A one-size-fits-all solution can't provide the depth that consultative selling demands and is too expensive for the transactional sale. It's an even less appropriate solution for enterprise sales. Because enterprise relationships require an organization-wide approach uniquely configured to each strategic customer, only a dedicated sales effort based on deep commitment, top management involvement, and cross-functional teams has any hope of success.

CHANGE LEVER 2: STRUCTURE FOR VALUE CREATION

Organization structure has always been a powerful change lever. A shift in reporting relationships, or a combining or separating of sales forces captures everyone's attention as no other change lever can. Despite fashionable cynicism that "changing the boxes" enriches consultants more than it impacts performance, there's no doubt that the wrong structure can make the best strategy unworkable. Conversely, an organization structure that reflects the value creation vision will be a key ingredient in successfully changing the sales force. Structural change, of course, has a powerful impact on the economics and cost of selling groups, on accountabilities, and on the ability to build or leverage capability. Further, because of the high visibility and "news" value of these events, these changes can serve as very powerful signals to the organization of management priorities, direction, and implicit strategies.

In this new era of selling, organization design issues, which were never simple, have become even more complex. Sales forces in the new era can no longer exist in isolation— they must be an integral part of the company's value creation and value delivery chain. So structure decisions have to include the linkages with these wider elements of the business system, such as R&D, design, manufacturing, or logistics. The history of business system design is littered with cautionary tales about the dangers of losing market focus. But even today, and even in companies that should know a great deal better, organizations give in to the seductive logic that the business system begins with the product. So they readily fall into the trap of starting with product design, progressing through manufacturing and—only toward the end of the chain—introducing the customer. They'll tell you they are market driven, they'll say they are customer focused, but the sordid truth is that their systems and structures are designed from the product to the customer and rarely vice versa. At best, most business systems and the structures that support them start with research into what kinds of products customers want.

We would argue that, in the new era, it's no longer enough to design the value creation capabilities of your company merely in terms of what products your customers want. In the good old days, when products were unique and differentiated, perhaps customer-centered product design was a sufficient starting point for creating a business chain that delivered customer value. But, as we've seen in dozens of cases throughout this book, products and services have become commoditized and product differentiation increasingly hard to sustain. The new customers care crucially about value. And, as we've also seen, they define value in very different ways. Consequently, the business systems and structures of the future must be designed to deliver the kind of value that these new customers demand. Except for intrinsic value customers who buy transactionally, the product is no longer the most important element in value creation. Our structures need to recognize this. We must design the business chain—its systems and its structures—from a perspective that starts with the value needs and expectations of the customer and works backward to align the elements of the business system to create value for that customer set.

Design must start with the customer's value expectations, then look at the sales force structure required to deliver that value. From there, work backward through the business chain of order fulfillment through manufacturing and, finally, look at the structure of research and development. Some readers will find this counterintuitive. After all, business chains are conventionally described as though they move in the opposite direction, starting with R&D, not ending there. But that's a product-focused view of the world—how do we design a product, then make it, then sell it. Starting with the customer's value requirement necessarily reverses the conventional flow. The first element in the business chain that most customers meet happens to be the sales function. There's a compelling logic to a design sequence that starts with sales.

We'll start with a discussion of the simpler case of serving a single type of customer, and then tackle the more difficult issues of serving multiple types. Because we're writing about sales forces, we'll look at structure more from a sales perspective than we would normally do. Of course, there are other factors that come into play in undertaking total organization design, but this perspective of an organization's being designed around the customers' concept of value provides interesting new models to effect change.

Structuring for Transactional Selling. For those companies whose customer base consists of a single type of value buyer, whether intrinsic, extrinsic, or strategic, the structural issues certainly aren't trivial, but because there is only one type of customer, the structural issues are relatively straightforward. Basically the task is to match the structure to the target segment's value requirements, considering both the structure of the sales organization and the alignment of, and linkages to, the other functions in the business chain.

Let's start with the structure of the transactional sales force. At its simplest, there are three ways to organize the sales function: around geography, around product, and around customer or industry. All these dimensions are important because every sale involves all three of them. The key question is which of these dimensions should be the primary organizing axis, and which secondary or tertiary. In general, the answer depends on the type of sales mode involved. In the transactional sale, the emphasis is on efficiency and execution—stripping out all unnecessary cost and making the acquisition process as fast, convenient, and hassle free as possible. From a structural perspective the objective is to find lower-cost sales options such as telesales, electronic commerce, or shared channels. If a direct sales force is involved at all, it will likely be structured primarily along a geographical axis, which generally turns out to be the most cost-efficient alternative. Accordingly, in a given piece of geography, one salesperson will be responsible for all products and all accounts. Using this low-cost geographical model, transactional sales organizations will consciously avoid the redundancy of separate salespeople calling on the same account, which constantly happens in sales forces organized by product. Similarly, there are not likely to be account-specific selling teams of the kind you find in sales forces organized primarily by customer size. If it's a true transactional sale, these extrinsic benefit resources will be able to create little or no new value in the eyes of the customer and will simply erode existing value by unnecessarily raising costs.

Working backward from the customer value demands, the rest of the organization must be aligned to compete in this transactional environment. Manufacturing must be driven for cost-efficient production. To support the high level of price sensitivity, order fulfillment, delivery, and service functions must be lean, but also they must be designed to make the customers' acquisition process fast, convenient, and hassle free. R&D and design must also be aligned, with a substantial portion of the effort focused on cost reduction.

Structuring for Consultative Selling. Any company, and any sales force, needs to operate efficiently. But a consultative sale, in contrast to a transactional sale, must shift more attention to effectiveness. The distinction between efficiency and effectiveness is an important one that may not be readily clear in the context of a sales force. Put simply, efficiency is about opening doors—covering as many customers as cost efficiently as possible. Effectiveness, in contrast, is what happens once the door has been opened, whether the seller can create enough customer value to win the business. The effective consultative sale has potential to create value at many points in the buying process—not just at the transaction itself—and can justify much greater sales investments if the result is higher value for customers. A direct sales force is likely to be the preferred model. If it's augmented by telesales, electronic channels, or shared channels, these will often be added to improve selling effectiveness, not just to lower selling costs. Further, the direct sales force in a consultative sale will often be organized around products or customers and/or industries, rather than the cheaper geographic axis of the transactional sale.

One way to reconfigure for consultative selling is around accounts. For example, the sales force might be organized around global account teams that would be responsible for the customer's needs across all products around the world. This account team model might include a secondary geographical axis, with individual sales reps in different countries as part of the account team, rather than part of a "local" selling organization. Such a structure helps drive deeper knowledge of the customer's operations and develops the insight into customer problems and potential solutions that is a prerequisite for consultative selling. Alternatively, where products are complex and customization routinely expected, the sales force might be separated into individual product sales organizations. Within each sales force, salespeople would be focused on helping customers understand their needs relative to their product category, and they would help get products customized to meet those needs. Consultative selling organizations can also be structured around specific industries, or vertical markets, which, as we'll see in the next section, can greatly accelerate the long learning curves that are so characteristic with newly hired consultative salespeople.

Once again, working back from the value demands of customers, the other elements of the business must be aligned to be effective. To continue with our example, let's assume that customers require global capability, and the selling organization is structured primarily around global accounts and is responsible for all products and geographies for each account. Then the other functions in the business chain must be able to support that structure effectively. Order fulfillment, delivery, and service will need global capability, as well as the ability to integrate smoothly across product lines to seamlessly meet global customer needs. Manufacturing must be flexible enough to satisfy unique account requirements around the world. R&D and design must be focused on product linkages, and global standards and/or interfaces. On the other hand, if the sales organization is focused around products, then the other elements need to be aligned accordingly, to facilitate the product customization, service, and support that will provide real value to consultative customers.

Structuring to Target More Than One Type of Customer. Some companies can afford to focus on just one type of customer—transactional or consultative—but for others, especially large companies, this level of focus isn't practical. Most major organizations need to cover both types of customers to achieve their financial goals. For these companies that target more than one type of customer, the principles are the same, but the application of those principles becomes more complex. Take, for example, a metal producer who has half of its business with customers who fit a transactional sale (standard product buyers, focused on price, delivery, and supply risk factors), and half with customers who fit a consultative sale (value creation potential in product customization, services, technical support, and so on). Understandably, it is unwilling to focus exclusively on either set of customers, but the company also recognizes that trying to serve these distinct customers with a one-size-fits-all approach is bound to fail. A better path is to structure the organization with separate and distinct approaches for each customer type, sharing elements where that makes sense, without compromising the ability to serve distinctly different value creation needs.

Figure 9-1 illustrates a possible approach to "dual" systems. Starting with the sales organization itself, you need two separate approaches—an efficiency-driven structure to serve transactional customers, using low-cost elements (telesales, electronic commerce, and so on), and an effectiveness-oriented structure for consultative customers, organized around key accounts, vertical markets, or products. Why, you might ask, would we urge the creation of two separate sales forces? Surely, if they are selling the same core set of products or ser-

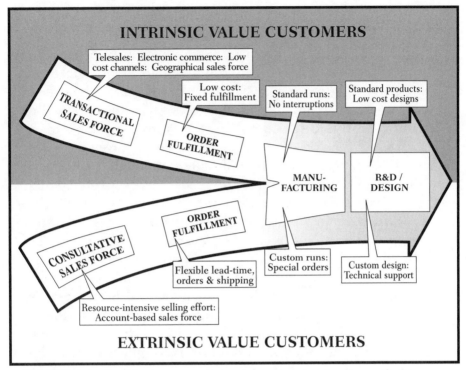

FIGURE 9-1   Dual business system to serve transactional and consultative customers.

vices, all that a double sales force will do is increase costs and overhead. The practical reality is that we've never seen a sales force succeed in the split task of selling to two radically different customer types where the value creation needs of one customer are contradicted by the requirements of the other. A dual structure lets sales forces build capability to deal with each type of customer and avoids the seemingly impossible task of training salespeople to be consultative on one sale and transactional on the next.

But sales structure is only the first step—working backward from the market, the other elements of the business system need to be aligned to be able to deliver against the distinctive needs of each segment, with a set of operating "rules" that distinguish between them. Order fulfillment, delivery, and service should, of course, be run as efficiently as possible, but the system for transactional customers must be driven by cost and convenience considerations, while that for consultative customers should build in more flexibility and capability to adapt to specific customer requirements. For transactional customers, this might mean electronic order entry covering a given set of standard products with set lead times, delivery modes, and service offerings—all designed to minimize cost, and hence reduce prices, to these customers. The system for the consultative set might have these elements, but it might also include alternatives that could add flexibility and respond to unique needs. Hence, the consultative customers might have the option of order entry through a representative in addition to electronic means. Product options would expand to include custom items with flexible lead times and delivery options for emergency or rush orders. Manufacturing and operations would also be adapted to each set of customers, even if the company served both from the same facility. Consultative sales would get priority treatment: Production schedules wouldn't be interrupted for transactional customers, but they would be for important consultative customers. Customized products would be produced for consultative sales, but only standard products for the transactional set. R&D and design would also be aligned to the two sets—special technical support and/or formulations for those who valued it, and would pay for it, but not for the price driven. The key here, of course, is not simply offering choices to customers but tying those choices to the ability to create value and to capture a share of it that value to make it economically viable. The trap to avoid is to just *assume* that customers are consultative. The acid test of whether they do in fact recognize the value being offered is whether they are willing to pay for it.

Structuring for Enterprise Selling.   We've never met an organization that serves only enterprise customers. The extraordinary value demands of strategic customers means that it's very difficult for even the largest corporation to have more than a handful of deep enterprise relationships. So enterprise relationships exist alongside consultative or transactional relationships. Because enterprise sales are made to a very small set of unique customers, they do require a separate structure from the ones that best serve other customers. The nature of this sale, as we discussed in Chapter 6, is all about leveraging distinctive competencies and the full range of corporate assets for mutual strategic advantage. Hence, these sales will always be organized around the account axis. However, leadership for this type of sale has to come from senior management rather than a typical salesperson, account executive, or even account team. The enterprise sale has to be led by a person with the clout to marshal the full range of capabilities of and resources in the corporation. Further, these types of sales will also involve cross-functional teams. Rather than aligning the various functions against a market segment, enterprise sales create effective function-to-function linkages. So an R&D department works with an R&D department, shipping works with receiving, and there are joint operations swat teams or initiatives. Staffing is likely to be shared with representatives from both companies, and corporate boundaries are likely to blur. The structure of successful enterprise relationships shows a wide variety of models. One of the most common success models treats the joint enterprise as a *strategic business unit* in its own right, with mutually agreed budgets, profit targets, and objectives. The constraints of a general chapter such as this prevent us from looking at enterprise structures in depth. Readers with special interest in this topic should review the research study of 200 partnership relationships reported in the book *Getting Partnering Right,* by Rackham, Friedman, and Ruff (McGraw-Hill, 1996).

Structural changes, such as the ones we've described in this section, are an essential second step in executing the value creation vision that was our first lever for change. As we've seen, these structural issues affect the whole corporation and not just the sales function. Of all the dangers facing those setting out to change sales forces, perhaps the gravest is to design sales force structure in isolation from the total business system. But, even if the structure encompasses and integrates the whole business chain, these structural shifts and realignments are only a part of what's required to change a

TYPE OF SALE	KEY OBJECTIVES	TYPICAL SALES STRUCTURE	ORGANIZATIONAL LINKAGES/ ALIGNMENT
Transactional	• Sell the product. • Minimize cost. • Facilitate acquisition ease and convenience.	• Telesales • Electronic commerce • Indirect channels • Geographic field force	• Low-cost manufacturing • Efficient order fulfillment • Standard product-service mix
Consultative	• Sell the problem-solving relationship. • Support individual customer value creation.	• Account- product-, or industry-based direct sales force	• Flexible design and delivery • Customization capability
Enterprise	• Sell the institution. • Leverage core competencies and total assets for strategic customers.	• Senior management led cross-functional and cross-company teams	• Function-to-function relationships • Joint staffing • Top priority from both parties

FIGURE 9-2   Summary of structural guidelines.

sales force. Done well, structural change can play a very important role both in signaling the new direction and/or strategy and in facilitating the capability building and new metrics that will also be required to effect change. Figure 9-2 summarizes the general structural guidelines for each selling mode.

CHANGE LEVER 3: CAPABILITY BUILDING

Let's assume that you have a viable vision—you know what kinds of customers you want to attract and how you can create value for them. And let's also assume that you have put into place structures that support your value vision, so that the whole of your business chain reflects the kinds of customer value you seek to create. Now all that remains is to align the sales force and to build any additional skills or capabilities they will need. It sounds as if your troubles are almost over. After all, compared to redesigning your whole business chain, how difficult can it be merely to change the way the sales force sells? Alas, as we said earlier, it's harder than you think. Which brings us to the third of our change levers: building sales force capability.

Improving Capability in Transactional Sales.   In transactional sales, we've seen that sellers create little of the value that customers seek. Transactional customers neither want nor welcome help, advice, or problem solving from salespeople. Because sellers add very little value, the primary value creation strategy in the transactional sale is to reduce cost and make acquisition easy. Taken to its logical extreme, the best transactional sales force is no sales force at all. But it's never that simple. As we saw in Chapter 3, when competing products have similar capabilities and price—in the zone of indifference—then the competitor who puts in a face-to-face presence is likely to have an advantage. So it's rarely a practical proposition to do away with the sales force altogether or to drastically reduce its coverage, unless the savings are both considerable and can be passed directly to the customer in the form of very substantial price reductions. The trick in most transactional sales is to use the sales force more efficiently and to find cheaper ways to improve coverage.

Improving the selling skills of transactional salespeople is unlikely to be an effective strategy. We saw in Chapter 1 the case of a transactional sales force selling packaging materials. They spent heavily to develop their salespeople into "packaging consultants" only to find that customers didn't want anything more than low-cost, convenient packaging supplies. As a result of their efforts to upgrade their selling, the company's costs increased, they lost money, and they were ultimately absorbed by a competitor. Stories like this one are common.

If it's ineffective to invest in building sales force skills, then how *can* you improve your capability in transactional sales? One cost-effective method is to embed knowledge in systems rather than in people. Most sales forces spend an inordinate amount of money and effort trying to teach product knowledge to their salespeople. It's a cheaper and better approach to put product knowledge into an easy and accessible electronic format. Although this is especially true of transactional sales, it's probably good advice for sales of all kinds. As Jeff Raikes of Microsoft says, "The days of *push* information are over. We can't afford the cost or the time it takes to stuff salespeople's heads full of information. We have to develop *pull* information that's quickly and conveniently accessible when salespeople need it. That takes more than just putting a product feature dump on to CD-ROM. Pull information has to be designed. If it's not well thought out it won't be used." Good systems that make knowledge easily accessible to salespeople are an essential part of transactional selling. A good system lets less experienced—and therefore cheaper—salespeople understand products, pricing, and delivery options in a way that is efficient for both seller and customer.

Another way to improve capability in transactional sales, as we saw in the last chapter, is to move to cheaper channel delivery options. So low-cost channels, such as the Internet, telephone selling, or affinity-group marketing take over from face-to-face selling. However, many organizations believe that the absence of a face-to-face selling presence will put them at a competitive disadvantage, particularly if they are in the zone of indifference where they have product and price parity with competition. What can they do to maintain a face-to-face presence at lower cost? One option is to move to nontraditional salespeople. Retirees or part-timers can provide the same coverage at an overall cost saving of 25 percent or more compared to a conventional sales force. The use of part-time salespeople becomes a particularly attractive option for companies that have developed user-friendly sales information systems. In the past a barrier to the employment of part-timers was the effort and cost required to fill their heads full of product information. As the vice president of sales of an office products company told us, "We have a dozen core products and each has maybe 10 configurations or versions. That means a new salesperson—just for starters—has to learn more than 100 alternative specifications. We don't get results until people get up the learning curve, and that can take months, even with dedicated full-time people. We can't make that kind of investment in casual or part-time salespeople. It would take them forever to get up to speed." A good sales information system can make product, pricing, and delivery details available at the touch of a button and enable part-timers to be effective more quickly.

A logical extension of user-friendly information systems in transactional sales is to put the systems directly into customers' hands. So the Fed-Ex or UPS tracking systems, for example, allow a customer to see the status of any package in transit. This not only creates real customer value but also reduces costs for the carriers, who no longer need to have their salespeople spending time tracking lost or delayed items for customers. By putting real-time information on pricing, availability, or product specifications into buyers' hands, customer convenience increases and selling costs fall.

Another source of cost that can be stripped from a transactional sales force is supervisory and managerial overhead. If salespeople require less coaching and less strategic help over how to create value for individual customers, then it follows that they require less supervisory time. We've seen organizations whose primary sale has become transactional, who have reduced their face-to-face sales force without a corresponding or greater reduction in sales management. It's an elementary mistake but one that's easy to make. Management has plenty of plausible rationalizations. "We don't have product superiority right now, but as soon as product development comes up with the promised silver bullet, then we'll need to expand the sales force, and that will require a full sales management infrastructure." Or "sales are down and times are difficult, so we need a strong sales management to make sure that salespeople perform." Whatever the excuse, the fact is that success in the transactional sale requires a slim managerial and administrative overhead. If competitors can succeed with a supervisory span of control of, say, 25:1, then it's hard to justify the cost of one supervisor for every 10 transactional salespeople.

Improving Capability in Consultative Sales.   Building consultative selling capability sometimes requires just the reverse of the actions needed to build transactional capability. Supervisory span of control ratios are a case in point. As a rule of thumb, an effective consultative selling capability requires a salesperson-to-supervisor ratio not exceeding about 8:1. Ratios of 20:1 or above are common in successful transactional sales forces. Unfortunately, because most sales forces are not structured around a value creation model, they often adopt an uneasy middle ground. There are too many supervisors for optimum transactional economics, yet—with ratios of, say, 12:1 or more—supervisors are too thin on the ground to implement an effective consultative selling model.

Why is it so important to have more intensive supervision in consultative selling? There are several reasons. For one thing, selling is more strategic and requires real problem solving and resource management skills. An experienced supervisor can ensure that such scarce resources as technical and customer support are available and deployed when they are most needed. The supervisor is also likely to have a direct selling role. Most consultative sales, based as they are on advice and customized solutions, require authority beyond an individual salesperson to configure and deliver the promised end product. The presence of the supervisor in the account at crucial stages of the selling cycle is an essential ingredient for competitive success. But, most important of all, the supervisor is the coach who, more than any other single influence, develops the skills and competence of the sales force.

One of the most consistent characteristics of successful consultative sales forces is their strong emphasis on coaching. "It's almost an obsession with us," says John Thompson of IBM. "We're passionate about coaching." Other leading sales forces have a similar coaching focus. This raises an interesting question: Why is coaching so important? Surely a well-designed training program could have a similar impact in terms of performance improvement. Look more closely and the question becomes even more interesting. Building a given level of skill through coaching costs roughly five times as much as developing the same skill through off-the-job class-room training. Most supervisors don't like to coach, and many of their people aren't exactly enthusiastic either. Why then, if it's both expensive and resisted, should coaching be given such importance by the world's most successful consultative sales forces? For one thing, skills acquired through training alone will evaporate fast. The sad fact is that new skills—whether in selling, in sports, or in, say, playing a musical instrument—will quickly fade away without constant reinforcement and prac-tice. The role of coaching is to provide the reinforcement needed to maintain and enhance skills.

That's not to suggest that training is unimportant. In fact, a well-designed combination of training and coaching is *by far* the most effective and economical way to develop consultative selling skills. Training is the most efficient tool for creating initial proficiency in a skill. Coaching is an essential tool for maintaining and refining the skills that training has started. Coaching doesn't come easily to most sales supervisors—even those who are from organizations that have a coaching culture and a reward system that gives supervisors an incentive to coach. Part of the problem is that many supervisors don't know what effective consultative selling skills look like. You can't coach a skill unless you understand it. Unfortunately, the majority of sales managers have a very inaccurate picture of what specific skills they need to develop to ensure an effective consultative selling performance. A good shared and widely understood skills model is an essential first step in building skills.

It's helpful to divide coaching in the consultative sale into two distinct types:

- *Skill Coaching,* where the purpose is to improve the face-to-face skills and behaviors of salespeople. To be effective, skill coaching has to take place on a fairly regular basis—as a rule of thumb, skill coaching is unlikely to bring about change if it is less frequent than once every two to three weeks. To coach a skill, supervisors must travel with their salespeople, watch how they sell, and give them helpful feedback. It's a time-consuming process. With travel, a coaching call takes up most of a working day. And that's one of the problems inherent in skills coaching. Just do the math. Assume a sales manager has 10 salespeople and decides to travel with each once every two weeks. If each coaching visit takes a day, then coaching has literally become a full-time job. Few sales managers are idle in this day and age. Most are already fully occupied with administration, meetings, forecasts, and reporting, not to mention customer demands. With the best of intentions it's hard to get out in the field to skills coach at sufficient depth to be useful. Most sales managers get out when they can, which means being with each salesperson once every couple of months if they are lucky. Studies carried out of effective sales skill coaches in Xerox Corporation, reported in *Managing Major Sales*, Neil Rackham and Richard Ruff (1991), show that this low-intensity coaching just doesn't cut it. So how do successful managers coach skills in the real world? The Xerox study showed that high-performing coaches didn't try to coach their whole team at once. Instead, they chose two or three people and coached them intensively for several months before moving on to new team members.

- *Strategy Coaching,* where the purpose is to improve salespeople's ability to plan calls and create account strategies. Unlike skills coaching, strategy coaching can be done in the office, making a much more economical use of sales manager time. What's more, it can often be done—on the call level at least—in just a few minutes. Both strategy and skill coaching are essential for improving consultative sales performance. One is not a substitute for the other. But whereas skill coaching is limited by the number of *people* that can be coached at one time, strategy coaching is limited by the number of *accounts*. In order to coach strategy successfully, the coach must have a fairly good understanding of the customer's business and the players involved. Less effective strategy coaches spread their "help" superficially across dozens of their people's accounts—making suggestions based on a perilously slender understanding of the account. The more effective coaches limit their coaching to fewer accounts where they take the time to really understand the customer issues and players in depth.

One final observation on coaching in the consultative sale: The Huthwaite study of effective sales coaching in Xerox Corporation showed that the coaches who were most successful at increasing their people's sales applied their coaching effort early in the selling cycle. Less successful coaches didn't coach until later in the cycle. Another study by Huthwaite in IBM showed a related finding. When IBM managers accompanied their people into calls early in the selling cycle, the overall length of the selling cycle was shorter than when managers became involved later in the cycle. It seems that early coaching effort speeds sales and sets them off in the right direction. Most managers don't become involved in a sale until it nears the point of decision. The research evidence suggests that this is not only too late to influence the specific sale but also fails to coach the most crucial element of consultative sales performance—the early parts of the selling cycle that center on uncovering and developing needs.

As coaching has the most impact in terms of improving sales performance in the early parts of the selling cycle, it's reasonable to suppose that other sales enhancement tools might also have a greater impact on improving sales skills and capabilities if used in the initial stages of the sale. We believe that there's a promising future here for new automated sales tools developed specifically for the early stages of the consultative sale. We've seen how, in transactional sales, automated sales tools can play an important part in improving performance. A different class of sales tools is starting to prove its value in the initial stages of consultative selling. These tools are diagnostic in nature, allowing less experienced salespeople to do a better job of understanding customer problems and configuring customized solutions to specific customer needs. So, for example, automated asset analysis tools help financial planners and consultants to diagnose client needs and to generate a range of options and possibilities that, without the tools, would require the expertise of an extraordinarily knowledgeable financial planner. Simulation software allows customers to play with configurations and alternatives, seeing a virtual-reality version of their selected options. This makes customization easier for an increasing range of consultative sales organizations from furniture designers to aircraft manufacturers.

Diagnostic tools like these address one of the central issues for building consultative selling capability. Consultative talent is expensive and scarce. Even if you can afford it, you may not be able to find it. As companies are increasingly forced to grow their own talent, they are finding that the learning curve is longer and slower than they had imagined. Coaching, training, and diagnostic tools all play an important role in enabling salespeople to learn faster. Sometimes the very structure of the sales force can also act as a learning accelerator. So, for example, sales forces that have organized themselves by verticals, or industry focus, have found that by dedicating salespeople to a single industry, it's easier for them to learn about customer issues and problems. Rick Beller, formerly director of Asian business development for Universal Instruments Corporation, describes a typical case: "Sales talent is often scarce in emerging markets. In Taiwan, for example, we had an inexperienced sales force, and the issue was how to get them up the learning curve fast in a technology marketplace that itself was evolving with confusing speed. By taking a vertical industry focus, we were able to narrow the amount of information salespeople had to learn and build their visibility and credibility." Even in markets that move more slowly, or where talent is less scarce, industry verticals can accelerate the learning process and develop the level of expertise necessary for effective consultative selling.

Improving Capability in Enterprise Sales.   Enterprise sales are fundamentally different from either transactional or consultative sales in that the sales force constitutes just one component of the value creation process. Consequently, to improve capability in the enterprise sale means improving the capability of the overall enterprise and not just the capacity of the sales force. "Improve the whole company" may be the most accurate advice, but it's hardly the most satisfying. What concrete steps can an organization take to improve its enterprise capability for key customers? In our experience the following three specific actions most often help improve the effectiveness of enterprise selling capability:

1. *Cross-Functional Competence.*   As we saw in Chapter 6, it's hard to leverage the assets of the enterprise to create customer value unless the organization has the internal ability to work well cross functionally. A sales force that doesn't work well with its own design, manufacturing, or information technology functions, for example, will have difficulty in marshaling these corporate assets to meet the needs of enterprise customers. Unfortunately, sales functions are among the worst corporate silo culprits. They are more likely to have a history of cross-functional warfare than cross-functional teamwork. Organizations that have allowed the sales function to control enterprise relationships have sometimes failed to create the extraordinary value that enterprise selling demands. The "sales unit" in the enterprise sale should be an effective cross-functional team led by a senior executive. One of the best ways to improve enterprise-selling capability is to look long and hard at how well your cross-functional teams are working.

2. *Zippering or Player Mapping.*   One way to assess whether the right cross-functional team is in place is to map your team members against key players in the customer's organization. To take a very simple example, if you have opportunities to add value to an enterprise customer's research effort, you are more likely to be effective if you have a team member from your own research function. Simplistic as

this may sound, it's a vital part of successful enterprise selling. Companies like McGreggor Cory, the contract distribution specialists, have developed a detailed strategy for mapping their enterprise players against their equivalent functions and levels within the customer. Under a variety of names, including "zippering" and "player mapping," organizations like McGreggor Cory frequently review the match between their team and the range of significant customer contacts. We're surprised at how often a failure to consciously review the team composition can lead to missed opportunities and wasted resources. It's relatively effortless to carry out periodic player mapping. We would recommend it to any organization looking for easy ways to increase the effectiveness of their enterprise relationships.

3. *Alignment with a Common Value Creation Model.* Because so many people in an enterprise sale play a part in creating customer value, it's important that everybody involved with the customer, from the humblest assistants to top executives, understand that their role is value creation. Just as important, it's vital that they make that role very visible to the customer. We saw in Chapter 6 how effective organizations train their teams in common problem-solving and customer relationship models. It's not enough to train salespeople or executives. The everyday customer interaction by those doing the work has a make-or-break impact on the effectiveness of the enterprise relationship. Alignment around a common customer-handling model is an important part of creating consistent value that the customer will recognize.

CHANGE LEVER 4: METRICS FOR VALUE CREATION

Metrics, and the reward systems linked to them, provide an essential change lever for creating improved performance in any sale, whether transactional, consultative, or enterprise. Unfortunately, there's no other area of selling that generates so much heat with so little light than reward systems.

Compensation is usually the first change lever that managers reach for—usually with disappointing results. The one reliable outcome from changing the compensation system is a wave of unhappiness and protest from the sales force. As Pat Kelly, who designed many of the Xerox compensation plans, used to say, "The only time salespeople don't hate your new plan is if you're paying them a lot too much." The sad truth is that while compensation can make salespeople sell harder, there's little evidence that it can help them sell smarter. And in today's world, particularly in consultative and enterprise selling, smarter is what it's all about.

There is such a universal obsession with the compensation system and with the various schemes that can be used that it's easy to miss the much more important underlying issue of what it is that we should be measuring. So that's what we're going to focus on in the remainder of this chapter—what metrics you should use to change sales performance. If you get the fundamental measures right, there are a wide range of choices in terms of creative compensation schemes. Virtually no one fails because they didn't use the latest clever compensation system, but virtually no one succeeds without the right set of metrics.

So what *are* the right metrics? That depends on the type of sale; metrics for transactional sales are different from those for consultative or enterprise selling. But there are some basic principles of measurement that apply across all sales. Metrics that succeed in creating performance change tend to possess most, if not all, of the following characteristics:

Measure Less to Get More.   Measures that have a powerful impact on performance tend to be simple and few in number. As a general rule, measuring just two or three important results leads to greater performance change than measuring five or six. As consultants, one of the first things we do when we review sales force metrics is to prune the existing measures drastically down to the critical few that really matter. Metrics, left to themselves, tend to proliferate. The best practice is to keep metrics few in number and never measure anything unless it's absolutely central to success.

Measure Results, Not Activities.   Perhaps the most common measurement sin is to fall into the temptation of measuring activities rather than measuring results. For example, many sales forces are measured on the number of calls their salespeople make per day. Call rates are an activity, not a result. This story, told us by a divisional head of a major New York bank, is a typical cautionary tale:

> We had some concerns that our calling officers weren't making enough customer calls, so we instituted an activity management system to track call rates. We found, on average, they were only making 1.3 calls per day. We intended to at least double, or treble that. If we could get three times as many calls, common sense said we'd get a big increase in sales. Maybe not three times the sales but a big increase. With the new system we certainly pushed up call rates to about 2.5 per day. Unfortunately, sales didn't increase the way we expected. In fact, the strange thing was, sales actually went down.

This tale is common enough—including the fall in sales results. Salespeople measured on activity will produce activity. They'll make more calls, at the expense of strategic sales opportunities. One major manufacturing company based in Chicago introduced metrics to measure salespeople's call activity. They found that, following the introduction of the activity measurement, calls increased and so did overall orders. But the average value of each order fell by 18 percent—a clear sign that salespeople were responding to the measurement of call rates by making easy and quick sales at the expense of larger strategic ones. Overall revenue fell by 1.5 percent, and the activity metrics were abandoned. The moral of stories like these is, if you measure activities rather than outcomes, don't be surprised if you get lots of activity but no outcomes in terms of sales results.

Align Metrics with Rewards.   At the risk of the obvious, metrics and rewards need to be aligned. All too often they are not. Companies measure the profitability of accounts but reward their salespeople purely on volume. Or they introduce customer satisfaction metrics, yet penalize their people for spending time on customer care. The value of alignment is obvious enough, but where do you start? Do your metrics come first, or does your reward system? Few companies ask themselves this question, and, in most cases, metrics and rewards tend to be designed simultaneously. That's a mistake. Design your metrics first, and design them independently of the reward system. Test metrics before introducing associated rewards or compensation—it's far easier to collect valid data if your measures don't begin their life colored by compensation issues.

Measure the Important Rather Than the Urgent.   Urgent issues usually get attention with or without metrics. Every sales organization has its share of fires to fight and customer crises to handle. Urgent problems like these get attended to immediately—usually at the expense of the things that people know they should be doing but, because they aren't so urgent, can be put off until the crisis is over. And, naturally, because new fires are lit with predictable regularity, the crisis continues forever. In most sales functions, things that don't have to be done by Friday will be perpetually put off until next week and will never be finished. Metrics are at their most useful when they bring attention to these important longer-term performance issues that are victims of the urgent. A good example is coaching. Coaching is unquestionably important, probably the most important single activity of the average sales manager. Yet, for most sales managers, coaching is a pious intention that they hope to get around to when the never-ending stream of urgent issues has been dealt with. It's here that metrics, in the form of clear coaching targets, can help an important performance issue compete for time and attention with day-to-day urgencies.

Use Metrics That Salespeople Can Influence.   If you measure things salespeople can't control, then your measures will never result in improved sales. Yet that's so often what happens. Take the case of a food company that measured its sales force on sales volume, or units of product sold—a typical metric for many sales forces. Company salespeople calling on grocery chains and retail outlets had very little control over units sold. They couldn't influence key elements that controlled volume, such as pricing or marketing expenditures. As a result, the metric didn't directly relate to anything salespeople could change. Their bonus system, based on sales volume, failed to motivate or improve sales performance. The company introduced new metrics based on things that salespeople could more directly control, such as number and location of displays, shelf position, and distribution level of products. As a result, performance significantly improved because the new metrics measured areas that salespeople were able to influence. More sophisticated packaged-goods manufacturers have solved this problem in an even more effective manner, by broadening the scope of what salespeople control. First they built capability for local salespeople to manage key profit drivers, like price and promotion funds. They then shifted responsibility and accountability for these elements to the local sales district, and finally, they focused metrics on the profit each district generated. These new systems and measures have dramatically improved overall profit performance and sales motivation.

Measure What Matters, Not Just What's Measurable.   Too many metrics focus on what's easily measurable rather than on what's important. There's a fundamental principle here: A rough measure of what counts beats a precise measure of what doesn't. Most metrics gravitate to the easily quantifiable. We measure calls per day because it's easy data to collect. Customer satisfaction, on the other hand, is harder to quantify, and—although it's unquestionably more important—it often goes unmeasured. In our experience, struggling to measure the important is one of the most worthwhile of all management activities. Customer satisfaction is a good example. Most companies who try to measure customer satisfaction report that the process of creating satisfaction metrics, although frustrating and difficult, turned out to be immensely worthwhile as a way to clarify and sharpen their thinking about an area crucially important to their business success.

Involve Salespeople in Metrics Design and Data Collection.   If struggling to measure the important is helpful at a management level, it's even more useful at the level of individual salespeople or sales teams. Continuing with our customer satisfaction example, one of the authors once worked with a key account team in the process control industry. They were responsible for selling to the company's biggest account, an account that provided more than 10 percent of overall divisional revenue. During a strategy meeting, it became clear that members of the team were divided in terms of their perception of customer satisfaction from the key account. Opinions ranged from "they love us" all the way to "they think our responsiveness stinks and they're ready to pull the plug." We asked the team to come up with metrics to test out the true level of customer satisfaction. The team designed a structured interview with a points rating where perfect satisfaction would score 100. They aimed to achieve a score of 90 or better. They were devastated to find, when they went out to collect data, that they were running at 74 and were indeed vulnerable. So they instituted a series of corrective actions and repeated the satisfaction metric quarterly. At the last count they were performing at a satisfaction level of 92 and had both retained the account and grown its business.

A couple of morals from this story: First, metrics can be a valuable sales tool if salespeople are involved in their design and collection. Second, it's sometimes better not to link metrics too directly to rewards. Organizations that have tried to pay their salespeople based on customer satisfaction measures have invariably found considerable faking of data. In this case, the sales team wasn't compensated directly for satisfaction. Their plan was based on a mix of overall revenue and profitability. The satisfaction metric was their own tool to get them to their revenue and profit goals and, being separate from compensation, remained an honest measure.

Focus Metrics on Improvement.   Metrics in manufacturing underwent a revolution starting in the 1970s with the development of techniques that moved measurement away from its traditional policing function of inspection to the new role of continuous quality improvement. As a result, manufacturing productivity took a great leap forward. Sales is overdue for a similar shift. Metrics are still used in selling today as inspection tools to police the sales force. Sales measurement systems look uncomfortably like the old and discredited manufacturing metrics of 40 years ago. Before instituting any new metric, ask the crucial question, "How will this *improve* the quality of our selling?" Particularly in enterprise selling, metrics are the guidance system that permits continuous improvement and the creation of extraordinary value for both supplier and customer.

These are some general principles of metrics design that have worked well for many organizations irrespective of whether their sale is transactional, consultative, or enterprise. However, the different types of sales each have some unique metrics issues of their own.

METRICS FOR THE TRANSACTIONAL SALE

Success in the transactional sale revolves around cost control and around satisfying customers' need for ease of acquisition. It's in these areas where the metrics for transactional sales must focus. The good news is that many traditional metrics make sense in transactional sales, including sales cost per customer, cost per transaction, and E/R ratios (expense to revenue). These cost-based metrics focus the sales force on the right set of issues. Transactional sales are made to intrinsic value buyers, who see value in the product or service itself, not in the information or insight that a salesperson can give them. Salespeople need to be cost conscious in transactional selling, and that's where many traditional metrics have their greatest strength.

For the other dimension of transactional sales—the customer's desire for ease of acquisition—there are also widely used and time-tested metrics that work well. These tend to be traditional customer service measures, such as time per transaction, order to delivery lead time, or percentage of "perfect" orders—on time and complete. One caution: Be sure that the measures truly reflect the *customer's* perspective. A few years ago we worked with an industrial equipment manufacturer who had a horrible delivery reputation in the marketplace and lots of customer complaints, but their internal measures reported that they fulfilled 98 percent of the customers' orders on or before the customer due date. Of course, customers' perceptions can be at odds with true performance, but the gap between internal measures and the external view was so great, we were skeptical. When we looked into it, we found that indeed, the factory did meet the "customer due date" 98 percent of the time—from the factory perspective—but less than 50 percent of the time from the customer perspective. The difference was definitional. *Customer due date* in factory reports indicated the date that the factory agreed to. It had little or nothing to do with the date the customer requested. Lead times varied widely over the course of a year, and salespeople, trying to placate customers, frequently made commitments without the factory sign-off. The factory didn't want to miss due dates, so they committed to delivery times only when they were very sure they could meet them. In this case, customer due date was useless as a metric because it didn't relate to real-world customers.

It's also useful to measure and track the resources invested in the sale. In general, it's good practice to limit the resources committed to transactional sales—the risk of overinvestment is far greater than the risk of underinvestment. Hence, you need to keep tight measurement and control over "investments," be they capital, sales resources, or discounts, and make sure that each investment is fully justified by real cost savings or real improvements in customer service that the transactional customer will pay for. Too many companies, trapped in a transactional selling environment, have persistently higher cost of sales than their competition because they lack adequate metrics to measure and control their sales investment. The old joke of "I make a loss on each item I sell—but I make it up on volume" is sometimes uncomfortably true in transactional sales forces that lack adequate cost of sale metrics. Successful sales forces avoid specific customer investments that take a long time to pay back because the transactional customer is by definition a fickle buyer who will jump at tomorrow's best deal. Good metrics will monitor and control the dangerous practice of "investing" with heavy discounts to gain customer loyalty. Most sales forces find to their cost that, when the discounts disappear, so do many transactional buyers.

A final trap to avoid in the transactional sale is the excessive focus on measuring activity levels, which has long been used to police the unseen work of the sales force out there in the field where management has an uneasy feeling that something isn't happening. These activity measures were designed to ensure that individual salespeople were actively working. Call activity reports, introduced in the late 1800s were a typical example of these metrics. Some of the problems of activity metrics were apparent from the start. In 1924, Russell and Beach wrote:

> Most companies ask their salesmen to send in daily reports or letters. These usually contain such items as the number of calls made, the names of prospects sold, and names of those whom he was unable to sell, together with a reason for such failure, business conditions in the community, total sales for the day, and expenses incurred. A few firms ask their salesmen to fill out reports that are virtually work tickets, accounting for every hour of every day. There is a tendency for the report forms to increase in size and number as more facts are wanted from time to time by an official at headquarters. They may become a burden to the salesman, who may be justified in raising the question whether or not all the facts requested are used. . . .

Little has changed in the last 75 years, except that advances in technology have automated the reports—usually with little positive effect. If anything, the automated reports have tried to capture even more information than their manual predecessors did and consequently take even more time for salespeople to fill out. This incessant demand for information—under the guise of metrics—actually destroys value in transactional sales because it increases selling costs in two ways. First, it wastes selling time. Second, it requires investment in costly sales automation tools that add little of value to supplier or customer in purely transactional sales. Yet, like lemmings, transactional sales force after sales force falls into the trap of believing that they must equip their salespeople with high-powered laptops and sophisticated activity measuring software. It's very easy to get "wowed" by the nifty things technology can do, but often the bells and whistles that seem so sexy increase the cost of transactional selling, yet add little or no value. Our advice is to maintain your skepticism and use metrics to prove the cost savings in pilots before committing to large-scale implementation and expense.

METRICS FOR THE CONSULTATIVE SALE

Metrics for the consultative sale are considerably different from those for transactional sales. While traditional cost and customer service measures can suffice for the transactional sale, they will get you in trouble in the consultative environment. In the consultative sale, cost is no longer the primary value driver. There are much greater opportunities to create value by helping customers understand and meet their unique needs than there are in cutting cost and lowering prices. In contrast to transactional selling, the risk in consultative selling is one of underresourcing; of failing to invest enough to develop insight about customer needs, or of failing to develop customized solutions to capitalize on those needs. Measures that focus salespeople and sales management on cost control only increase the risk of underresourcing the sales force in the consultative mode. That doesn't mean that your metrics totally ignore sales cost in the consultative sale, but you should change the perspective—and measures—away from sales as an expense to be continually whittled away to one of sales as an investment that needs to be optimized.

We are also advocating a shift away from the traditional emphasis on measuring value created for the seller to a more balanced view that also considers the value created for customers. Metrics along the lines of individual account targets, sales volume, or account growth reflect what a supplier may be getting from its sales force, but they totally ignore the customer's value perspective, and they will not suffice in the emerging value-driven marketplace.

Sales forces who want to get metrics right for consultative selling will focus on three key areas, each of which represents considerable change from most current practices. These are process-linked measures, team-based measures, and value creation proxies. Let's look at each one:

PROCESS-LINKED MEASURES

As we discussed in Chapter 7, sales process will take on increasing importance in the future, enabling ordinary mortals to replace scarce rock-star talent. But process is unlikely to take hold in a sales organization without the reinforcement of metrics. This doesn't mean a new set of activity measures— consultative sales measures need to be focused on results to be effective—but it does mean a set of measures that tracks progress through the process, and not just at contract signing or the overrated "close." For example, you might have measures at three or four points in the selling process. The first would focus on customer needs assessment and measure the size of the problems (or value opportunities) uncovered during the needs assessment phase. The second measure might focus on the proposed solutions for the customer and the value expected to be created for the customer by those solutions. The third measure might focus on the contract-signing phase and measure how much of the value to be created would go to the supplier and how much would be retained by the customer. Finally, during the implementation phase, metrics could turn to tracking the actual value delivered—either in costs saved or new revenues generated—as well as the new opportunities uncovered to fuel future sales. This series of measures keeps the selling process on track and permits course correction or recovery from a misstep. In contrast, those whose metrics just focus on the end of the selling process, or sales close, can learn about sales process deficiencies only when they lose the sale and it is too late to do anything about it.

TEAM-BASED MEASURES

Salespeople are a fairly independent lot, with an ingrained "lone-ranger" mentality. Whether it's because that's the type of person that has historically been attracted to a sales career or alternatively because that's how generations of salespeople have been shaped by decades of individual metrics and other "solo-performer" reinforcements is an interesting question. Whatever its cause, the lone-ranger notion of sales has to change for consultative sellers to succeed in the future. We have argued in this book that sales forces can no longer exist in isolation—that they must become an integral part of a company's value creation and value delivery system. And a key element of that change will be to shift away from individual- to team-based measures, recognizing the interdependencies that will drive successful performance.

There are two types of team measures that will become increasingly important in driving account team rather than individual performance. One type of measure is aimed at the multiproduct team and the other at the multifunctional team. In the multiproduct team, account teams are made up of salespeople from different divisions, or product forces, where each team member represents a product or a set of products and the team works together to sell the whole product range to a single customer. In the multifunctional team, team members come from the different functions involved in delivering a customized solution to a customer. The multiproduct sales team is not uncommon in large companies with a number of different product lines or divisions selling to the same customer base. As we discussed earlier, in the consultative sale it often makes sense to organize sales forces by product to facilitate customization of products to better meet customer needs. Traditional measures of each individual product sales force in this type of structure aren't adequate here—they fail to measure the entire account relationship and how well the company is serving the account across all of its product lines. Worse, metrics that focus salespeople only on their own product lines can be divisive and can restrict cooperation. In addition to encouraging collaboration among different product sales forces, smarter suppliers who are organized by product groups are developing measures around total account performance, and they are tracking how well total customer needs are being met.

Multifunctional team measures are more difficult to put in place, but they are increasingly important. Shifting sales from a role of communicating value to creating value requires new and different linkages with other functions in the company such as R&D, manufacturing, or service. Measures must be developed to understand how well the entire business system is meeting account needs and creating value for the customer. These are not readily available measures because most companies' measurement systems have been oriented around products or around functions, but not around accounts. However, multifunctional team metrics of this kind need to be developed to successfully shift to the new consultative selling.

VALUE CREATION PROXIES

Perhaps the most important, and clearly the most difficult, metrics to put in place are those that measure the value that has been created for customers. Creating value for customers is what the new selling is all about, but how do you measure it? Some have suggested customer satisfaction surveys as one possibility. We're not against surveys of this type—it's never a bad idea to measure how customers feel—but surveys alone are inadequate. They measure customer perceptions, not true performance, and customers may be wrong about the value they are receiving in either direction. Customers who believe they are getting more value than you are really delivering may lull you into complacency and leave you vulnerable to a competitor who opens a customer's eyes. On the other hand, customers who don't recognize the value they are really getting can drive you to take unnecessary corrective actions to increase benefits or reduce prices, actions that will needlessly lower your profitability. So, while customer surveys can be helpful for understanding what customers *think* your performance is, you need another set of measures that can give you a sense of your actual performance.

In the consultative sale you should try to measure the value created for customers directly, and, when that isn't possible, you should use proxies that can at least give you a ballpark estimate of where you stand. So, for example, if you deliver products in half the time it takes your competitor to do so, you can measure the resulting inventory savings that speed creates for your customer. If the custom formulation you developed for a customer increases their line productivity by 3 percent, you can measure what that means in terms of cost reduction. If you helped a customer develop and launch a new product line, you can measure what value was created in terms of incremental revenue and profit. These measures aren't precise, are not readily available, and often require assumptions as well as estimates. But despite these drawbacks or imperfections, and in some cases because of these imperfections, they are enormously powerful. They require salespeople to engage customers in fact-finding about productivity improvements or new revenues, and while the salesperson learns, so does the customer. The facts drive warranted actions. They don't just track customer perceptions; they help shape them, and they provide the foundation for further value opportunities. Further, they focus the interaction between customer and seller on the full value delivered and help to diffuse confrontational discussions about price.

METRICS FOR ENTERPRISE SALES

Metrics for the enterprise sale, as you might expect, are substantially different from those of transactional or consultative sales because the enterprise sale is a unique model. Remember, enterprise sales are appropriate for only a handful of customers. They are relationships between equals, they have strategic goals rather than simply profit goals, and they are not just a device for pushing more volume to a big account. The best way to think about metrics for the enterprise sale is to treat the relationship as a discrete *strategic business unit* (SBU) in its own right. Think of it as you would a separate division, with two owners—the supplier and the enterprise customer. The specific measures will vary somewhat from relationship to relationship because each is fairly unique, but the following guidelines can help set the parameters for effective enterprise sale metrics:

TRACK INVESTMENTS OF BOTH PARTIES

In an enterprise sale, the investments each side has made must be made clear to everyone. This includes dedicated or reserved production capacity, human resources such as dedicated R&D resources, or cash such as funding for special projects. It's important to capture investments from the buyer as well as the seller—if the seller is making all of the investments, then it may be an important sale, but it's hardly an enterprise sale. The investment measure is essential to determining the true ROI of the relationship to each side. Further, the investments in this type of sale tend to be considerable for both parties, and generally they exceed the level that most executives believe is being invested. Fact-based measures of the investment are key to periodically assessing whether the relationship has enough potential to continue to justify its high costs.

TRACK VALUE CREATION FOR BOTH PARTIES

Measuring the value that the parties have created mirrors the measures of investment and must similarly be made clear to everyone. This is a shared relationship, and, like a partnership, both parties need to benefit from it. The benefits to each party shouldn't be secret or hidden. In addition, good measures of value created provide the other half of the ROI calculation and are probably the primary determinant of whether continuing with the enterprise relationship is justified. Measuring value in this sale poses similar problems to those of measuring value in the consultative sale, although it may be simplified somewhat by the small number of accounts involved. Needless to say, value creation metrics have such a central role in guiding the relationship that they must be created and collected jointly by the enterprise partners. Unilateral metrics of value are a symptom of a poor enterprise relationship.

DON'T OBSCURE STRATEGIC GOALS

The primary objective of an enterprise sale is strategic—on both sides—and measures should reflect that. But developing strategic measures is easier said than done. Enterprise sales, with their inherent cross-functional structure and multiple points of contact, often generate considerable improvement in day-to-day interactions, as well as incremental operating improvements. This is all to the good, and such improvements should be captured, but don't let these day-to-day measures obscure the real intent of the relationship, which is strategic. It happens all too often. The day-to-day improvements seem more concrete, are more readily quantifiable, more readily tracked, and their progress is more easily observed. Strategic goals, on the other hand, are often vague and certainly take longer to achieve, and progress toward those goals is more slippery. That's why you need to be especially diligent about putting sufficient time and effort toward getting a good handle on measuring these strategic elements. Otherwise, you may find that you've developed good working relationships but failed to achieve the real strategic breakthroughs that were essential to justify the effort and cost of the enterprise sale.

SUPPORT CONTINUOUS IMPROVEMENT

Another key element of the enterprise sale is continuous improvement and the learning that underpins a continuous-improvement methodology. To learn, an organization has to understand not only what happened but it also must gain some measure of why it happened. It also has to understand how much the outcome varied from expectations. It's a curious thing, but our memory of what we expected to happen is heavily colored by the outcome itself, and unless those expectations were carefully documented, it's virtually impossible to go back and re-create them. Hence, to support the learning for continuous improvement, measures need to document these expectations and the assumptions behind them. Only then will you be able to look at the real outcome and understand which assumptions held and what needs to be done to make further improvements. One outcome of the quality movement in manufacturing has been extensive literature on metrics. These developments in manufacturing metrics are becoming increasingly applicable to enterprise sales, and we're likely to see more of the type of metrics used in manufacturing to measure the continuous-improvement aspects of enterprise relationships.

BUILD IN REVIEW PROCESSES

Performance metrics are the guidance system that steers value creation in the enterprise sale. Many enterprise relationships are based on continuous improvement models where quality and cycle time metrics are deeply embedded into the collaboration. But, even where the enterprise relationships don't have embedded metrics, a regularly updated set of performance goals and measures is essential to success. As many organizations have found to their cost, incomplete metrics can damage or destroy the relationship. One control systems manufacturer told us the story of the disintegration of a long-time enterprise relationship with a large customer. This customer, in an increasingly commoditized market with diminishing margins, was forced to review every element of their supplier agreements. When the manufacturer's relationship came under scrutiny, there were no unified metrics to prove how much value the supplier had created. In fact, because the manufacturer's accounting system was unable to roll up expenditures by account, it wasn't even possible to show how much cost the manufacturer was investing in the relationship. Reluctantly, the customer disengaged from the relationship, telling the manufacturer, "We probably got a wonderful deal from our relationship with you, but there's no way for either of us to prove it—and we can no longer do business that way."

Metrics might not have always had such an immediate life-or-death impact on a relationship, but they are crucial to today's enterprise sale and are usually poorly designed and executed. The fact is that the enterprise sale is based on the proposition that extraordinary investment of institutional effort will yield extraordinary new value. The inability to measure this value is a fatal flaw in the proposition. So review your metrics carefully. Ask yourself, and your partner, whether you have sufficiently clear value creation goals and equally clear measures to track achievement toward the goals that you've set.

One final point on why metrics provide such a powerful lever for improving enterprise selling capability. The process of measurement itself reveals new opportunities for value creation. The most powerful purpose of measurement is not to prove but to improve. In the Huthwaite studies of 200 successful partnerships (see *Getting Partnering Right*, Neil Rackham, Lawrence Friedman, and Richard Ruff (McGraw-Hill, 1996), we came across case after case of how a focus on metrics led to unexpected avenues for new value creation. For anyone looking for ways to significantly improve their enterprise relationships, a careful review of metrics isn't a bad place to start.

WAKE UP RIP VAN WINKLE!

We opened this book with the fanciful tale of a Rip Van Winkle salesman waking up after a 30-year sleep to find that sales was the only function in his organization that was still recognizable. And we warned that he woke up just in time. As we've seen in each chapter, selling, as we've traditionally known it, is disappearing fast. Sales forces are in the early stages of changes that are altering every aspect of what we once called "selling." From the simplest transactional sale that now takes place electronically without a single millisecond of human involvement, all the way to massive enterprise relationships that are transforming the total business strategies of the participants, these changes are profound and irreversible. And they are gathering speed. Individual salespeople are inevitably feeling alarmed, confused, and uncertain, but, unlike Rip Van Winkle, their alarm is more likely to keep them awake than asleep.

We wish we could say that the same were true for most sales functions. Too many of them seem to be dozing, oblivious of the forces that will ultimately drive them out of business. Everywhere we look we see transactional sales forces with unsustainably high-cost structures, we see consultative sales forces that just don't sell deeply enough to win the business, and we see would-be enterprise players who lack the cross-functional capacity to create enough value to cover the huge costs of enterprise involvement. We see household-name sales forces who are firmly convinced that their mission is to be value communicators—and who seem oblivious to the fact that some of their smarter competitors are already learning to become value *creators*. It's true: The majority of sales functions are sleepy at best. Our message is plain: wake up—and wake up fast! Rip Van Winkle may have slept for 30 years, but any sales function today that drops off to sleep for even a few months will not be worth waking. Think in value creation terms. Understand how to structure and manage transactional, consultative, or enterprise elements of your sales effort so that each creates new customer value.

This is a time of unprecedented opportunity for thoughtful players. In the past, selling offered high rewards to those with the energy to sell hard and the tactics to close deals. Today, in the new era we're entering, selling will offer even greater rewards to those who can sell smart and who can understand and implement the strategies for creating customer value.

INDEX

INDEX

ABOUT THE AUTHORS

NEIL RACKHAM is the founder and CEO of Huthwaite, Inc., a leading sales consulting, training, and research firm, and author of several leading books, including *SPIN Selling, The SPIN Selling Fieldbook, Major Account Sales Strategy,* and *Getting Partnering Right.* Recognized as a pioneer in sales force effectiveness, Mr. Rackham is widely credited with bringing reasearch and analytical methods to the field of sales force management.

JOHN DEVINCENTIS is an independent sales and marketing consultant based in both Solebury, PA and Washington, D.C. He was previously a partner at McKinsey & Co., where he led the firm's Sales Force and Channel Management practice from 1986 to 1998. Mr. DeVincentis works with major multinational companies in a broad range of industries to build sales capability for strategic advantage.